The Amazing Danis!

A hidden mountain tribe becomes a modern day people of faith!

by David L. Scovill

Dave and Esther Scovill share their inspiring story of personal experiences among the Dani tribespeople of Papua, Indonesia

Ex Líbrís

DELORES ALT

—✺—

Dedicated to:

My family who have been active participants in the unfolding of this story.

The many friends whose fervent prayers and sacrificial gifts have sustained our ministry in Indonesia for nearly half a century.

And in loving memory of:

Son, David Brian Scovill, whose birth was an answer to the Danis' prayers and who loved the Danis. His Heavenly Father called him HOME on December 28, 1983.

Table of Contents

—༄—

Part II: Faith in Action

Acknowledgements:

—〰—

Special thanks go to so many who have been a part of the stories in the following pages.

To our colleagues with whom we served among the Dani: Among the many who have ministered to the Dani church for various lengths of time, with eternal gratefulness we mention Ralph and Melba Maynard and Leon and Lorraine Dillinger. As the archives will testify, these two families saw the potential in us, this young couple who arrived on the field right out of Bible School; they made deliberate decisions not to hold us back, but to mentor us along in ministries and opportunities which would maximize the gifting God had given to us.

To our fabulous, faithful supporting constituency: Many have already gone on ahead of us into Glory, yet to those churches and individuals still encouraging us, still praying for us and still giving to our ministry, we are eternally grateful. This story is your story as well as ours. You helped make it happen! Our career has been abundantly rich in fruitfulness and fabulously satisfying in fulfillment because of your participation. You have shared your homes with us in generous hospitality, your time in faithful prayer, and your funds in liberal giving—yes, to the mundane financial needs of our lives, but also to those special needs which we have had as vision drove us to new heights of involvement in wider ministries. We agree with the comment made by one family who gave a sizeable gift toward the printing of the

Scriptures translated into Dani, "We feel we have been a part of your ministry to the Dani these many years, and would like to give." How appropriate!

To the leadership and staff of our mission, UFM International now known as CrossWorld: They worked faithfully here at home, serving in the mundane of missions, so we could be free to enjoy the sensational and make it happen out there in the field. These men and women provided firm, sacrificial leadership and created a family atmosphere of which we were proud to belong, and which held us firm in the many crises of missions.

To those who have encouraged us to pen these stories: These are many and without them we probably would not have taken the time to complete our story, or we would have been sidetracked into other activities.

To those who have given their time, literary knowledge and experience to read and to make suggestions on the content of the volume and the flow of the story: We make special mention of Mrs. Grace Davies and Mrs. Gwen Plut. Both willingly turned their microscopic literary lens, loaded with training, skill, experience, and profound perseverance, onto the text, making it more readable.

And lastly, to my wife and our two children who have been a major part of this career: Though our son, David, slipped off to Glory ahead of us, Dawn is still very much a product of those early years among the Dani where she grew up. While the Dani's claim could not be realized that since she was born among them she must return to them, she was a part of our ministry during those early years, enjoying life with us among the Dani at Mulia. A Divine call led her with her husband, John, and our four grandchildren, to a different part of Indonesia for a time, then on to Thailand where they are now in ministry.

Words fail me, and my eyes get teary when I try to express God's goodness in providing me with a mate who has stuck with me these many years. My call was her call; her call was my call; and together our call was God's call taking us to the Dani in 1960. Together we arrived in that strange land and among a strange people; together we learned the language and served; together we raised our children; together we worked our way through the normal struggles of married life; and together we are growing old. I am most grateful!

An Introduction:
some explanations!

—〜〜—

A s the years of our missionary career continue to increase, and stories of our personal involvement in the lives of the peoples to whom we ministered continue to be told, increasingly people are saying to us, "Dave and Esther, you need to write your story." This we have attempted to do in the following pages.

In contemplating an appropriate title for these memoirs, we felt that no better name could be found than the simple statement: **The Amazing Danis.** And that is what we have used, feeling it best pulls together the events, the experiences, and the people who have been a part of our rich and rewarding missionary career spanning nearly fifty years of service.

This is not a documentary. We have not worked alone; others have shared in the events of this story. And wherever possible we have included them. However, it is impossible to make mention of all of them with their stories. Written here are those experiences in which we have been personally involved and which have shaped us and our ministry during our career.

During our nearly 50 years of ministry, many changes have occurred which complicate the telling of this story, especially in the name changes within mission organizations. In those early years of our ministry, the Unevangelized Fields Mission became UFM International, then more recently, CrossWorld. UFM Australia became The Asian Pacific Christian Mission (APCM), and has more recently merged with the Pioneers mission. The Regions Beyond Missionary Union became RBMU International and some time ago merged with and is now known as Worldteam.

For reader clarity, though our mission has recently changed its name to CrossWorld, I will use the banner of our organization under which we served for nearly 50 years and the one with which most of you are familiar, UFM International.

Numerous name changes also have occurred with the island where we have served. In 1960 when we began our missionary career, that island located directly north of Australia was called New Guinea, but was actually two different independent countries. The eastern half, controlled by Australia, was called Australian New Guinea, while the western half, controlled by the Dutch, was called Dutch New Guinea. Several years later, the eastern half of the island was given its independence and renamed Papua New Guinea, while the western half of the island was taken over by the Indonesian government, made a part of Indonesia, and renamed Irian Jaya, which is probably the name with which my reader is most familiar. However, during the latter 1990's, in a strange concession, the Indonesian government allowed the people of Irian Jaya to change their name to Papua.

Through this name change, the Papuan people of the western part of the island of New Guinea are making a statement. They want the world to know that, though still governed by Indonesia, they rightly are Papuans and belong to the eastern half of the island now known as Papua New Guinea. And you can guess where this is taking them!

Confusion could also occur in my use of the word "Dani." Linguistically, there are two main branches of the Dani tribe. The Dani people inhabiting the large fertile valley drained by the Baliem River in the heart of Papua (Irian Jaya) are known as the Baliem Dani.

In the early 1960's, the number of Baliem Dani speakers was estimated to be some 75,000 who were very resistant to the Gospel. Whereas the Dani people residing on the western edge of the Baliem Dani population in the Baliem Valley and moving westward nearly an hour's flying time from the Baliem Dani, became known in mission circles as the Western Dani. They were estimated to number about 150,000 at that time. Acceptance of medicine, along with teaching on better hygiene in the villages and the introduction of more nutritious foods, has greatly increased that number. Some of us believe the current number of Western Dani speakers to be around 200,000. It was this tribe, the Western Dani tribe, which has been very responsive to change in general, and to the Gospel message in particular. It is about the Western Dani that our story is written.

And it was to the Western Dani that five missions directed their activities beginning in the mid-1950's and on into the early 1960's. These were The Christian and Missionary Alliance, the Australian Baptists, RBMU International, and UFM Australia with UFM of North America. Each had a slice of the geographical area populated by the Western Dani tribe, determined largely by the topography and the availability of personnel at that time.

And we respected each other's ministry in our separate geographical areas, feeling that since it was all the Lord's work, we would be better stewards of our time, our funds, and our personnel by not duplicating our efforts in the same geographical area. In this way we were able to maximize the total mission team effort as we minimized the tag, i.e., the banner of our organization. And we are sort of proud of that!

All this is my attempt to clarify the larger picture of missions among the Western Dani of Papua, the location in which our story is set. I also want to inform my readers that unless specifically mentioned, my use of the term "Dani" means the "Western Dani" not the Baliem Dani.

There is one further feature about the Dani that I want to mention. They (the Western Dani) have no "s," "c," or "v" sounds in their speech, nor do they have laterals ("l" sounds) at the end of words. Thus, how does one handle our name: Scovill? Well, it comes out as "Kobo," pronounced like "Hobo" but with a "K" (no comments please!) and that is what will be seen in the following stories. I also ask for your understanding in my generous use of Dani words in the text. Somehow the stories seem better expressed with the use of Dani words and phrases.

Finally, I must add that our career can easily be broken into three phases. We worked with the Dani at the interior station called Mulia from 1960 until 1980. At that time we felt it best to move out of their area to allow nationals to transition into leadership roles within the church/community. We had also been elected to the responsibility of field leadership by that time, and felt it best to move to Sentani, a more central location on the coast, to be more easily accessible to the total field.

While carrying on this responsibility, our vision took us into new outreaches in the coastal areas with special emphasis on an area along the north coast of Papua. In our mission strategy planning, this area became known as the Dark Triangle due to the disease and dissipation of the people living along those large crocodile-infested rivers. Several times a year we would make trips into this area to give member care to our national missionaries placed there, as well as to assist them in the development of leadership for those isolated villages in that area. This was the second phase of our career.

The third phase began with our move to Jakarta, the capital of Indonesia, in 1987. Jakarta is a mega city of over 13 million people set in a third world country. Visas were getting more difficult to obtain and our mission wanted increased positive input in and better relationships with the offices through which we obtained proper documents to reside in Indonesia. So we were asked to move to Jakarta where we set up an office then spent 16 years as advisors to faithful, committed, responsible national staff who operated it. In addition, we were involved in a church planting ministry in that city and its suburbs, as well as in other cities in the greater Indonesia.

This book is the story about our work among the Western Dani people in the interior of Papua. It does not touch the other two locations of our ministry where we have also left strong churches under the direction of national leadership, nor does it include other stories which scream to be told — perhaps sometime in the future.

But for now, read on.

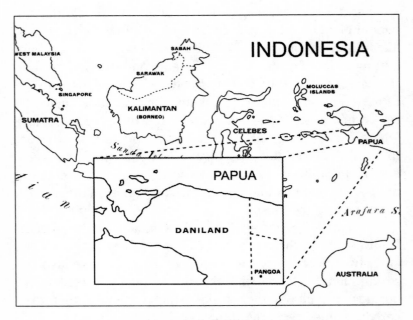

Map of Indonesia with Papua inset

Prologue: The Dani

—ᔕᔕᔕ—

A son is born

The infant shivered in the dampness of that chilly evening. His chest and lungs expanded, drawing in the cold night air, and then he cried—his very first sound—and it was a cry of rebellion against the world into which he had come. Fate had determined this one was to live and his breathing continued after the first few gasps of cold air.

Breathing he was, but unaware was he of the blackness of the night around him, and of the cold rain beating against his little body. He was unaware that his mother, coming home in the evening hours with a heavy load of sweet potatoes on her back for her family, feeling the pangs of childbirth, had merely stopped along the trail, bent down into a squatting position and given birth to him. And there he was, still wallowing on the wet ground.

The rain was coming harder now. Hence, without cutting the cord, since the afterbirth had not yet arrived, the mother picked up the shivering, slippery child with her cold, wet, dirty hands and, holding him closely to her bosom, went on down the trail to her village. Once there, some of the older women experienced in traditional methods of midwifery were quickly called. They would have helped in this birth as well, by wrapping their arms tightly about her abdomen and squeezing the baby out.

While these were coming, some of the younger women went out into that dark, wet night and gathered the *ndooli* tree leaves, the only type of leaves used by the women in childbirth. Others of the women called the husband who brought more firewood into the house, then slipped quietly out. He was happy that his wife had delivered the baby, but afraid to look upon his own child for it had not yet been wiped dry. Had he seen the blood on the baby, he knew he would lose his eyesight.

When the women returned with the leaves, some of them were placed under the mother where she sat with the newborn infant on her crossed legs in front of the fire. She was waiting for the afterbirth to arrive so she could cut the cord; it was making handling of the child difficult because of getting tangled in the leaves. While waiting, she put other leaves about the fire to be dry and warm to place on the child to keep him comfortable. Later, some would also be placed in the net bag where the newborn would be cradled.

While these women hustled about seeking to make the mother as comfortable as possible in her sitting position, from about the fire in one of the nearby houses came a voice calling out above the sound of the raindrops now reduced to a gentle pitter-patter on the grass roof, "Is it our kind, or your kind?" ("Is it a boy or a girl?") Back came the answer: "It is your kind, but pay attention you men there in the house. The afterbirth has not yet been delivered!"

The insinuation was most evident and one of the men in the house immediately aroused himself and came outside. Standing under the eaves of the house where the newborn was with its mother, he took two rocks and, while striking them together, said: "This woman has not paid me sufficient bride price; hence, it is forbidden for her to bear a normal child. The payment which I have desired causes my teeth to chatter." Over and over this phrase was repeated as the rocks were struck together.

Still the afterbirth had not come, so others of the men took turns striking the rocks and repeating that phrase until the announcement of the coming of the afterbirth. Then, one of the women helping with the birth, with a small bamboo knife, cut the cord close to the little tummy and, while the others in the house covered their eyes, she took a forked stick and wrapped the afterbirth in leaves and grass. Then, placing it near the wall boards of that tiny house, she burned it and the smell of burning flesh permeated the air both within and without the house.

The newborn son, now warm from the fire as well as from the warm leaves placed around his body, cuddled against his mother's breast. He slept soundly and breathed deeply of the air of this strange world into which he had come.

The mother remained sitting on that pile of leaves, adding to it when necessary to ensure that none see the blood. Here she remained, with the other women bringing her food, until the bleeding subsided.

There was much happiness over the birth of the male child. One of the older women reminded the rest that she knew the child would be a boy. As one empowered to predict the sex of the unborn child, had she not taken the mother down to the stream and, after placing a certain leaf in the stream, taken water and poured it on the mother's stomach? The water had run straight down off the stomach, she had noted, promising the birth of a son. Had part run down on one side, and part on the other side of the protruding stomach, a girl would have been born. In payment for this, the mother had given her a very valuable shell and two newly woven net bags.

The mother, too, joined in the happy conversation about that fire; she boasted of the ease and swiftness of her delivery. She did not know that her husband, while cooking the potato vines the evening before due to his wife's imminent delivery, had added a special leaf potion that would assist her in the delivery. These were leaves to prepare the birth passage for the swift exit of the child—leaves which ensured she would have as little pain as possible when the pangs of childbirth came upon her and which would protect and stimulate the newborn youngster to cry.

By this time, the women who had gathered to help in the birth of the child began to disperse, going back to their own homes to rest. The mother, however, knowing that she was still bleeding, continued through most of those long night hours in a sitting position, adding more leaves as necessary. Toward morning, feeling that her bleeding had stopped, she lay down on the hard dirt floor with the newborn at her breast close to the fire, and she slept.

As she slept the sleep of one as drugged, she dreamed she had given birth to a son who was lying tenderly at her breast on the dirt floor beside her. She reached out to cuddle him, and then became aware not only of movement at her breast, but heard the cry and felt the coldness of his little form. Instantly she awoke, aware that the fire had gone out in the night. Stoking it with dry wood from the wood hanger above the firebox, she then blew on some of the live coals to produce a flame. In a few moments, the flames lifted their arms in warmth to the mother with her small son seated there beside its flame.

Morning had come, and the mother, refreshed by her rest, quickly gathered up the leaves on which she had been sitting. Taking them outside, she burned them before the village came to life. Then, going back inside and finding several uncooked potatoes in a net bag hanging against the boards of the wall, she scraped back the ashes of her fire and buried them, her breakfast, in those ashes.

While waiting for these to roast, she tucked her grass skirts, now stained with the blood of childbirth, under her and reached for her newborn son already whimpering in his bed of leaves hanging in the net bag against the boards of the house. She knew what he wanted, for already her breasts were full with sustenance for him. Opening the net bag, and picking off the leaves from his little face, she held him to her breast and he drank deeply of life's nourishment.

****

It was now several days later and she was feeling her strength return. Already she had begun to cook the family potato vines and, as per custom, for two days she had cooked the vines, then, thrown them away without eating them or giving them to her husband. This was part of the purification ritual at the birth of a child. Today, after feeding the child, she placed him fondly back into his net bag, swung him to her back, positioning the net bag securely on the back of her head and, picking up her weeding stick, she deliberately and slowly made her way to her potato garden. This time the weight of her son hanging on her head, the movement of his precious little body upon her back, and the love and tenderness sensed in her heart, gave her momentary pleasure as she returned to the routine tasks of the women in her culture.

Struck with a spirit arrow

It was several weeks later. Since midmorning the mother had been in her garden. Throughout the afternoon hours she had been bending over those sweet potato plants, stirring the soil around them with a small pointed stick, the only implement which she had in her culture. Her arms were beginning to feel the fatigue of the day's work, and her back was beginning to ache. Several times she stood up, stretching her back and adjusting the net bag hanging on the back of her head which held the child she had birthed.

This time as she adjusted it she felt movement in the leaves and then heard the furious cry of the little one. Realizing that he was probably hungry and since she, too, wanted to rest, she sat down on the ground, swinging the little fighting monster in the bag off of her head, and laid him across her thighs as she sat cross-legged on the ground.

Reaching through the leaves in the bag, she lifted out the child and, leaning over him, cooed softly and with pleasure as he hungrily suckled the breast offered to him. Looking about, the mother realized the sun was setting and noticed in the distance a cloud bringing the normal afternoon shower. Hurriedly she fed him, and, after making him comfortable in the leaves of the net bag, she hung him up on a broken-off branch of a nearby tree. Then, picking up her digging stick, she quickly began hunting for and digging up the sweet potatoes for the family's evening meal.

Placing these potatoes in one of several net bags the Dani mothers always carry with them in their daily duties, she swung the heavy bag of potatoes to her back, positioning it to hang properly from her head and horizontally across her lower back. Then, picking up her baby and hanging him likewise from her head on top of the bag of sweet potatoes, she began walking slowly back to her village some distance away.

Bringing home sweet potatoes

Nearing her village she stopped to wash her potatoes in the small stream which ran down from their village site. With the baby still lying comfortably across her back, she dumped the bag of sweet potatoes in the stream and began scrubbing off the dirt with her hands. She was not aware that all the refuse from the village, both from the pigs running through the village as well as from the place out in the long grass which the people used for their toilet, drained into that water. Indeed, she did not think, for, after washing and putting the potatoes back into her bag, she bent down and drank deeply from the stream before she climbed out of the steep ravine.

Still a distance from her village, she quickened her pace fearing that the rain would soon catch up with her. And it did! The cold blast of that torrential shower not only chilled her but soaked the small child she carried on her back.

On reaching her village, she slipped quickly through the small door of her round house and pulled down some kindling from the firebox above the fire. Though it was only a few minutes before the warmth of its blaze enveloped both her and the child, who now lay across her thighs as she sat drying out in front of that fire, the consequences were soon to be felt.

Realizing that her husband would soon be coming bringing with him the evening firewood, the duty of all the men, and that he would be hungry, she immediately placed the cooking rocks on a small rack on top of the fire she had made. While waiting for them to heat, she prepared the small pit—dug out of the ground near the wall within the house—by lining it with leaves she had gathered on her way home from the garden.

Then, taking a small forked stick and working it as one works a pair of tongs, she carefully placed the hot rocks, one by one, in the pit and around them placed the sweet potatoes and sweet potato vines she had brought home. Then, using other more common leaves and grasses, she placed a covering over the pit, her "stove," and waited for her evening meal to steam cook.

It was not long before she heard the crash of an armful of firewood outside the doorway. Her husband slipped inside, pulling the firewood in after him and placing it in the hanging rack above the firebox to dry. He, too, was soaked from the rain and began immediately to scrape the water off himself using a small chip of wood. His long waist-length hair, tucked into several net bags his wives had made for him, was also wet. Stripping his head of those bags and hanging them up to dry, he let the warmth of the fire dry his long greasy locks.

After eating their potatoes together, he placed his long hair back into the net bags, reached for his stone axe and slipped quietly out into the night. He dare not stay longer or sleep with his wife, for his son was not yet walking. It was forbidden to spend the night with one's own wife until such a time as the child was weaned. Hence, he made his way through the pigs that were waiting at the doorway of his wife's house to the *kunume* "men's house" where he spent the night.

The wife, having forgotten to put the pigs in earlier, called out to them. Immediately they jumped through the doorway of her little round house looking for their sweet potatoes which she had prepared for them. These she tossed on the dirt floor of her hut and waited until they had scrounged for the last little tidbit. Before bedtime, they too, needed a gentle caress. So they came rubbing up against her and she, clutching her son in one arm, turned and rubbed them about the underbelly, giving each a gentle pat as she shooed it into its tiny hutch on the far side of the fire. Then she closed the boards after them. Here, with her, they spent the night hours.

After again nursing her infant, the mother stoked the fire one last time, and then lay down, the child at her breast, to spend the long weary night. The fire burned brightly, warming the house so that all perspired freely. Then, slowly and silently, as a thief slipping out into the night, those long-fingered flames glowed less and less until only a few red coals remained. For a time these continued to warm the contented, grunting pigs, as well as the mother with her child lying on a rough piece of bark in front of the fire.

Several hours later the mother awoke—her body hot and perspiring. Sitting up, she looked about to see who had built such a hot fire. Feeling the tiny infant at her side whose body did not share that intense heat, she realized that she was being consumed with a fever. Reaching up for another piece of firewood, she became aware also of intense pain in her chest which made her breathing labored and difficult. "A spirit has struck me," she muttered as she clung to two of the four upright poles on which the roof rested, rising out of the corners of that small firebox in the middle of the hut.

By morning, she lay prostrate on a piece of bark in front of the fire, intermittently hacking from congestion deep within her chest, her body racked with pain. The little one at her side began to cry. Love reached out to him and, summoning all her strength, she pulled herself into a sitting position, lifting the child to her breast. He drank, but alas, already the sickness had depleted her milk supply and the hungry child angrily cried out.

At this point the father, wondering where his morning sweet potatoes were, slipped into the house. There he found his sick wife leaning against the upright poles rising out of the fireplace in the house, holding the screaming tugging infant at her empty breast. The pigs, anxious to be let out, squealed and grunted their disapproval. Reaching over to their pens, the father took out the boards which held them in. And each pig went bouncing out of the house to relieve itself and to begin its daily search for food.

He took the infant son from his wife. As she told him that sometime during the night a spirit came in and struck her, she indicated with one hand that the arrow went in right above her shoulder, between the shoulder and the collar bone and, with the other, that it came out below her lower rib on the other side. Flipping her empty breast with her hand, she indicated to her husband the reason for the child's crying. Then, her strength failing, she lay over on the floor, close to the fire to keep warm, while the husband thoughtfully and, with a certain amount of anxiety, took a stick, pushed back the ashes of the fire and buried several potatoes in those ashes. These would be his breakfast.

Fear gripped his heart as he wondered who could succor the infant now that the mother was sick. He wondered which "spirit arrow" had struck his wife; he wondered if this was in retribution for some sin she had committed and if it would prove fatal as it had to several of his relatives. He also wondered if the spirit that caused it could be appeased so that his son, the pleasure and prestige of his family, would have a mother to care for him.

Unable to quell the crying of the infant, the father took him out to some of the other women in the village asking if they would nurse him since the mother was sick. There was instant response as one of the women reached out for the young child and placed him at her breast. The husband then went slowly back to his wife's house. Taking his sweet potatoes from the ashes, he returned to the *kunume,* the "men's house."

Into the fire

It was several days later that the mother, sufficiently recovered, could again nurse her baby. This particular morning, several hours before "the singing of the early morning birds," the baby, being hungry, had awakened and began to fuss. Picking up the little tot, she reached up for some firewood and, after stoking the fire, sat close to its blaze, warming and nursing the hungry child.

She was not aware of how it happened; she was aware only of the agonized screaming of her child. Feeling on her lap where he should have been, she could not locate the squirming body. Then suddenly, aware that she had fallen asleep there in front of that blaze, she jumped up to find that, after nursing, the child had rolled off her lap into the fire.

She picked him up out of the hot ashes where he had fallen and with an anxious heart stoked the blaze to create enough light in the house to see. Fortunately, he had fallen feet first into the ashes burning only his right leg and knee and, in struggling, had gotten his little hand burned and blistered. The severe pain was most evident from the terrorized cry of the infant, and the mother, now wide awake, cuddled him close, repeating the *wa-wa-wa-wa* sounds to quiet him.

When his screaming subsided and, exhausted, he drifted off into a restless sleep, the mother took out several clean leaves from the net bag in which she carried him. After placing her saliva on the leaves, then on her son's ugly burns, she took a piece of string and tied those leaves over the burn on his leg and, as best she could, over the blisters on his hand.

Sitting there in front of that fire with the child on her lap, she could not help but feel sorry for him. She also thought of how fortunate she was that he had not burned to death. Was not his little cousin several months older than he, burned to death only a few weeks ago? It seemed that the mother likewise had fallen asleep in front of the fire with the child on her lap. He had rolled off into a bed of red-hot coals. His entire body had been burned; his hair had been completely singed off; his nose, eyes and lips had so puffed up from the blisters of the flames that his face had been nearly unrecognizable. He was still weakly crying when his mother had awakened. Quickly she had gathered the little one into her arms, but it was hopeless. Several hours later, that little life had slipped away with the mother cuddling only a small burnt corpse which the family had cremated that afternoon. She shuddered at the thought, thankful that her son was still alive.

The birds were beginning to sing, and daylight began to push back the dark shades of night. It was not long until her husband stepped into that little house and, after letting the pigs out, scraped back the ashes and put the sweet potatoes into the fireplace to roast. Since his wife's sickness, he had been doing this himself while waiting for her to recuperate and take up the routine tasks of a wife and mother.

After covering the potatoes with ashes and stoking the fire, he glanced across the fire at his wife and son, and then noticed the leaves tied about his leg and hand. *"Nonggop eekerak?"* "What happened?" he asked. Simply and tearfully she told her husband how she had fallen asleep while nursing and the child had rolled off into the fire.

A moment of resentment and hot anger burned within his breast. He could not understand why his wife could not take better care of his son. *Indeed these women have only a pig's dumb nature,* he thought. Seething inwardly he muttered, *"Wam ore abet aret o!"* "Indeed the woman is the other half of the pig," and, picking up his sweet potatoes, he stepped outside, adjusted his gourd, then returned to the men's house. Taking his bow and arrow from the carrier hanging from the ceiling in the men's house, he made for the forests. He wanted to be alone; frustrations of life had driven him out this day to hunt. He had no other way to relieve the pressures built up inside him.

The mother, still holding the child, ate her potatoes in silence. Then, remembering that the leaves in the child's bag smelled of urine and feces which needed her attention, she carefully took the child and slipped out the door to give him to one of the women in a nearby hut. Taking the bag of leaves out to the edge of the village enclosure, she dumped out the dirty leaves. Nearby were a few shrubs of the type whose leaves were soft and pliable. These she plucked, placed them in her net bag and trudged back to her little house.

After retrieving her youngster who was now wide awake though whimpering because of his burns, she untied the crude string which held the leaves against the burn. Taking new ones, with a fresh supply of saliva, she again bound up his sores. The blisters on his hand had already broken; it would be only a matter of time until they healed. After feeding him, she made him comfortable again in his bed of soft new leaves, then, swung him onto her back. Fastening the net bag securely on her head, she reached for her digging stick and stepped outside into the brilliant sunshine. *Due to my illness, the weeds in my garden will be bad,* she thought as she made her way up the steep mountainside to her garden spot.

Late that afternoon, she arrived back at her village with a bag of sweet potatoes and a bag of sweet potato vines for the family. Placing these to cook in the small pit with the little bit of firewood she still had in the house, she picked up the hollowed-out gourd, her water pitcher, and went off down the trail to the stream a short distance away to fill her container with water. Having filled the gourd and drinking deeply herself, she made her way back to her small house.

Her husband still had not arrived and, since the potatoes were already cooked, she opened the pit and ate. Then she fed the pigs that were clamoring at her doorway for their food. After eating, they very obediently went into their small hutches inside her house and, grunting their satisfaction, settled down for the night.

Not knowing if there would be any wood for the evening since her husband, disgusted with her, had gone to the forest to hunt and, since dusk was settling in, she went outside again to pick up a few dry branches to keep the house warm during the night. These she tied in a bundle and, balancing them on her head, made her way back to her little house. Nearing its doorway, she noticed the flames rising up from the fireplace, giving light in the house, and her husband, who had just arrived back from his hunting trip, sitting in front of the fire.

She slipped in with her little bundle of firewood and greeted him. His eyes were sparkling as he pulled two small possum from the bag hanging on his shoulder. These he lay out on the floor saying, "Shall we cook them tonight or save them for tomorrow?" His wife and he, always hungry for meat, were anxious to cook them, so he began at once to singe the hair from the animals by turning them over and over above the fire, then, scraped off the hair with a stick.

They thought they could enjoy them in the privacy of their own little round house. However, as the smell began drifting out into the village yard, reaching other nostrils, the secret was out. "Hey, you there, what are you burning?" came the cry across the village yard. "*Lek o!*" "No, we are not burning anything," the answer was shot back.

But it was not long until little eyes and big appetites could not resist seeing and tasting what the occasion was all about. They watched from outside the doorway as well as through the cracks and slats of the house. Sensing the irresistibility of the moment for the younger ones, and knowing the custom of the tribe to build one's own prestige through acts of generosity, the father invited the children to come in.

After the possums were cooked, with a bamboo knife he cut the meat into little squares, dividing them equally with those who now filled his small house. A large portion he gave to his wife saying, "You have been sick and need this to make your veins strong."

While the meat was being eaten, someone noticed that the father himself had given away his own share, and offered the father a piece of his. The father however, knowing the meat hunger of the children, merely turned away saying, "You eat it, my son. I am a man." Nevertheless, after all had slipped out and gone back to their own sleeping quarters, a tiny thought of self-pity rose in his heart as he bid his wife goodnight and returned to the men's house. Placing his bow and arrows back in the community arrow hanger, and shedding his hair of the outer layers of the net bags, he crawled upstairs, found a place to lie down, and slept.

Meanwhile, his wife, after eating a good portion of the meat, wrapped the remaining part tightly in a leaf and placed it in her bag hanging against the boards of the wall—except for one small tender piece. This she placed in her mouth and chewed it slowly and deliberately. When it was thoroughly masticated, lifting her son to a sitting position on her lap, she placed her mouth next to his and spit portions of this meat into her infant's mouth. This was new to him but he thoroughly enjoyed it, swallowing furiously until that piece of meat was gone, then, yelling lustily for more.

That was it, however; his meager diet of meat had begun; now it was more milk. Again, the mother nursed the child and, while doing so, pulled down more firewood. After stoking the fire, she with her child lay down close to it to spend the evening hours.

This is the beginning of the life of the yet unnamed child, for his real character had not yet been discovered.

****

No one really knows when it all began for the Dani people. Their legends vary. Though some sources say the men came out of a cleft in the mountain, most accounts indicate that two men came up out of a hole in the ground near the interior city of Wamena, in a place called Taakobak. As they crawled out on the rim of this hole and endeavored to walk upon the ground, they sank in mud and water. Quickly they buried the stone axes which they carried, whereupon the ground immediately solidified and they were able to walk upon it.

Some time afterward, and fortunately for the men, two women appeared out of the same hole in the ground. One, so the legend goes, carried a banana shoot; the other carried the shoot of the sweet potato. Somehow a dog managed to squirm out of the same hole with the women and in its ear were found lodged a cucumber seed and a gourd seed. Those seeds, with the banana shoot and sweet potato shoot, they planted and life began. What happened next is obvious.

Briefly—since I will give more detail in the following pages—the two men took the women and thus began the two main branches of the moiety system within the Dani culture in which it is forbidden to marry one of the same clan. This would be considered incest, marrying one's sister or brother, and was punishable by death, for the consequences of such an act would cause all the potatoes in the valley to rot, precipitating an area-wide famine.

Like ripples in the water, these people moved out from Taakobak; for some strange reason, the movement was always toward the west. Ever westward their adventurous natures carried them. Often there was no choice; they were driven by their enemies. More often, however, it was in search of more and better land where one could raise bigger and better gardens which in turn would allow them food to raise more pigs, which necessitated more wives to care for those pigs, which produced more posterity and wealth, and thus brought a man to the apex of the Dani culture: more power and prestige.

Villages were almost always comprised of the two moiety groups which provided marriageable partners for the other. The *kunume* "men's house" occupied the most central and strategic position in the village with the houses of the wives built in a loose semicircle around the men's house.

In that the Western Dani practiced pluralistic leadership, a single village could boast several such men's houses, depending on the number of that man's extended family members who were looking to him for leadership.

Without question, the *kunume* was the hub of the village. In it and behind the *kunume* in a small hutch, approximately three feet wide and five feet long, built up on posts, was kept the spirit fetishes which the men would use to maintain the normal religious routines and spirit rituals of life in that village.

It was here, in the men's house, that the weightiest of all community decisions were made, along with plans to execute those decisions. Here it was that the boys, newly weaned from their mothers' breasts, at 4 to 5 years of age, would move to be with their fathers, joining their older kinsmen in the life of the *kunume* and would sleep with them around the fire.

All Dani huts are round and constructed with boards approximately six feet in length, crudely hewn (split) from larger logs, formerly with their stone axes. These boards are driven several inches into the ground to give the house stability, with an inner and outer wall between which grass and leaves are tightly stuffed. Then two horizontal saplings, one on the inside and one on the outside near the top and bottom of the upright wall boards, are placed into position and lashed together with very strong vine, snugging the inside and the outer wall together in a tight sturdy manner.

The bottom end of the poles serving as roof rafters are placed at the tips of the upright wall boards and rest on the top horizontal sapling, then move up, with a rise of about three feet, to form an apex in the middle of the house. This apex, formed by the poles of the roof rafters, rests on four upright poles spaced in a square about 30 inches apart in the middle of the house. On the ground level, the inside of the square serves as the fireplace, with those four poles moving upward serving as posts to which the upstairs floor joists are tied, the firewood box above the fire is hung, and upon which those sitting around the fire can lean. There was only a dirt floor with scattered pieces of bark on which they sat around the fire; sleeping was done upstairs.

An upstairs floor is made of slender, bamboo-type reeds tied to larger poles bisecting the diameter of the house which in turn are tied to the four upright center poles around the fireplace. These four poles extend upward to support the roof rafters which provide the necessary construction to which the grass roof is fastened.

The small round hut being built

The dying embers of the fire downstairs, plus the handful of large live coals they would place in the smaller upstairs fireplace, provided the warmth necessary for the tired bodies that climbed the five feet to the upstairs floor, using a notched pole at the edge of the house. Here, lying down with feet to the fire and head to the wall, they would spend the night hours. If one could stand a reasonable amount of smoke which would eventually pass through the grass of the roof, the trapped heat of the fire underneath the roof provided about as cozy a comfort as possible for the bodies that sprawled like spokes of a wheel around that fire.

The typical Dani round house when completed

The difference between the men's house and the women's house was basically size and function. The men's house, always taboo for the women due to the fetishes of the men kept there, was spacious and roomy to accommodate the number of men who would gather there to sleep as well as to discuss important community events. There was a front and also a back door to the men's house.

The women's house was rarely more than eight feet in diameter and normally boasted the pig stalls at the far end, opposite the only door in the house. As can be deduced, the woman was the caretaker of the family pigs. Hers was the responsibility to feed them, to nurture their young—even to suckle them herself should the mother pig die in giving birth or be killed—and to place them in their stalls in her house at night. She would then spend the night hours with them and her family in the same quarters. Hence, the title: *"Kwe ti, wam ore aret o!"* "The woman is the other half of the pig."

And sad to say, her role in life was not much better. In a way, she was the chattel of the man—given in a business deal to a man, normally an older, wealthy, polygamist—by the father if he was living, or by the older brother, to pay off a family obligation or to increase his social standing: his power and prestige in the community.

****

The Dani's world is conceptualized as an overturned dish. On the top of its dome lives a race of small dwarflike creatures having little effect or influence on earth's creatures below. Underneath the dome exists their world of spirits with their various hierarchies which do influence his life.

The bottom of the earth is flat with a long dark tunnel underneath through which the sun passes from west to east during the night hours, then, it slips out of its tunnel to dawn upon the world of darkness and to begin the cycle of another day. The darkest part of the night just before dawn is when the spirits within the Dani world gather just inside the entrance of that tunnel to discuss the direction of the day's activity.

The long night of the Dani is broken by a variety of sounds and senses which arouse the sleeping forms who groggily sit up to put more wood on the fire keeping the house comfortable. Often it is the cry in the night of a hungry baby needing to be nursed, or of a sick child needing attention. Often is heard the unhurried exit of flatulence, the natural result of a diet of sweet potatoes on which the Dani survives. Other times it is just the slow slender finger of cold which moves into that little round hut and, in the receding warmth of the untended fire, makes those sleeping bodies so uncomfortable that one will wake up, poke around in the ash until he finds a live coal which he then blows upon until a tiny flame shoots out from its blackened remains. With this, the groggy sleeper works until a blazing fire again warms him and the house, whereupon he topples over on the floor to continue his sleep.

This ritual occurs normally twice during the night, at midnight (*oonikiya mbere eeke paga* "when day and night meet"), and again about three o'clock in the morning *(towe oone iyaalok eeke paga* "at the first chirping of the birds"). As the sun moves eastward to burst out of the mouth of its tunnel to bring dawn to another day, the short boards which fit crosswise into the doorways of both the men's and the women's houses can be heard opening as they make their way to the toilet area to relieve themselves. For some, it is just a few steps away from the house; for others it is to move deeper into the grass. The point is that there are the normal allocated, acceptable places in each village setting. And the people are to take care of this matter before being exposed and embarrassed by the coming of the dawn.

And it is at this moment in time that the role of the women and the role of the men in the normal Dani day move in different directions.

As the woman tucks her underclothes—a few strips of her grass skirt—underneath her, and makes her way back to the warmth of her fire, the pigs are already creating a fuss to be let out of their stalls. One by one, she pulls the boards out of their slots and the pigs make their way quickly out of the house and into the grass to also relieve themselves, then to forage for any fresh fecal material left either by mothers who tossed the soiled leaves of their tiny tots into the grass, or by others who had relieved themselves a few moments before. Such is the strange twist of nature which requires that all life survives on that of another.

By this time a roaring fire in the fireplace will be spreading its warmth throughout the hut. Enjoying its comfort and, while waiting for a good disposition of coals into which the morning sweet potatoes can be submerged, the mother will nurse her infant, or mend her net bags to take to the garden later on that day, or perhaps she will work on a new one in anticipation of the next child.

It is not long before the quantity of red-hot coals indicates it is time to bury the sweet potatoes in those hot coals and ashes. Taking a short board, the women will scrape back the coals and the ashes, placing in that indentation a layer of sweet potatoes whose skins had earlier been glazed in the flame. These she will cover with the ashes and red-hot coal mixture and stoke the fire to a hot blaze.

Meanwhile, the men and boys a short distance away in the men's house busy themselves with rekindling the fire to warm themselves. While waiting for their women folks to come with the potatoes, some men sharpen their axes, others make handles for them, and others carve the hardwood points of the arrows or fit them into their bamboo shafts. Still others, risking being laughed at by the other men, go right to their wives' houses where they will play with their children while waiting for their sweet potatoes to cook.

That initial burst of direct sunlight from behind the mountain peaks is the force which breaks into the sleepy life of the village alerting all that the day has officially begun. Now there is no reason to loiter about that cozy fire. The sun's rays are enough to bring the necessary warmth into the Dani's world, and the grass is now dry for the traveler.

The noise level in the village noticeably heightens. The men yell for their breakfast—another sweet potato; the women yell back that the potatoes are on the way. Pigs squeal as they are kicked out of the way to make room for the occupants of the house making their way out the small door. Dogs bark; babies cry because the attention of the mother is temporarily given to other duties; and the occasional infant throws a temper tantrum, writhing on the ground and screaming at the top of his lungs. The day has begun.

Some of the men with their axes make their way to the forests to cut boards for a fence or a house being built; others move off to their gardens with their digging sticks to prepare the soil to be planted by the women; others, with bow and arrows in hand, slip out to the forest to hunt possum or wild pig; still others, with simply their net bags slung over their shoulders and bow and arrows in hand, wander off to visit a friend or kinsman in the next valley.

The woman's preparation for the day in the garden begins. Untangling her several grass skirts she had slipped off the night before, one by one she carefully winds them about her waist, swings her newborn to hang from her head with it lying horizontally in the net bag across the flat of her back, calls for the younger brother or sister who will accompany her that day, picks up her digging stick, and heads for the garden.

Across rivers and ravines, up the steep mountain slopes she climbs to her garden. Once there, the sleeping infant is hung in the shade of a bush within hearing distance of the mother as she, with the older child, moves to the green potato vines which carpet the ground. Bending over, stick in hand, she begins the toil of the day—working around those tender sweet potato plants. She loosens the ground around the new vines taking root; she mounds the dirt over the potential sweet potato in development; and at the same time she prunes the vine so it will produce more and bigger potatoes.

By now it is high noon, and beads of perspiration can be seen on her furrowed brow. Only once has she heard the baby fuss, but now he is screaming. Even the sapling on which the child hangs is set in furious motion by the angry gesticulating child hanging in the net bag below. It is nursing time for the infant and resting time for the mother.

She picks up the net bag full of potato leaves she has plucked while weeding, swings this to her head, and makes her way to the crying infant. The tender sapling immediately rights itself as the mother relieves it of its burden. In its shade now sits the mother; her cry of *wa-wa-wa-wa* immediately soothes the frustrated and irritated antics of the infant as she swings the net to her crossed legs and pulls him out of the soft leaves which, while these leaves kept him warm and comfortable, did not supply the necessary nourishment to abate his hunger.

Lovingly the mother plucks off the soft leaves clinging to the infant's wet, perspiring body, then coddles him to her breast. Hungrily, he drinks and is immediately soothed and satisfied.

The scene is a happy one—the mother sitting comfortably under the shade of the bush and, in the quietude of those tall trees around her, nourishing the life she has birthed. A smile of contentment is on her face and love radiates through her being as she looks at the nursing infant, then reaches out and tenderly pinches his fat cheeks.

But wait! From whence comes that odor? And she remembers the diaper problem. Holding the infant in one arm, she uses the other to open the net bag in which the baby lives, to get a better look at the leaves. Sure enough, there are the obvious signs that the baby had relieved himself. Maybe that was why he woke up so unhappy!

Carefully, she sifts through the leaves in the net bag, picking out the dirty ones and tossing them into the grass. Within her reach is a bush of the type of soft leaf needed to replace the ones she has discarded. These she plucks and replenishes those in her bag which is open now and ready for the satisfied, cooing infant.

She picks him up, nipping his cheeks and, as she does, a trickle of warm liquid hits her chest then runs down her breast. She points him to the grass where he completes that body function, then gives him another nip on the cheek and lays him back in amongst the leaves. The dampness of her breast and thigh as well as the net bag which has caught some of the stream of urine will soon dry. No one worries much about such things. Life goes on because the natural life processes go on.

Enjoying the bliss of those happy moments with her child, the mother has lost track of the time. Already dark clouds are blotting out the sun and in some of the upper valleys a light rain is beginning to fall. She must hurry or she will be caught in the afternoon rain.

Quickly she hangs the infant on the head of his older sister, adjusting the length of the net bag to fit properly across the sister's small back. His sister then walks about, "rocking" the infant back to sleep as she taps the net bag and sings the *wa-wa-wa-wa* song. And the mother, picking up her digging stick and empty net bags, makes her way to the older garden area.

It is not too far away and, once there, she slips the extra net bags from her head and begins searching for and digging up the sweet potatoes she intends to use to feed the pigs and her family their evening and morning meals. The corn has already been harvested, but she does find some cucumbers that will make good munching for the men who invariably come in hungry and thirsty. These will be used to quench their appetites until the potato vines and the potatoes are cooked.

Upward of an hour later, she straightens up to rest her back and to survey her work. A bag of potato vines and some cucumbers, a good-size bag of sweet potatoes, and a smaller bag of culled sweet potatoes for the pigs—it looks to be enough. All three bags she hangs from the back of her head and makes her way back to her older daughter who is still caring for her infant. Both are fast asleep: the son amongst the leaves in the net bag; the daughter lying on the grass and leaves of the forest.

"Mbet keenik aru, mayu wage me!" "Hurry, wake up! The rain is coming," she screams at the daughter, who immediately jumps to her feet. The mother hangs the bag of sweet potato leaves on the head of the daughter, shooing her down the path, while she herself swings the now whimpering infant onto her back on top of the two bags of potatoes. Together they head for the village as the rain begins to fall.

Part I:

Faith Embraced!

—⟀—

Chapter 1:
This moment was mine!

—⁓—

I stood with legs quivering; my hands holding the piece of paper were shaking. Around me sat nearly a thousand Western Dani Stone Age tribal people; their bodies—greased with a mixture of pig fat and soot—glistened in the bright midmorning sun. As the heat intensified, some covered their heads with their net bags, others flicked the perspiration from their brows, a few of the older men dozed, leaning on their *wanggun* "walking stick," while still others just waited.

People were still gathering and, as they burst from the smaller paths leading on to the airstrip, calls announcing their arrival pierced that cool air, and the thud of hundreds of bare feet on the rocks and grass of the airstrip mixed with the chants of a happy people gathering to worship.

Today was Sunday, "the day we meet to pray" as the Danis say. And as they approached the area at the top of the airstrip where we were waiting, the women with their babies and small children slipped quietly into the group with only the swish of their grass skirts announcing their arrival. The men hurried over to the rock fence—built around the airstrip to keep the pigs from getting mixed up in an airplane prop—and leaned their long 10-foot spears, and 6-foot bows with arrows against that fence before they too came, seating themselves among their friends within the group.

Today was my day. As a youth walking behind the horses in the field on our farm in Minnesota, I had dreamed of this moment; as an eighth grader in junior high, I had written an essay imagining this moment; as a sincere young person in my early teens, I had slipped out of the pew during an altar call in our church—kneeling at the altar committing my life to Jesus Christ—to experience this moment; and as a student at Prairie Bible Institute, I had prayed for this moment. Now it was mine!

Though only six weeks among the Dani, I had practiced the sounds of the words and flow of the grammar in my story before I stood, that piece of paper shaking in my hand. On it was a very rough paraphrase of the story about the parable of the wheat and the tares as found in Matthew 13, which I had worked over with my language informant.

Slowly and mechanically I began to mouth the strange sounds on the script held in my hands. And as I read, the restlessness of those steaming bodies at my feet ceased; the men yelled for silence; the older men looked up from dozing; and the women tried to quiet the fussing of their babies. A spirit of interest and quiet expectancy came over that large group and I was ecstatic. They were listening; they were understanding.

Having finished the page and a half of my story, I carefully folded those pages, and sat down with a great sigh of relief. I had given my first message in the Dani language and I was overcome with emotion. I waited for the group to move so I, too, could get out of the hot sun. But no one stirred. The air, pregnant with expectancy, was broken finally by the voice of an older man sitting near the fringe of the group: *"Tuan Kobo wae. Wone ti, obeelom aret me, ambinom yo'niru o."* "Sir/Mr. Scovill. Concerning those words, they are good words. Tell them to us again."

Since I did not yet have enough language to know what he had said, the men around me motioned for me to stand up and read the story again. Amazed but elated, I stood again and read through the story. Again, quietness! As I sat back down, I could feel nearly a thousand pairs of eyes on me. A moment or two later an old woman near the front of the circle blurted out, "Tell us, just once more."

I rose for the third time to read my story. And as I read, I became aware of a low mumbling sound throughout the group. Looking about, I noted that they were memorizing the phrases as I read them. With utter fascination, I watched them count the phrases on their fingers, one phrase at a time. When they ran out of fingers, they moved to their ten toes. When their fingers and toes ran out, they transferred the phrases to their neighbors' fingers and toes to begin counting again with theirs. In this way the story was recorded (we learned later) to be recited around the fires that evening.

A crowd under the big tree where services were held

These tribal people then made their way back to their villages in the valleys and along the mountainsides. And my wife Esther and I, with hearts filled with unrestrained excitement and unbounding praise, returned to our little home, built out of round poles and tree bark, with chicken wire and plastic in the windows, and a grass roof. We had launched our ministry, and this launching was to take us through nearly a half century of ministry with the Western Dani tribe in the heart of Papua as its focus. It was also a ministry destined to bring a deep sense of fulfillment to us personally as well as blessing to hundreds of supporting individuals and churches in North America.

But preparation for this moment had begun years before.

Chapter 2:
Influences which shaped me
to become a missionary

—ᨠᨠ—

I was the second of eight children born to Gordon and
Dorothy Scovill, who farmed in northern Minnesota.
The farm was small and the soil was poor, a major portion
being a large peat swamp. Yet I cannot write disparagingly
of this piece of geography because it was home and because,
I believe, it was God's provision for our family, shaping our
values and eternal perspectives in preparation for our future.

The land produced the necessary crops to feed our cattle;
the soil near the house responded to our gardening efforts
giving us a variety of vegetables; the woods yielded all kinds
of wild berries and nuts; and the peat swamp grew large
delicious blue berries which we were able to pick and sell
for small cash revenue as well as to enjoy in pies and other
pastries throughout the year.

By anyone's standards, we were a poor family; the old car
forever needed repair and its tires fixed to take us to church
and Sunday School. We would leave home with at least one
and, more often, two spare tires to go the six miles to church.
But more often then not, we would end up driving home
on the rim, having used all the spare tires we had prepared.
Though gasoline sold for only 12 or 13 cents a gallon, cash
to purchase a gallon or two to get to church became a weekly
challenge. But getting to church on Sunday was a family
priority and we seldom missed.

Inside plumbing and bathroom facilities in our home were only dreams! The toilet was an outhouse behind a small shed we had built; the bathing facility in the spring and summer was a large tub behind the lilac bush near the well and, in the winter, in front of the stove in the kitchen. Water for needs within the home was carried in pails from the nearby well by one of us older children. We endeavored to keep the wash tubs in the kitchen full.

Electricity was something the neighbors enjoyed and we wondered if it would ever light our house and barn. The day an electric pole was placed in our yard and a transformer wired to it made history for us. And then the flow of the current! My, we had fun with those switches, and we began to dream of some of the conveniences which could be ours in the years ahead.

I can still see Dad sitting in his chair in the corner of that small, two-story, non-insulated, cold, three-bedroom house heated with a woodstove made from a 55-gallon drum. His ear would be tuned to an old battery-powered radio to catch whatever news he could retrieve from the loud static coming over the air waves.

Though poor by others' standards, we were never hungry! There was always good food on the table. We raised our own meat and produced our own milk and vegetables. Without a refrigerator or its predecessor, the ice box, mother did a lot of canning during the summer. A cellar full of hundreds of jars of canned fruit and vegetables and a 55-gallon drum with a bear-proof lid, set out in the snow to keep our meat frozen during those subzero winter months, provided all the wholesome food we needed.

We farmed with horses: two teams we used in the fields. At about 9 years of age, raking the hay we put in the barn to feed the cattle during those cold winter months became my responsibility using the older team. My brother Don, two years older than I and the obvious family horseman, would take the younger team into faraway meadows and swamps to mow hay. Breakdowns required creative repair; obstinate horses had to be coaxed into shouldering their load; runaway teams had to be quieted and returned to their task; thunderstorms complete with striker lightning knotted our stomachs with fear. Yet it was in this context we learned creativity, responsibility, and the discipline of perseverance, as well as the fun and wholesomeness of hard work. And I am forever grateful.

The Scovill brothers were known and respected throughout the community for these qualities. Young though we were, when the threshing rigs made the rounds through the area to thresh the grain providing food for the cattle, our hayrack and horses were among those that snaked from field to machine, bringing in the oat bundles to be threshed. We could keep up with the best, pitching those oat bundles into the throat of that noisy threshing machine. We loved the excitement and the thrill of those community events.

The bean patch was another summer family activity, and could we pick those tender green and yellow beans! When the beans were ready, the entire family moved to the bean patch as soon in the morning as the dew would permit, each with straw hat and bucket. Mother, of course, was the number one picker; she could move down a row of beans filling her pail so quickly that we all marveled at her speed. Her hands literally flew from bean bush to bucket but she also used those moments with her children to build relationships and to keep us encouraged as we moved from one row to the next, doing our best to preserve the vines for a future picking.

Any dislike we harbored to this family activity could be noted by the degree of destruction seen in the bushes of the particular row we had picked. My older brother Don and I much preferred to be out in the field doing something with the horses, but Don especially had a special dislike for the bean patch. He would express his frustration by straddling the row of beans and sliding along the row on his bottom, leaving the vines broken and wilted after being relieved of their beans!

Often we would compete to see who could fill his pail first, running back and forth to fill the sacks which dad kept in central places along the rows. The secret of course was being able to pick with both hands. Dad was the slowest picker of the group and was loaded with indisputable reasons as to why he could not keep up with the rest of us: his back, his hernia, his hands, but the full picking crew of us children with mom could fill the sacks so quickly dad was normally kept busy tying them up and carrying them to the end of the row. Then, in the late afternoon we would load them into our old pickup and dad, with a big smile on his face, would coax that old truck to the cannery while we started the evening chores. With full crew and good beans in the patch, we could pick a ton of beans a day. A good bean crop meant clothes and shoes for school as well as funds to pay on the farm mortgage. Hence, all of us respected the bean patch as an important though, at times, a distasteful part of our lives.

After those busy, often hectic, summer days, we looked forward to winter. With the barn full of hay, the silos full of silage, the cellar full of cabbages, potatoes, carrots, turnips and hundreds of jars of canned fruit and vegetables, when the snow came we headed for the woods. Chain saws had not yet made their appearance, but armed with axes, two-man saws, horses and sledge, we hauled in firewood to keep the potbellied stove fired up, and brought in logs to saw on our small homemade sawmill to provide rough lumber for any building or repairs needed on the farm.

After the chores were finished in the evenings, we enjoyed skating on the frozen ponds and rivers, sledding on the snow-covered slopes, skiing down the hills, or being pulled along by the rope tied to our saddle horse's tail. These were all family fun times.

Music made its special contribution in shaping our lives and future ministry. When the snow fell, and the wind howled, we would stoke up the old potbellied stove which heated the entire house, pull out the music, and sing and play our instruments. Mother rather enjoyed those times of practice, coaching us on; dad faked enduring them sitting in his corner, often with his fingers in his ears, but we knew he was proud of our musical abilities. The discipline of practice was not only beneficial in shaping us but resulted in many invitations to provide both instrumental and vocal music within the church, as well as for special ministries such as street meetings and visits to senior rest homes.

Though mom and dad came from very nominal Christian backgrounds, following their marriage, each had made a personal decision to accept Christ as Savior and a commitment to raise a family that would bring honor to God. And though times were hard, money scarce, and farming discouraging, they held on to the spiritual values they wanted embedded in the lives of their children.

Family altar was very important to us as we grew up. This was part of our normal breakfast after milking, feeding and watering the cattle, and before we ran off to meet the school bus. We always kneeled and each of us children prayed during this time. How well I remember that my chair at the table was a five-gallon milk can at which I knelt and waited my turn to pray.

I'll have to be honest and say that not always were those efforts times of spiritual insight and help to us. The chores would have taken longer than usual, the bus would be honking for us at the end of the driveway, or mom and dad would have had a spat and dad would leave us to pray alone, slamming the door on the way out. But the value was planted; family altar was important. We believed that indeed, the family that prays together stays together!

With no television, videos, or DVDs, books enlarged our small world and shaped our future. Biographies of David Livingstone leaving his mark on Africa, of David Brainard's ministry to the American Indians, of Hudson Taylor's attempts at cultural identification in China, of William Carey's amazing life, linguistic ability and ministry to the peoples of India—all impacted my young life.

While walking barefoot behind the horses in the field one day, dust billowing around me, the thought that I, too, could follow in the footsteps of some of these other pioneer missionaries I had been reading about, could reach a people who had never heard of Christ, pushed its way into my thoughts. If they could do it, why could not I? And the seed of foreign missions was planted in the heart of this farm lad.

The thought surfaced again when we, in the eighth grade, were each asked to write a short essay on what we wanted to do when we grew up. I knew, but struggled to write honestly of that desire for fear of ridicule from both my teacher and my classmates. In the end I did and, with fear and trepidation, anxiously awaited the return of my paper and what I felt would be my teacher's caustic remarks. My head was bowed low over my desk as the teacher went around the room, passing out our essays. As she slipped my paper back to me, I felt her hand on my shoulder then a quick squeeze as she went on. Looking down at my paper, I noted across the top corner she had written, "A very fine vocation; God bless you!"

Missionaries often stopped in for a meal or to encourage mom and dad in their efforts to raise eight children for the Lord. Their special calling, their love for the Lord, their obvious joy in serving Christ where the Gospel had not yet penetrated, and their stories—oh, how I loved their stories— these all made an impact upon the direction of my life.

Chapter 3:
The call confirmed

—◊◊◊—

With ministry on my heart, I went to Prairie Bible Institute in Three Hills, Alberta, Canada. Here, the study of the Word forever changed my life and influenced my walk with the Lord. And it was here the Lord led me to the one who was to walk beside me during our missionary career of nearly 50 years.

Esther is the daughter of the late George and May McKerihan, missionaries who served the Lord in Cuba and Haiti for many years. She grew up in the Caribbean speaking Spanish, but came home to North America to take her high school and subsequent Bible training at Prairie Bible Institute.

The rules of the Institute did not allow one to build any close relationship with the opposite sex. Prairie was not against marriages within the student body but its students were urged to keep first things first. We were there to study the Word of God, to be good soldiers of Jesus Christ, and to be able to endure the disciplines of missionary life.

But, "the way of a man with a maid"! As nature would have it, the unplanned happened. During our Bible School days, this one pretty young lady stood out above the rest, and I began making this known to her, Prairie-style. My eyes could find her anytime and anywhere in that large tabernacle and she always seemed to be searching for me! It was amazing how often we would coincidentally pass on the sidewalk. The rules did not mention secret codes so we worked out a code between us. The flash of two fingers, or three fingers, or sometimes four: all had "lover's" meanings. Oh yes, there are always ways!

We also used the same music practice building, and Esther was amazed at how often she would find an apple or an orange waiting for her on the piano in her practice room. But it was the summer I traveled in a male quartet that sealed it. I would be traveling for over four months; I just had to say good-bye!

So shortly before leaving the school on our itinerary, I slipped into her practice room where she was practicing. I bent over her, looked her in the eye, and that delicious yet unexpected first kiss sealed everything for life! The secret was out. She knew and I knew that we were meant for each another. Even the matronly dean of women was to learn of our relationship and to assist us in our courtship at Prairie.

During this time, the studies in the Word, my private prayer times, and the many speakers who came through Prairie Bible Institute to share their missionary experiences, only confirmed that feeling in my heart: I was headed for an unreached tribe to analyze their speech, to share the Gospel in their tongue and, eventually, to translate the Word of God into their own language. And I never doubted that call of God on my life—except once. Believe it or not, that was during the summer AFTER I had graduated from Prairie Bible Institute.

Having now settled on the young lady who was to become my wife, I was excited to learn that she also was interested in serving the Lord overseas, particularly in the island world. At the end of that summer, Esther and I had made plans to drive to Los Angeles to take a one-year course in missionary medicine, not only to protect our own health in the isolated yet unknown places we were to serve, but also to be of general medical assistance to those within those tribes to whom God was calling us. To obtain funds for that training, I was working in the wheat fields of North Dakota during the summer months while she was working in a resort center in Alberta, Canada.

My employer, also a firm believer, had to leave his home for several days and I was left alone to work those long wheat fields. Over the weeks working for him, I had become involved in the music ministry of the church which we attended. When the youth pastor, who was also musical, tuned into my musical ability both in singing and on the cornet, he urged me to rethink what I felt was God's call on my life. And I began to question God's leading. *Maybe it is just the excitement of reaching a primitive people; maybe, in my youthful zeal, I have mistaken God's direction on my life. Certainly I could be used in molding the lives of young people here, and probably better use my musical gifts in a ministry of music here in the States.*

This so bothered me that on this particular Monday morning, since the house was empty, I took my Bible downstairs into the family room to struggle through this issue with God. The sun was shining through that large picture window looking out over the lawn as I pulled the footstool into the warm sunshine. Placing my open Bible on it, I fell to my knees to, like Jacob, "have it out with God".

As I began to pour out my confusion before the Lord that morning and, before I had even begun to read the Word, the almost audible voice of our Lord came reminding me of Isaiah 30:21(NIV): "Your ears will hear a voice behind thee saying: 'This is the way, walk ye in it.'" And directly into my thoughts came the words, *I've been preparing you these many years; why do you now doubt me? My will for you is still to GO!*

"Hallelujah!" I shouted to the walls and the windows. "Thank you, God, for this your answer to me," and I closed my Bible without having read it, grabbed a bowl of cereal, climbed up on that big tractor, and with incredible peace and joy raced up and down the fields that day. I never again doubted the call of God upon my life.

Through missionary medical training, through marriage to Esther, through candidate school, through linguistic training, then through deputation, there was always the excitement, the momentum and the clear "push" of God upon our lives: that Voice BEHIND us, reminding us of our destiny, and we never wavered. We identified with the apostle Paul's expression in 1 Corinthians 9:16(NIV): "Woe to me if I do not preach the gospel."

By that time, we knew His will for us was a people in what was then Dutch New Guinea. And in this confidence we went—prepared and called!

Chapter 4:
On our way!

—◆◆◆—

It was June of 1960. We had raised our support of $350 per month (which included a $5 monthly assessment to be set aside for special emergency needs, and an additional $50 per month for Missionary Aviation Fellowship airfreight costs on goods flown in to help us survive in the interior), and we had received approval from our mission to leave for the field.

It was time to head west! We would load our 1951 Chevy sedan and small trailer with all the household goods we had acquired and depart for Los Angeles. There, we would pick up our passports and visas, finish purchasing and packing any other household goods we assumed we would need, and board a ship which would take us to Australia. Once in Australia, we would transfer to a smaller ship which would take us past Papua New Guinea and, following the coastline, on to Dutch New Guinea.

Our actual departure began on that little farm in Minnesota. We were young, and we were inexperienced, but His call upon our lives and the joy of finally being on our way was only temporarily dampened by the tears of my dear mom. She had given us a long hug, and then released us to do what she knew God had planned for us in answer to her prayers. She was not about to hold us back. For this moment she had lived and prayed, and had often reminded me of it following the miraculous healing of a hernia I had experienced during my years in junior high school.

Dad was never one to show his feelings or to flaunt his spirituality, but he, too, gave me a bear hug. Then, as I reached to open the car door to be on our way, he slipped a small folded piece of paper into my hands. On it he had penned a verse of Scripture from 1 Thessalonians. The exact verse, time has erased from my memory. But this was a very special gesture between a father and his son. It was dad's official way of saying, "Goodbye, David. We love you, and release you to do what God wants you to do. We will be praying for you." I knew he was searching for some way to identify, for something significant by which to send us on our way, and I loved him for it.

****

We were not strangers to the big city of Los Angeles, for we had taken our one year of Missionary Medical Training at Biola in downtown LA. During that time, our Christian Work assignment had led us into contact with a small interdenominational church in Pico Rivera where we worshipped and served, endearing ourselves to the congregation and them to us. They were waiting for our arrival and send-off.

The women helped Esther with her last-minute shopping. Since she was several months pregnant with our first child, purchasing baby clothes was her main concern. These she carefully packed in the tub of the gasoline engine-powered Maytag washing machine we had acquired, while several of the men in the church, who were our spiritual mentors in this adventure, helped in finding several drums in which to pack. They worked with me making crates for larger items: our four-inch-thick $39 dollar foam rubber double mattress, a knockdown baby bed, a fold-up high chair, and perhaps other things I have since forgotten.

Using their pickup trucks, we had already taken our outfit, consisting of three drums and two crates, to the ship before our departure hour arrived. Last minute teary phone calls made, we were driven to the ship terminal by those dear California friends to find, when we arrived, it seemed that the entire congregation had come to send us off.

Three honks of the ship's horn indicated we were pulling away. As we waved goodbye, the strains of those great old hymns, "No Never Alone," and, "God Be With You 'Til We Meet Again," wafted over the widening gulf between the dock and the ship. We were on our way; alone yes, but loved and sent by that body of believers.

Eventually their voices ceased and their forms grew dim in the distance. Then, it was the lights of the harbor receding, until we were out to sea with only the darkness hiding our tears, and the gentle splash of the ship's wake, created by those massive diesels moving that large ship towards Australia, filling the emptiness we felt in our hearts and reminding us that we were on our way at last. An entry in my journal on the 29th of July 1960 recalls those moments:

We stood leaning over the ship's rail and waved our last goodbyes to the folks at home. This was a strange feeling for a big fellow like me to be so utterly alone. We were glad for each other as we saw the last of the lights disappear on the horizon. And I was glad for a precious life-companion with whom I prayed as we stood on the top deck huddled there in the darkness.

The 21-day boat trip to Australia was very memorable for this young couple. Having grown up in Cuba, Esther was somewhat used to sea travel, but I expected all sorts of sicknesses to descend on me…though tough farm boy that I was! At first we chafed that we were not able to be together in our own cabin. The rates, however, were cheaper in the larger multi-passenger cabins and after the first couple days, with all going well, we began to enjoy it. The wonder that this was

happening to us—a young farm lad, with his new bride pregnant with their first child, on the way to that strange, far-off
storybook place called Dutch New Guinea—was awesome.

That certainly was the "end of the world," was it not? It
was cannibal country, no doubt about it! And one dear lady
in North Dakota in all sincerity had given us several cartons
of those small Morton salt containers, advising us to take
them with us when we went on trek in the mountains and to
use them when in dangerous situations! "Who knows," she
had said, "sometime maybe this will save your lives!"

Upon our arrival in Australia, we prevailed upon a taxi
there in the harbor to take us to the UFM headquarters in
Sydney. With our three drums and two crates in storage there
on the dock, our suitcases loaded into the taxi, and Esther
already situated in the back seat, I slipped around to where
the taxi driver stood with the door open, presumably being
polite to me his passenger. Hurriedly, since I thought he was
probably impatiently waiting for me, I slipped past him and
into the seat, but on the way down I noticed the strange look
on his face, then my arm bumped up against something that
should not have been in my space. I looked up to find that I
had slipped into the driver's seat. "Oh, yes," I remembered,
"this is the place where they drive on the left-hand side of
the road." We laughed together as I slid out of his seat, raced
around to the other side of the taxi and took my place beside
him in the passenger's seat.

We enjoyed the generous hospitality shown to us by our
Australian brethren; we even enjoyed sleeping in one twin
bed to keep warm since central heating was rare in the normal
Australian home. Our one concern now was that, having
arrived in Australia, we needed to find booking on the Royal
Dutch Inter-ocean Lines to take us on to Dutch New Guinea.
So, the next working day, we took a taxi to their office.

To our dismay we learned that all the ships going to
Dutch New Guinea were fully booked for the next three

months! Our only hope was to wait it out, or perhaps to consider taking an airplane. However, flying was expensive and beyond our missionary budget. And, what about our drums and crates we were bringing with us?

In the end, we were given no hope that we could continue our journey to Dutch New Guinea for several months. Disappointed, disheartened, hopes for a quick booking dashed, and cold (it was their winter), with heavy step we made our way slowly toward the door of that long, dreary building, praying, "Lord, what next?"

I opened the door and, as Esther slipped out, I heard a strange noise from the desk a good distance behind us in that long room. Looking around, the booking agent was motioning us to come back. As she placed the receiver back on the phone, she called out, "Well, there's your cabin! A cancellation has occurred on a ship that leaves in six days. Can you be ready to go by that time?" We could, and we did. And what a trip up along the coast of New Guinea! The beautiful tropical beaches, the islands we slipped past, the active volcanoes casting a red glow lighting up the nights, the knowledge and excitement that we were nearing our destination—all endeared us to that island world, and fuelled our anticipation for ministry among the peoples of Dutch New Guinea.

The beauty of that island was indeed breathtaking, but so were the friends we made along the way. We were able to lead several to the Lord during that voyage. Rob was a young man of the crew with whom we had long discussions about the things of the Lord. An entry in my diary on August 31, 1960, records that for us:

We are just a few hours away from the land of Dutch New Guinea. Amidst letters, reading, Bible Study and so on, we had a good time of fellowship with Rob. The battle now is whether or not it is necessary for him to give up drinking and smoking to be a good

Christian. We spent over two hours studying the Word today with him. Never have I seen such an honest, open, young man. After reading 2 Corinthians 6:14-17 he knew in his heart what he had to do. We know not the result as yet, because we want the Holy Spirit to do the convicting.

On September 1st I recorded the following:

I got up at 5 a. m. to catch my first glimpse of Dutch New Guinea. There it was with its rough rugged mountains rising high into the heavens. Here and there small columns of smoke rose up through the trees probably from the fires of villagers living beneath them.

Rob did not come up this afternoon, so I went down to his room and found him desperately trying to get his diary for engineering in order. Then he said, "Well, Dave. You see no more beer cans in my room. Last night I threw three cases of beer and a carton of cigarettes overboard while the third engineer and second officer laughed at me!"

What a rich experience to witness this miracle taking place in his life. I almost wept for joy.

We are making over 12 knots an hour and should arrive in the Port of Hollandia, the capital of Dutch New Guinea, by tomorrow evening.

And we did—on September 2, 1960—having spent two weeks enroute from Australia. In Hollandia, we were met and given accommodations by missionary colleagues of our sister mission, the Regions Beyond Missionary Union

(RBMU), who had preceded us. We were both 24 years of age; Esther was pregnant with our firstborn; and we were ready to get located and into a language.

Those few days on the coast began the culture change in us that was to mark us for life! We had moved into another world: a world of pioneer missionaries who were driven to discover unreached tribes in the highlands of that large island and who dared danger to stop that attempt; a world of plane talk: flying small airplanes, hazards of weather patterns in the mountains, airdrops to teams trekking into unknown areas, crashes that had occurred or nearly occurred, and airstrips that needed to be built; a world of new cultures, unknown languages and utter frustration because one could not communicate. This was a world where men and women, having left their comfortable homes, convenient kitchens, financial security and cozy relationships, had arrived with the bare necessities of life and valued not their lives in the excitement and privilege of serving their Master. We thrilled at being a part of that noble band.

We were preceded by several missionaries from UFM Australia as well as from UFM North America who, by that time, had pioneered several airstrips in the mountainous interior. The most recently opened by UFM North America was called Mulia. Ralph Maynard, Dave Cole, and Leon Dillinger of UFM North America, with Bert Powers of UFM Australia, had trekked into this valley toward the end of 1958 and built the airstrip.

(Several months later, Dave Cole had retraced his steps two days trek back to a large plateau they had noted on their way to Mulia. There, at a site called Ilu, Dave, with the help of the Danis in that area, had built another airstrip and, with his wife Dina, faithfully served the Dani for many years before pioneering into other unreached tribes located in the Eastern Highlands of Papua with Dani missionaries.)

Ralph Maynard with his wife, Melba, and a UFM nurse, Rie Dedecker, were there at Mulia and waiting for us when we disembarked from that little yellow Cessna 180. And though we did not know it at the time, there was a young man about 12 years of age watching us from behind the rock fence that had been built around the airstrip to keep the pigs from rooting up its hard surface or from getting caught in an airplane prop. As we had loosened our seat belts then slipped out the door of that small plane to place our feet on Daniland soil, totally astounded, this youth had muttered, "That's the man and woman I saw in my dream several nights ago!" And off he ran to his nearby village.

We had arrived! And we looked out upon incredibly beautiful mountains on each side of the valley with the occasional terraced garden enclosed in a wooden fence; upon small, round, grass-roofed huts clustered in villages along those mountainsides; upon a rugged, unfinished, though partially useable airstrip; upon people whose bodies, smeared with pig fat and soot, gleamed and sparkled in the early morning sunlight, and whose fingers tightly clasped bows and arrows.

Though we had seen pictures, we did not know whether we should be embarrassed at the men dressed only in gourds covering their private parts or at the women scantily clad in short grass skirts! They seemed to be at ease with one another in that dress, so we too accepted it as the norm. The men had their hair bundled up in net bags, we noted, and the women had the same type of larger net bag hanging on the back of their heads and down their backs, many with infants or sweet potatoes in them. But they seemed friendly. Several braved the distance and a bit warily extended to us the knuckle of their index finger grunting, *"Nogoba wa,"* then awkwardly waited for us to respond.

What does one do? What does one say? How could we share this moment of ecstasy with them? We couldn't. Later we were to understand that they were saying, "Welcome, my father. Welcome, my mother." But not understanding what they were saying or what we were to do, we clumsily grabbed the entire outstretched fist, smiling and shaking it in the good old American way.

Fortunately, that awkward embarrassing moment for both of us was broken by someone yelling, *"Kineebe! Kineebe!"* "Move back! Move back!" And we watched fascinated, as the pilot revved the single engine of his little plane and checked through the take-off procedure. Then, with a grin and wave of his hand, he buttoned down the little window, released the brakes, raced down the short airstrip, and lifted off to the accompaniment of hundreds of voices whose yells of glee at the phenomenon taking place before their eyes mixed with the noise of the engine echoing off those mountainsides.

What a day! What a world into which we had moved! It was at this point we realized there was no running from the scene. We were locked in those mountains and with those people with no way out, be it danger, sickness, or death. That airplane, now becoming a speck in the distance, was our life-line with the outside world. It was now just ourselves and our colleagues, with God and some 15,000 tribespeople spread out in the valleys around us. We picked up our suitcases and supplies of flour and sugar brought in on the plane and, led by Ralph and Mel, moved towards that little house that was to be our home. Framed with round poles, it sat on posts five feet off the ground. Rough boards split from logs with stone axes were used as siding on the outside; tree bark was used to panel the inside walls. A grass roof kept out the rain; chicken wire and plastic in the windows kept out unwanted guests! We were home!

Let me share an entry in my journal of our arrival on September 13, 1960, so you can catch our mood.

Reaching Mulia we flew over the airstrip, made a long circle and came down on the rocky runway. We were met by the Maynards, Rie Dedecker and several dozen of these Dani people. They are actually worse than the pictures have shown. Pig grease, gourds and filth. We love them though, because He loves them.

This afternoon I assembled the washing machine... works like a charm thanks to Howard Lane and John Gronewold. Then, I made a crude bed frame out of poles and we now have our new mattress and linens (our wedding gifts) on it. We are HAPPY!

Bark floors, wood stove, kerosene lamps, no sink, no toilet, a bucket shower, bark walls and ceiling, pole rafters, grass roof, and a filthy people to work amongst! BUT a God who is real and precious and who loves them and us! What could be more satisfying? This is HOME: our first since being married. We are happy and LOVE it.

Chapter 5:
Home at last: some early experiences

—ɷ—

Disregarding the chatter of dozens of nationals outside and under our house, and the eyes staring at us through the plastic and chicken wire in the windows, we went to work. Water was available from the roof drain-off, or carried in a bucket from the nearby stream and dumped into a 55-gallon drum outside the house. Into this Esther dipped to begin the cleaning process. Our colleagues, Ralph and Melba Maynard, had built and used that small bark house during the building of the airstrip. Upon hearing of our coming and need for accommodations, they were in the process of building a larger more permanent home a few feet away, leaving the smaller temporary one for us. This was our mansion.

My first task was to build a bed frame out of a supply of round poles Ralph was using to build his house. On this we unrolled our four-inch thick, double bed, serofoam mattress, made quite homey with the sheets, pillows, and blankets Esther had pulled out of our drums and boxes flown in. We lay down that evening in the privacy of our own little bedroom, far from home, family, and friends, but feeling pleased with our day's accomplishment and the pure joy of being there. What we did not know until some weeks later was that we were not alone that evening. Outside a pair of eyes, peeping through the cracks, had watched us get into our nightclothes and slip under the covers before we blew out the kerosene lamp! And the story circulating was, "They are just like we are!"

Being a farm lad and knowing, I thought, all there was to know about lighting fires, the next morning I was up bright and early to light the fire in our woodstove to heat some water for breakfast. My point was to have that fire roaring in the firebox before the arrival of the Dani lad who had been asked to come make us a fire. Certainly I did not need a "native" to come build my fire! Carefully I put in the wood with the kindling, and tried several times, unsuccessfully, to produce the flame.

During my struggle, who should walk in but the Dani lad sent by Ralph and Mel. He looked at me, waved away the smoke that was filling the room, smiled and, pointing to himself, said, *"An eeri."* "Let me do it." I backed away, then, watched him take out all the wood and kindling I had so smartly placed in the firebox and begin all over. In just a few minutes, the small flame became a roaring fire. Lesson number one: In his world, he knows more than you. Learn from him!

Several days later, while we were still settling in, the door of our little pole and bark house burst open, and in the middle of our kitchen stood a young lad of about 12 years of age with a big smile on his face. Gesturing wildly, voice animated, obviously he had a story and he was intent on communicating it to us. But when he saw we were not sharing the ecstasy of his moment, disappointment registered on his face, so he tried again, raising his voice as if turning up the volume would help.

Unfortunately it did not. However, when he pointed to the empty space under the stove and, with his hands, asked for an axe, we figured out he was probably asking if he could find us some firewood. We quickly found and gave him an axe and shortly that space was filled with good dry firewood. He then found a bucket and filled the drum outside with water from the stream. Then it was a broom which he found and began sweeping the floor of the wood chips which had fallen. Pointing to himself, he said (we assumed), "Let me help you in the house."

Along with all this and, in addition to the preliminary help given to us by Ralph and Mel, this young lad was very interested in teaching us his language, carefully pointing to and articulating the names of things with gestures if we indicated we did not understand. We noted his desire and clear pronunciation, and realized here was God's answer to learning the language, so we began in earnest to take several hours daily to work with him in mimicking, recording, and listening to the words and phrases he would give to us. He was quick to demonstrate when a verb was used: *"An kani mbangge,"* "I cut firewood," and he would point to himself, axe in hand. *"Kat kani mbangge,"* "You cut firewood," and he would thrust the axe into my hand, directing me to cut. In this way, not only was our vocabulary increasing daily, but we began to pick up personal pronouns as well as personal pronoun prefixes on words: *"neenggi"* was "my hand," *"keenggi"* was "your hand," *"eenggi"* was "his hand," as well as verbs with their various subtle inflections and tenses.

In addition to emphasis on language study, we found ourselves involved in a lot of other activities as indicated by the entries in my journal of September 30, 1960:

Rain is bouncing noisily on the aluminum roof here over the kitchen; Esther is helping Rie complete a delivery. My thoughts and moments have been spent on language.

Today was the first time I pulled a tooth. Poor fellow and poor me! He did yell and wince a bit but I locked arms around him and went to it. Was a thrill and relief to see the rotten thing come out without breaking!

Warriors are gathering for another strike somewhere. Almost all day they have been coming in, even from different valleys to prepare by feasting on sweet potatoes prior to the attack. We certainly need the intervention of the omnipotent God. We long to see Him work in our valley.

Ten days later I wrote:

I pulled my third tooth today. Almost had to bodily throw a cheeky native out of the yard. Still I like the fellow and we are friends. . . I think!

A man came in today from the fighting with the point of an arrow embedded in his neck.

And three days later:

A profitable day having spent nearly 5 hours in language study. Felt ashamed of myself and prayed for cleansing after almost bodily throwing another native out of the yard. Probably could have done it in a more Christlike way!

Washed our house-help's hair today and literally had mud in the bottom of the bucket after the first soaping. After the third wash it came out reasonably clean except for the lice.

Today when paying for work done on the airstrip with cowrie shells, their currency, one hot-headed old gent threw his shell back at me, grabbed a slab and was about to spear-throw it at me. I really had the scare of my life but at the same time was so angry

I almost ran and grabbed it from him. I finally was able to pacify him with a larger shell.

The entry of the 2nd of November gives another glimpse of our interaction with the Dani during those early days.

What a day! Live and Learn I would entitle it. Tonight was the only night so far that I forgot to count the bush knives before paying the men who were preparing the bark for paneling in the house we were building for our nurse. When putting them away, I noticed one missing, but too late. From some of the men we learned that a man from the Yamo (village over the mountain) had stolen it. Seeing him leave, I called him back and he, to my face, denied it, saying probably one of the young men who was dissatisfied by my giving him only salt for his work, had taken it.

I headed up to that young man's village in the rain even though it was fast getting dark. The people of each village I entered told me he had gone on to the next village. Eventually, feeling they were probably protecting him, I retraced my steps in the rain. And I had just finished supper, when some men, over an hour's walk away, came in to tell us more about the Yamo man. He was sleeping in one of the villages right off the end of the airstrip, they said, and they wanted to go down to confront him about the missing knife.

I pulled on my already wet pants and shoes and we left the house. Finding the house in which he was sleeping, we called him to come out to speak with us. Again he denied having it, but the two men with me probed about, they said, and learned he had hidden it hoping I would not miss it. He intended to come back the next day to take it.

Early the next morning the knife was found underneath some of the bark. The man from Yamo did return sorely angry that I had accused him of stealing the knife. As he left, he expressed that anger by running out to the airstrip with loaded bow, then swinging around, aimed the arrow at me. The kids ran for cover, but the men with whom I was standing held their place, so I did too and watched him finally leave.

To this day I do not know whether their younger sibling had indeed taken it, but fearing retribution of some kind, they had come and put the blame on the Yamo man. I suspect that is what happened, because that Yamo man, whose name was Tibenok, turned out to be a real leader in the church/community and a very close friend.

We worked with the hundreds of men and women who were completing the airstrip by carrying clods of dirt and rock, throwing them off to the side of the area marked for the airstrip; and we walked the paths of the valley locating and writing down the names of the villages with the names of the leading men in each village.

It was during one of those afternoon walks with Ralph that we came into a nearby village where lived a man whose eyeball had nearly been pierced by an arrow during a recent war. Ralph was telling me about the dead and wounded the warriors had brought back with them, one of them being this man. A missionary doctor from another station had been flown over to care for the wounded: this included minor surgery, extracting arrows from many who had been hit. Among those brought to him was this man called Ngganuk. Just missing his eyeball, the arrow had embedded itself in the muscle behind the eyeball, and the wound had been grotesquely swollen from infection. After examining him and, confident he would never see out of that eye again, the doctor had sent him back to his village, giving him no help and no hope that the eye could be saved. Disappointed, Ngganuk had left the clinic then disappeared from the community.

As we approached the larger round men's house in its prominent place in the village, Ralph stooped down and looked inside. Sitting there across the fire was this man, Ngganuk, whom Ralph immediately recognized and greeted. Then he stepped back from the doorway as Ngganuk slipped out of the house into the sunlight. Amazed that he was there and beginning to see out of that eye, Ralph had blurted out, *"Kat nggeeme wonagandak?"* "Where have you been?"

Briefly, Ngganuk told him the story: After the doctor had sent him home without being able to help him, one of his kinsmen had taken him out into the forest and, with a bone knife, had made several incisions in the flesh behind the eyeball, pulling out three large slivers of wood, the point of that arrow that had broken up on impact. Then he had taken a certain leaf known for its curing properties, spit on it, slapped it on the incision, and sent the man home to heal.

It had now been nearly a month and the wound was healing without infection, the swelling had receded, and Ngganuk was beginning to see out of that eye. Ralph was amazed. Over the following months, the eye continued to heal, eventually nearly hiding the fact that he had had surgery. Needless to say, I left that men's house that afternoon duly impressed with life in the jungles of New Guinea!

On another of our trips out into the community, we were met by a group of men fully armed and whom we could see were quite angry. Several in the group had painted their bodies; many wore the feather headdress, with leaves stuck in their arm bands. We watched as two or three of them raced off ahead of the others, then jumped into the brush intent on finding something, their fingers holding tightly to the arrow taut in the bow and poised for action. It was obvious there was a problem, so we slipped off the trail into the brush to let them go by. Ahead on one of the trees was a large grotesque knot formation and, as the group approached this tree, a call rang out as several of the men shot their arrows into that knot. We had passed under that tree a few minutes before, noticing the ugliness of the knot, and I had wondered about several old arrows sticking out of it. Now, they were again shooting it.

As we slipped back onto the trail and continued on our way, we were immediately met by another group of men, perspiration pouring from their bodies and glistening in that bright sunlight. They were carrying a sick person, laced to a pole, going down to the clinic UFM was operating. Again we stepped off the path, letting the group go by. As we continued, we asked the men traveling with us what was happening. In very simple Dani, they told us that the group we had first encountered was going ahead to secure the path for the sick person from the spirits who were intent on robbing the man of his soul. The large grotesque knot on the tree was presumed to be the abode of the spirits who were waiting for an opportunity to descend into that group to snatch away his soul and bring about his death.

Indeed, a few nights before that encounter, Esther and I had been awakened by shouting and a commotion outside our little house. It came from the direction of the small, round, sick houses which had been built for them and in which they could put their sick needing special and/or long-term attention. We had slipped out that night with a flashlight to find one of those sick-houses surrounded by men with arrows loaded against their tautly pulled bow strings; others were walking around the house, filling up all the holes and cracks with dry grass and anything else they could get their hands on. Questioning them the next morning, we learned that the dreaded Kuguruwo spirit who fed upon the bodies of dead people had visited. They had heard its cry in the middle of the night and were petrified, believing it was coming to snatch away the soul of their kinsman. Thus, they were "on guard" should she appear, for it was the dreaded female spirit. Such was the fear permeating their lives.

****

We continued to work daily learning the language, coached on by our young informant who also was a big help to Esther in the home. I was immensely enjoying those times, finding communication easier to the point where I was beginning to dare myself to give this young man some simple thoughts about the God we worshipped, even paraphrasing for him the occasional New Testament story.

This particular morning I had struggled through the main points of the story found in Matthew 13 of the enemy who had secretly come and sowed tares (weeds) in the master's wheat field. The servants had come and asked the master what to do, and he had replied, "Let them both grow together, and at harvest time we will separate them, putting the grain in the storehouse, and burning up the tares." He seemed to understand the story.

Several days later, as we were working, he reminded me that since my colleague, Ralph, had gone to visit another one of our UFM stations, the responsibility for bringing a story to those hundreds of people who came for the service on Sunday would be mine. "Skip the record playing," he said. "We already know all those stories. Give them the story you gave me yesterday about the man who came and sowed weeds in his neighbor's field."

Aghast, I immediately rejected the idea in that we had been there less than two months and no one would understand a word I would say. Ralph had been using the Gospel Recording records for the group, and then closed the service by giving a few comments and reading a short prayer he had worked through with some of the Dani men. Not me, man! I wanted none of the novelty attached to sitting there hand cranking that little machine to play records of fringe group Danis telling stories! I wanted to preach the Word in Dani. For this we had been trained; this is why we had come; this was the goal of our language study; and this was the way they could best understand and make a decision on the message we had come to bring them. We still exuded that "new missionary" untamed, untried enthusiasm which had not yet touched the pragmatics and reality of living in the mountains of New Guinea.

My young informant, however, would not easily be silenced. He broached the subject the next day, insisting that those hundreds of people who would be coming would be expecting me to give them something. Again, I resisted, insisting that my Dani was not good enough to be understood, and that I had no story for them. He again reminded me of the story I had told him of the wheat and the tares, and urged me to tell it. When I resisted a third time that my use of Dani was too poor, he grabbed my pen and thrusting it into my hands said, "O.K! If that is the case, I will tell you in good Dani the story you told me, and you just write. Write it as I will tell it to you, then you get up and read that message you put on the banana leaf."

I had no choice. He began retelling the story and I began writing—phonetically of course, since we had not yet firmed up the alphabet. When we finished he said, "Now read it back to me!" So I did, not once, but several times during the next couple of days in preparation for the service on Sunday. And Sunday arrived along with hundreds of dancing, perspiring Danis. I stood with my story in hand, knees shaking, and began reading.

And that is the background of the story reiterated for you in the first chapter of this book. That was the event which launched us into our nearly half-century of ministry to the Western Dani in the interior mountains of Dutch New Guinea renamed Irian Jaya by the Indonesian government and now called Papua. That was the beginning of God's super plan for our ministry to the Western Dani.

****

Days flowed into weeks, and weeks flowed into months so quickly that in our excitement from all we were learning, we hardly kept track of time. We continued to make language our priority; we enjoyed the increasing ease with which we could communicate as well as the interesting cultural complexities surfacing in our language analysis. Through it all, our young informant was just as faithful to teach us and just as insistent that we learn, though he too, at times, would weary of the pressure (and our ignorance!) and drop down on the floor for a quick nap.

During one such language session, he began to tell us what the people first thought about us when we arrived. Since they had spirit houses out behind their "men's house" in each village, those little shelters out behind our houses, our outhouses, which we visited at various times during the day, but especially in the early morning and at night before retiring, had to be our spirit houses where we communicated with our unseen powers as they did. So they never looked for us there! That little outhouse was sacred!

Even though perceiving pictures on paper was difficult for them, they had figured out the pictures on the cans of food. Normally, there was a picture of the contents of the can on the outside and often we would give them a taste of those contents. Wieners, corned beef, corn, even sweet pota- toes in a can—they could distinguish because of the picture. But it wasn't until later we learned why so few infants had been seen about the station and why so few women came to be helped through their deliveries by our nurse midwife. Someone had picked up an empty can of baby food and had seen the picture of the baby on it. Word had gone out: "No infants are to be seen at the mission station because the missionaries kill, can and eat infants!"

As we learned to communicate more easily, the young man helping us also felt more freedom in his attempts to communicate with us. During one such language session we were enjoying together, he reminded us of the story he had told us one of those first days after we had arrived. At that time, all we could do was to smile and nod, as we did not understand what he was trying to tell us. This time, as he told the story, we were at once overwhelmed and humbled.

The young man speaking was the same young man who had watched us step out of that airplane and, totally astonished, had murmured to no one in particular, "That was the man and woman I saw in my dream." We listened with incredible interest as he retold the story.

One night before we arrived, he had a dream. In that dream, he saw a big man with his wife step out of that little airplane. In the hands of that big man was a large book. As the dream progressed, he saw himself teaching that man his language; in turn, that big man was teaching him from the pages of that Big Book.

That was the message he had excitedly tried to convey to us a few days after we had arrived, but which we could not understand due to the language barrier. With tears filling his eyes, he went on to say that he knew the God of that Big Book wanted him to teach us language so that his fathers and mothers could hear the words of eternal life. Wow! We sat immobile on the floor of that little bark house, pondering the preparations made by our Heavenly Father for us to begin ministry among the Western Dani.

This young man, now in his late fifties, is still very active in ministry. Over the years, he has been a faithful informant, then literacy teacher, then Bible School student, then pastor, then translator. At this writing, he is the head of the Evangelical Church of Indonesia in the Mulia-Ilu area with over 150 churches under his supervision. "There was a man sent (prepared) by God whose name was...(Wa'lambuk)," who upon conversion changed his name to *Mbogut-Paga-Enegen* meaning "with eyes only on heaven." God was actively preparing the way for this Dani people to receive the Gospel, even prior to our entrance into that valley.

Wa'lambuk butchering a pig

Chapter 6:
Building credibility

—⚏—

Given his aggressive, confident personality integrated with deep longing for immortality which included physical life in a setting where all his material needs would be bountifully met, the Dani's desire to enjoy a better quality of life was soon in evidence.

Steel axes to replace stone axes for their gardening and building purposes the Dani felt to be a real necessity. The small white cowrie shell, valued according to its bumps and shape, meant more wives, more gardens, more sweet potatoes, more pigs, more power, and finally, more prestige—in that order. The small grains of white salt which they had tasted from the missionary's small plastic spoon filled their mouths with all kinds of juices and made even the sweet potatoes more enjoyable to eat. There must be a way to get these.

Killing the missionary and running off with his goods was discussed in muffled voices around the fire in the center of the men's house during the blackest hours of the night. "But if he is the source of these things," they reasoned, "then it did not make much sense to get rid of the source, for the flow would then dry up. We would again miss our chance at immortality."

Stealing was the next option considered. "Yet that little voice in the black box (our single sideband radio) the missionary keeps in his house which gives him all the answers to the unknown and *'abera'lek me'* 'at the drop of a hat' he can call in an airplane—that would surely reveal who among us dared defy the missionary's spirits and steal his possessions." They wanted his steel axes, his white salt, and those small cowrie shells!

Thus, when the missionary requested their assistance to bring in poles and grass for his house, or to build an airstrip, they were delighted. That work created unimaginable excitement in the valley. When a call went out for poles, bark, and grass, in came the poles—long ones, short ones, crooked ones, straight ones, soft ones, hard ones—and bark for the inside wall paneling along with innumerable bundles of the long grass for the roof.

Hundreds came to work on the airstrip. The trees were cut down; the ground was cleared of all stumps and grass; the ditches were made; the daily digging and leveling, with tons of rocks and dirt moved to cut down the high spots and fill in the low places, was accomplished. Each day brought new experiences and challenges which allowed both the missionary to learn about his people, and the people to find out that this stranger in his community was no pushover.

Principles which were to form the foundation of the church we had come to plant among this tribe were being laid. The principle of justice: you were paid according to your work. Of responsibility: if you came to work, then don't sit around smoking all day. Of honesty: if you are given an axe to use, you are expected to bring it back that evening and account for it. Of equality: even though you came from a distant village or valley, you will be paid the same type of shell. Of discipline: if you did line up to be paid, but didn't work, you would be kicked out of the line-up! The tricks were unbelievable.

One particular morning, 76 adults lined up to work. With them looking on, we counted out 6 axes, 12 bush knives, 3 steel digging bars, and 15 gunny sacks, and gave them to the workers, carefully marking the numbers on a sheet of paper.

Amidst much singing, shouting, and chanting, they moved out to the airstrip and began to work, occasionally stopping to puff on self-rolled cigarettes, or to eat cold roasted sweet potatoes they had brought with them. With an early start, normally by early afternoon they would be too weary to continue so the call to gather for payment would be given.

There was much excitement in the anticipation of having some white salt or receiving a shell. *Maybe my shell will have that special knob on it which increases its value of which obviously the missionary is unaware or he would have saved such shells for special purposes.*

They learned the procedure quickly. Before any payment was given, all the tools would be gathered, again counted and, with them looking on, placed back into the small storage shed we had built for such tools. Always there was a sigh of relief from the group when the furrows in the missionary's brow were replaced by a big wide smile. No tools were missing! They knew they would get their pay for the day. Quickly the word was shouted, *"Mbet mbigininip o. Mayu wage me!"* "Hurry and line up; the rain is coming." And normally a semblance of a line appeared as each scampered for a spot in the lineup. But again, having checked our paper, we would carefully count the number who lined up. We had begun with 76 adults that morning. Now there were 81.

Registering disappointment, we would inform them that five people had sneaked into the line and had not worked that day. Therefore, no one would be paid until those five culprits identified themselves.

"Oh no, Tuan," they would say. "We also counted this morning and all these people worked today. You have forgotten; maybe you did not count correctly."

Back to that little piece of paper we would go, informing them that there were only 76 who had begun work that morning and that the paper does not lie. "Someone is trying to 'climb our backs' (to deceive us)," we would tell them. "There will be no payment until those people identify themselves."

Then the shouting, threatening and interrogation of the group would begin. "Hey you! You were not here this morning." And one would slink off into the grass. "Hey friend, I saw you come stand in line just when pay time was called. Out you go. Can't you see that paper does not lie? You want us to lose our shell and salt for the day? Go quickly!" And another embarrassed pretender would leave the group, probably thinking, "It was worth a try anyway!"

In this way, the culprits would be weeded out and payment finally given to those who had worked. Normally, happy as could be, they would bounce off to their homes to return the next day, should there be more work to do.

At first, very quickly we could identify those who had sneaked into the pay-line by looking at their hands. If their hands were clean, they had not worked and we would send them off. But they soon caught on to that and would quickly rub mud and dirt on their hands and bodies.

Then we went to a ticket system, giving each worker a small tin ticket. If he had a ticket, we would pay him in the afternoon. If not, no pay. But then he would break the small tin ticket in half, giving it to one of his friends who had come later in the day to work, or he would latch on to an empty tin can and try to cut out his own ticket, which he would present to us.

So we went to pressing a small letter of the alphabet on the pieces of tin. Well, wouldn't you know it! Several days later some very interesting letters would turn up on those pieces of tin to be presented to us for payment for work that day—and this in spite of their ignorance of reading and writing!

One particular day four axes were counted and given out with the usual dozen or so gunny sacks which were used to carry the fill needing to be moved. In the morning we went through the usual procedure and in the afternoon the same— counting and bringing back the tools we had given out.

This particular afternoon one axe turned up missing and we got the runaround: "Oh, Tuan, you miscounted this morning. We, too, can count up to four. We watched you count and you gave us only three axes. We are sure of it. Even your piece of paper will tell you that. You better have another look."

We went and had another look. Plainly four axes had been given out. "Someone has taken one of the axes. We are sorry. No one gets paid until that axe comes in," we informed them. "But Tuan, look, the rain is coming. We haven't eaten since last night. We are potato hungry. Have pity on us. We are sure your writing is wrong this time. Please let us have our pay so that we can go home and get some food."

"Sorry folks," we had to say. "We can't work that way. We lose one axe today; we will lose another tomorrow until all our tools are gone. Stealing is wrong. The man who steals will never enjoy immortality in heaven with God!"

The thought that it may have gotten lost or perhaps been left in the grass or roots where they had been working brought several responsible men to their feet who ran down to the area to have a further look. Patiently we waited for their return. Nothing!

"Friends," we said, "we will pay you when the axe comes back." Closing the door to the tool shed, we walked off to our house. Then the cries went out: "You with the 'dried-up liver' (obstinate)! Can't you see we have worked hard all day? Our hands are bleeding; our bellies are empty. You don't know anything about pity for us."

And the women workers railed at the men: "You treacherous imbeciles. Give the white man his axe. Take pity on us. Can't you see the rain is coming? Our children here in the net bags will get sick and die and you will go hungry because we have not prepared your evening potatoes and potato vines. Can't you men understand that it is impossible to deceive that piece of banana leaf on which the white man writes these secrets? Come across with the axe so we can go home".

"Shut up, you stupid women, and go back to your raising of pigs. Potato-diggers and child-bearers should learn to keep their mouths shut," the men countered.

Thus, the tirades went on as we walked off to our home, hoping there was no hothead in the group who would put an arrow in our backs as we walked. From our windows we watched the group form a little huddle. After several minutes, a couple of the men jumped to their feet, raced down to the work site, and minutes later called, "Tuan come! We found it. Someone in the group forgot they had left it in the trees where they had sharpened their digging sticks."

Without further arguing, we returned, paid them off, and chuckled as they raced down the path to their homes. We knew someone had slipped the axe into the weeds where he planned to pick it up on his way home and leave the valley that night.

Such were the challenges of working with these people in those early days. Gradually they learned. But we had to be alert to their shenanigans believing it necessary for them to learn principles of right living, and for us to build bridges of communication to produce the respect necessary for them to eventually embrace the message we had come to share with them.

Chapter 7:
Shaping vision for ministry

—〜〜—

After familiarizing myself with the paths, the villages and the leaders in the immediate Mulia valley where the airstrip had been built, I began trekking out to valleys and villages on the backside of those mountains several hours walk away. Often I spent the nights in the villages, sleeping around their fires and with their pigs in those small round houses. One such day, trekking through a heavily populated valley called "Ngguragi," I was overcome with the rugged beauty in the valley. The villages and gardens built along the mountain-sides; the flow of the turbulent rivers; the stark towering peaks and vast untamed forests above me; and the warmth of the sun enhancing that beauty around me, was awesome!

Walking along one of those long low ridges, viewing the panorama below me, I stopped to drink in the beauty. From that elevation, I looked down upon at least a dozen villages spread out before me. The awesomeness of that moment ignited the passion in my soul. Tears filling my eyes, I cried out: "How, God? How can we meet the needs of these peoples about us? I'm here to reach the people of this valley with the message of LIFE. God, how can it be done?"

The answer was not long in coming. As I stood there mesmerized by the beauty of that setting, yet my heart aching for the people who inhabited it, into my mind stole our possible strategy. Each of these villages needed a clinic to improve their health, a literacy school where they could learn to read and to write, and a church in which they could gather to worship our God out of the sun and rain. At that moment, I pictured these three ministries with their appropriate buildings in each of the villages. Satisfied, I looked around at the Dani men walking with me and said, *"Nawi!"* "Let's go!"

We had walked only a few minutes when we came out on the crest of the ridge. Looking down, we saw hundreds of tribespeople in the yard of one of the closer villages, with smoke billowing up into that clear blue sky. Obviously there was a feast in progress. We could not resist the opportunity to be a part of it and to enjoy what we now know is genuine Dani hospitality. We grabbed our packs and started down the hill toward the village where we were royally welcomed with smiles, the typical Dani handshake and—when they opened the cooking pits—with piles of cooked sweet potato and sweet potato vines placed before us.

At that time, not knowing the excitement in the Dani ceremonial distribution of the pork, I sat fascinated by all that I saw: the carcasses of the pigs spread out in a long line before us, the man with the bamboo knife moving alongside each carcass to make the first ceremonial cut in the jowl flesh of that carcass, the owner of each pig cutting the carcass into large portions.

When this was finished, I watched the leading chief of that village walk to the center of the feast area with a nice-size piece of pork in his hand. Holding that toward heaven, he looked up into the sky and shouted out in a loud voice for all to hear, *"Ninogoba Wakkagagerak wae!"* "Our Father Creator. This is your piece of pork with which we honor you at our feast." Then, wondering if he had done the right thing, he slipped over and sat down beside me. "Is it all right that we offer to our Father God the first fruits of our feast?" he asked. "Did I do wrong in approaching Him in this way?"

Noting the sincere expression on his face, I could not tell him that God did not eat pork. I merely said, *"Op aret o."* "That was all right. We will teach you more about this

Creator God." He smiled, snapped fingers with me in the typical Dani friendship greeting, then went back to leading the activities of the feast. And I sat pondering what I was seeing and hearing. Here was a nearly naked Dani chief—his hair done up in a net bag the tail of which reached down to his heels, his nose displaying a large pig's tusk, his body greased with pig fat and soot—reaching out for understanding of and blessing from this Creator God about whom we had come to share. Here, indeed, was a people waiting to hear and to regain access to the eternal life they believed they had lost somewhere in their distant past.

****

The months continued to roll by rapidly, ushering in 1961. A month before, we had become the proud parents of a lovely baby girl. Nearing the delivery date, Esther and I had flown out to the coast where there was a fairly complete hospital with reasonably competent staff where our daughter, Dawn, was born, and never has there been born a daughter like this one!

A journal entry on the 7th of December, two days after Dawn's birth, conveys our feeling:

> *Our first baby, a girl fittingly named Dawn. Esther is so happy. It is good to see the radiance of her face as she talks about OUR baby. God has given me a super daughter and a super wife and mother; I am privileged!*

Communication was getting easier as we progressed in analyzing and understanding the beauty of the language with its many verb inflections. As well, cultural features captivated our interest and enlarged our understanding of the Dani world. More than my studies in apologetics in Bible

School, the beautiful structure of the Dani language breaking down into verb tenses complete with embedded person and specific time indicators, their use of indirect objects, and their vast vocabulary set in their world of reality, convinced me of a Divine Hand behind its formation. There was no way this complex yet beautifully structured, symmetrically predictable language could have evolved among this "simple" people. I marveled that even among the people of this Stone Age culture in the heart of Dutch New Guinea, God had his secrets; there was clear evidence and expression of the Creator. This could only be the product of a God of order and design.

Chapter 8:
The Dani conversion experience

—ᴍ—

Immediately upon our arrival we had noted a phenomenal attendance at the weekly Sunday services, where the Gospel Recording records were played with simple brief additions and explanations given by the missionary. Following this, other local leaders, who at the moment felt either inspired to contribute or compelled to explain in good Dani what they thought was being said, would rise to their feet to give their spontaneous exhortation and application of the message.

Awed, we had witnessed hundreds of heads bowing in prayer with father or mother forcefully slamming onto their laps their young children who wanted to "look around" during prayer, then, tightly covering their children's eyes with their hands. Amazed were we that the total group— often numbering up to a thousand people—fervently and in unison repeated the "amen" when the missionary finished his prayer. Most impressed, we concluded that God was obviously at work in the hearts of these people.

And while the basis of our evaluation (repeating the "amen") was wrong, the fact of it was not. God was at work. The hundreds who came bursting from the paths and dancing up the airstrip each Sunday morning, the orderliness of the way their bows and arrows were lined up along the rock fence surrounding the airstrip prior to their sitting down, the scuffle to sit as close to the "talking box" as possible in order to hear more clearly the words coming out of that box, the intensity of their listening, the shouts at the women to suckle their babies to keep them quiet—all indicated something unique was going on inside those Dani minds and hearts. The Gospel message, simple in presentation, was ringing bells of longing and hope. We were thrilled to be a part of it and, very soon, were able to assist in communicating it.

Not only on Sunday was this interest apparent, but now during the week. On a normal afternoon, men would gather under a banana tree in our yard, shouting out that they had come to hear more *"ki wone"* "living words." We would go out to sit and chat with them, but normally ended up giving them a nugget truth about God which they would memorize on their fingers, repeating it over and over making it theirs. Then as dusk set in, they would drift off to their own villages some 10 to 20 minutes walk away. We knew these words were being repeated around the fires in their small round houses that evening, prior to their sleeping.

****

It was the beginning of 1961, not long after we had arrived, when we became aware that big doings were afoot. One afternoon, a voice from outside our home called in to me, *"Tuan Kobo wonage ilik lek a?"* "Is Mr. Scovill there?" I called out, "I'm here!" "Come on outside," the voice said. "We want to talk with you."

I looked out to see several of the local Dani chieftains sitting on the grass in a circle near a banana tree in our yard, anticipating me and my colleague joining them, which we did, and listened to their request. The spokesman for the group directed our attention to the dark stains of human blood on some of the arrows he carried. He pointed to the small bag of fetishes in the larger net bag hanging from the shoulder of every adult Dani male. "My fathers," he began, "the things which we do and worship are in direct opposition to the *'ki wone'* 'living words' which you give us from that Big Book. We, as a people, have made a decision to do away with our life of killing one another and worshipping of the spirits; we want to live the way that Big Book tells us to live. To do that we must destroy our weapons and fetishes immediately."

Much more was said, and at different times. Our background as well as the training we had received was on how to plan for and handle the one-on-one method of evangelism. Here, some 12,000 people around us wanted to come to Christ, NOW!

We explained our reluctance. "These are new and heavy words we have brought you," we said. "You do not really understand them yet. When you comprehend the meaning, destroying your weapons and fetishes will be fine, but not yet." Their response: "Then don't bother any longer to teach us from that Big Book because there is a veil over the eyes of our hearts which does not allow us to take in any more truth. That veil is caused by these things in our net bags." And they would point again to their weapons and spirit fetishes. Frustrated, they would go back to their villages only to return a few days later to try to convince us with a different line of reasoning.

Let not my reader feel irritated with us for not jumping up and down with joy at their decision. Not only did we want them to think through this decision, to count the cost of what they were really doing, but we were buying time to be able to more clearly present the claims of the Gospel. In addition, there was the problem of communicating in a language that was not yet truly ours. We too, while seeing and appreciating their reasoning, but not yet sure of ourselves, approached it from the possible consequences which could result from such a dramatic rejection of their past along with the burning of their fetishes.

Several weeks before, Ralph and I had moved among groups of their *yigin unde,* their "warriors," pleading with them to abort their planned attack on their enemies two days walk down valley. They had listened politely, but in the end, had attacked and returned with their sick and wounded for us to treat. They boasted they had killed men, women, and children, driving them to the west and forcing some to jump to their deaths over a high precipice. We also knew these enemies had returned to their homes and were at that time rebuilding their villages and gardens—and planning!

"What if your enemies down valley hear you have burned your bows, arrows and fetishes?" we asked. "They will seize the opportunity to come up and return the attack. You will be powerless against them, fleeing like women out of your homes and sleeping like possums in the forest. Your villages will be burned, your pigs killed, your gardens ravaged, and your women raped and killed." We thought this line of reasoning would catch their attention and it did. In unison they nodded their heads in agreement: *"Abet aret o! Abet aret o!"* "That is true; that is true!"

Overwhelmed by the reality of this logic, silence ensued. Furrows knit their brows. Fact was fact. This was final. They drifted into smaller huddles and we could hear them weighing the issues as they plucked their beards, and deliberated. There was no answer to this one—or was there? A body turned our way, positioning himself to speak. His no-nonsense voice broke the silence.

"Tuan, you have talked to us from that Big Book. That Being up in the sky who made the world and who made us: He can heal the sick; He can cast out demons; He can raise the dead and quiet the wind and the waves. If He can do all that, can He not control our enemies so they will not attack us, or at best protect us if they do?"

What could we say? Our Bible School training had not given us the answers to this. They had backed us into the corner. Their logic had won the day! The word spread rapidly that the fetish burnings were on; the valley began to prepare.

It was Sunday morning. The evening before, few people slept. The night sky was red with the glow of fires and the valleys echoed with the screams of pigs being killed. During those evening hours, they had torn down and torched their spirit houses located behind the men's houses; spirit pigs were killed and upon these they had feasted throughout the night. It would not do to bring that type of activity into the morrow. These were pigs they had consecrated to the spirits to guarantee their care and protection from various malicious acts of those spirits, or to be used in a ritual placating that spirit for some future emergency.

Killing a pig dedicated to the spirits

Early in the morning, the call went out! From mountain peak to mountain peak, it reverberated through the valleys: "This is the day. Awake my kinsmen. This is the day we find eternal life. Hurry, prepare yourselves."

By midmorning, the paths were dark with thousands of people moving toward the burning site they had prepared at the top of the airstrip the day before. They had brought in the necessary firewood and branches to make the long pyre on which their fetishes would be disposed. The air was full of calls, bouncing back and forth across the valley, announcing the groups on the way. The atmosphere was filled with unbelievable tension. Our spirits soared to God in ecstatic joy and thankfulness, but mixed with apprehension and a tinge of fear.

Then, I felt it. The tiny bark house in which we were living about a hundred feet from the top of the airstrip began to shake. Our first thought was that an earthquake had hit. At the same time, I heard the thudding of hundreds of feet on the airstrip turf and looked out through the clear plastic window of our small house to see the paths, the grass, the foliage, and the stream beds actually and almost literally disgorging themselves of the people who had waited within their shelters. At a given signal, they poured forth onto the airstrip running, dancing, and chanting. Smaller groups merged and integrated with the larger groups until there was one massive group of some 8,000 black perspiring bodies that raced madly up and down the airstrip in their dance patterns.

Each one was decked out in all his and her finery of leaves, feathers, and designs—of red clay mixed with ashes—painted on their bodies. Most bodies glistened with a freshly applied pig fat and soot mixture. Some of the *abe aap,* the "real men" had let down their long hair from the net bags in which it normally hung, and were swishing it from side to side in celebration.

Bows and arrows with their accompanying long spears were much in evidence, along with the "spirit duster" made of cassowary bird feathers which they had waved back and forth to ward off the evil spirits. Others had their bags of fetishes tied to the end of long sticks which they proudly displayed above their heads. Above all, their chant caught my attention. Over and over again, it was sent on its way by thousands of happy, exuberant voices: *"Agi uugwe! Agi uugwe!"* "We want heaven! We want heaven!" They wanted the immortality which they believed they had lost centuries before.

We watched as this large, colorful mass of perspiring bodies drifted into their own village and *kunume* groups and prepared their fetishes for burning. Many of the leaders within those groups rose to exhort their own not to hold anything back. This was a "do or die" situation, and could work only if all participated. Specifically, we noted the intensity of the men's exhortation directed to the women and we immediately understood the tension between the two: the men feared the women, the women feared the men. If the men burned their protective charms and confessed their secret ritual, but the women did not, the men would make themselves vulnerable to the women and visa versa.

I recall several men, one in particular whom I had thought was a nobody in the community — perhaps a bit "different," — stand to his feet to exhort the group. In his hand he held a stick with an odd piece of old dried-up meat laced to the tip. A hush fell on the group as he began to speak.

Asking a few questions of those around me, I learned that this man was the shaman of the dreaded Kuguruwo spirit, the spirit which fed on the bodies of the dead which would somehow materialize from the ashes of their cremation. Often the death of a loved one was attributed to this spirit because it was hungry. And in the evening at dusk, her call — for it was a woman spirit — could be heard as it departed from its haunt, seeking nourishment for its nightly activity. Men working outside or walking on the trail to their homes, upon hearing the cry, would race to the protection of the nearest house, where they would spend the night.

I listened with interest as he vowed to the group that it, that symbol of his power which, some said, was a piece of actual human flesh, would be placed on the fire. He was finished with that sort of life. Other confessions and intentions were made by other men. I recall being impressed that this was the final round, the most important part of the ceremony, when each had to reassure the other, and be reassured by him, that he was coming clean. Each man's secret and supernatural power and influence affected the other. Only the total willingness of each one in the tribe to reject and dispose of his and her spirit paraphernalia (which threatened the other), would guarantee a positive communal end.

Having satisfied themselves that this was their community desire and decision, we watched as group by group came, placing on that pile of firewood their charms, amulets, relics of the past, bows and arrows, spears—all they had trusted in for centuries. Gone were the gods which controlled every area of their lives.

My colleague, Ralph Maynard, wrote a description of these things: "...innumerable bows, arrows, spears, stone and bone knives, shells, beautiful fur headdresses, pig tails, nose bones, bits of string, all sorts and sizes of feather bands, large and small bridal stones, pieces of cane, armbands, feather-dusters, necklaces, rare ornamental shells plus a host of wrapped items which we didn't see..." were brought and dumped on that pile.

Several made appropriate comments as they tossed their possessions imbibed with spirit power on the pile of firewood. One man, a very charismatic influential community leader, stood on the edge of that pyre that was already loaded with fetishes and in a very dramatic gesture began methodically to strip himself of all his paraphernalia: the bundle of arrows along with his bow in hand, the headdress on his head, the pig's tusk in his nose, the plugs in his ear, the necklace and amulets hanging from his neck, the pretty colored leaves and feathers in his armbands with which he wooed the women, the armbands themselves, gifts and special bracelets used in the free-love courtship ceremony held during times of community crises like war and death to annul grief with sensuous animal pleasure, his special net bag filled with shells and exotic pieces of stone, wood, and glass—all of it he stripped from his body, tossing it on the pile.

Then, in a moment of rare grandeur, he pulled a long bone dagger from one remaining armband. Loosing it from its sheath, he held it up for all to see, crying, "My fathers and my mothers! My brothers and my sisters! My children one and all! Look at this bone dagger. I've killed over one man's hands (plus or minus 10 people) with this bone dagger. Today, in the presence of you all, I'm burning it and taking eternal life. I don't need it any longer." And he flipped it onto the pile of firewood. Then in distain for that which had held him captive for so long, he turned and spit several times on those things he had placed on the pile to be burned, after which he returned to his place as leader of his group.

After all their relics had been placed in a huge pile on the firewood in preparation for burning, several significant things happened. First was concerning who was to light the fire that was to consume this huge pile of fetishes. The people sitting neatly in their groups looked our way; we, the missionaries, looked their way.

Again, Ralph wrote of this dramatic moment: "We had quite a discussion as we all tried to point out to them that it was their place to burn their own fetishes, but our admonitions were to no avail and for half an hour we were locked in a stalemate that looked as if Satan would claim the victory.

"At last I suggested that the chief and I together would set fire to that huge pile of fetishes. Everyone was pleased with this. The chief who was to set the fire to the pile came forward and held a bunch of dry grass. I set fire to the grass, and he in turn placed the burning grass in the kindling under the firewood. In a matter of minutes, the wood caught fire and quickly became a blazing inferno."

The chief involved was by birth the one through whom the right and power of lighting ceremonial fires was vested.

And therefore the responsibility for ensuring that the fire accomplished its designated purpose was his. In terms of his understanding of lines of authority and power, perhaps some of his reluctance was his thinking that Ralph, the superior spiritual personage at that ceremony, was also invested with the same power. Ralph's superior power would not only authenticate and complete the destruction of the fetishes, but it would also defeat the spirit power behind those symbols. At any rate the partnership was acceptable, and these things of their past quickly turned to ashes.

At some point during the burning, a group of men came up to Ralph, urging him to be responsible concerning his "badness" which needed to be placed on the fire with theirs. For a few moments, Ralph wondered just what they had in mind. Seeing the question and consternation on his face, they then volunteered the information. Had they not seen Ralph purchase some bows and arrows to take to America to show his friends? Were these not hidden in the attic of his house?

Quickly, Ralph responded, "Oh, but I'm not going to use them to kill people. They are to show my friends in my village in America what you folks here at Mulia did." "Nonetheless," the Danis argued, "those bows have been used in war, and thus imbibed with our spirit power along with the feathers on the tips of the bow and carvings at the base of several of the arrows. They must be burned." So, my missionary friend had to join the crowd that day and toss his artifacts on the fire!

The final impression I recall of this burning was the moment when the fire began to envelop the whole pile. Assured that all would be consumed, one of the leaders rose to his feet, giving forth a mighty call of victory: "Witness this fire consuming our badnesses (sins). Today is the day we embrace the living words. Today we exchange our mortal skin, to be clothed with His immortal one. Today is the day we take to ourselves eternal life, *'Ninogoba wa!'* 'Father, we thank you!'" And at that moment, some 8,000 voices joined in a mighty response of affirmation which resounded back and forth among those mountains. Then each group rose to their feet and, without looking back, raced silently down the paths to their homes, many of them spitting on the ashes of the relics as they passed.

The fire on which was burned their fetishes and weapons

The next day several of the leaders in the community returned, dug a large hole, and buried the remaining ashes and rocks which had not completely disintegrated—a beautiful and permanent memorial of what God had done. In addition, within the next several days, one of the men, Wogoriya'mban by name, brought a young tree and, planting it at the top of the airstrip, said to the tree, "May you confirm our decision by growing tall, spreading your branches, and providing shade and shelter for those who come and sit under you." In the years ahead, the Dani would often refer to this burning of fetishes as the turning point in their conversion experience.

Looking back upon this historical event, and understanding a bit more about their culture with its links to the supernatural where abode thousands of spirits which required intricate ritual, oppressive obedience to a zillion taboos, and wealth-eating sacrifices to keep those spirit beings positive and thus benevolent in the interrelationships, we realize how very superficial was our understanding of this event at that time.

Two overarching and overwhelming truths move out of that milieu: First, the terrible, distasteful, oppressive, wearisome bondage to those spirits governing their universe; and second, the deep, deep yearning to regain "eternal life" which they felt they had lost. These two truths, I believe, were the foundational pillars of their logic which led to their decision to rid themselves of that bondage and to embrace the freedom found in a commitment to Christianity. The objects thrown on that fire were not just what we saw, a bunch of silly things like sticks and stones. They were the undergirders; this was the bedrock of their culture; through these fetishes they could make contact with their gods whom they felt preserved them, protected them, fed them, and guaranteed their health and posterity.

Even now as I think again of the important place these objects—symbols of spirit power—had in their culture and worldview, I am awed that such a decision was ever made by the leaders of this people, and then was actualized in such a remarkable experience. This was definitely a "God-thing" and their subsequent growth in the faith has affirmed it. Those amazing Danis!

Chapter 9:
A power encounter

—ɯ—

The fetish burning which happened at Mulia had already taken place among the Danis in most of the other non-UFM areas several days walk from us. The Mulia-Ilu area, one of the last Dani areas reached with the Gospel, was only now responding to that message. Hearing that the people at Mulia had burned their weapons and fetishes, some 15,000 Dani people at Ilu, two days trek upriver, made the decision to do the same. Following the main burning of fetishes both at Mulia and Ilu, there were several smaller burnings in the more isolated population pockets throughout the area. However, between the two main areas there was one valley that resisted, claiming that their gardens were still producing food, their pigs were still having litters, and their wives were still giving them children. "What's the fuss?" was the word which drifted down to us at Mulia.

I do not recall being aware of such resistance until one day on trek through that area. We stood on a high ridge looking across the large Ngguragi River as the men pointed to several villages on the other side, saying that they were the *"iniki omaawi"* the "hardhearted ones," who had not burned their fetishes. What's more, our spokesman informed us that they were bragging about a large new garden they had made high on the mountainside which we could see from where we stood. Indeed it was huge, probably about 15 to 20 acres as I recall, with a beautiful new wooden fence built around it and new luscious green sweet potato plants and corn growing in that afternoon sun. It was beautiful and they had every right to be proud of it.

Hearing that they were the "hardhearted ones," and had resisted the burning of their fetishes, I said to the men with me, "Let's go on across and overnight in their village, sharing with them the message of the Gospel." While this was being discussed, for some were wondering if it was the safe thing to do, we saw a small group of men from the main village come out of their houses and, standing in the middle of their village yard, they called across the valley to us: "Don't come this way; we do not want the message you are bringing. The *'woneelom'* 'words of our ancestors' are still good words."

We further discussed the matter, and when one of the men with us who lived on the side of the river where we stood said, "I know every person in that village. There is no danger; let's go across!" I grabbed my bag and said, "Yes, let's do!" and we began slipping and sliding down the small trail to the river, crossed it, and started climbing up the other side.

It was nearly an hour later that we approached their village and, climbing over the gate—a small notched pole you walk up, then another you walk down, with upright poles you grab on your way over—we walked into their village yard. And it was eerie! There was an unnatural deathlike quietness hovering over the village. All the houses, including the men's house, were tightly boarded up as if the entire village had fled. I understood immediately what was going on, so deliberately walked past the large men's house where I was convinced all were hiding, and said loudly to the men with me, "Well, I guess there is no one here. We might as well move on!" Then I moved past the boarded-up front door of the men's house, stepped quietly over the fence ladder, slipped around to the back door, which was open, and stooped down to look inside. And there they were—men, women and children—sitting as quiet as mice around the fire.

I smiled, greeting them warmly, and then said, "My friends, we are not here to force you to accept the message of *'nabelan-kabelan'* 'eternal life' which we bring to you. If you want to continue to live according to the words of your ancestors, and die with that little *pirigobit* bird perching at the tip of the pole on which hangs your possessions at your cremation spot and screams, 'Ha, ha, you missed it; ha, ha, you missed it,' that is up to you. Even though you reject the eternal words we bring, we can still be friends. We will go now." And without a sound from them, I stepped back over the fence, joined our men waiting for me, and we went on our way back across the river to overnight in a village more friendly to us.

Several weeks later, I looked out the window of our house to see several strangers walking hurriedly toward our door. Wondering what was up, for I did not remember having met these men, I went out to welcome them and to hear their story. They were from the village of the *iniki omaawi,* the "hard-hearted ones," and they had come requesting me to come to their village the following weekend. Sensing something a bit extraordinary, I asked them why they wanted me to do that. They then proceeded to tell me what had happened.

"Several nights ago," they said, "during a heavy downpour in the middle of the night, a landslide occurred and our big beautiful garden was wiped out and dumped into the river below. The power of the spirits of our ancestors is no match for the power of your God; please come to our village this coming Sunday. We want to rid ourselves of our weapons and fetishes."

And that Sunday, when I went up, I saw what had happened. Almost within the very boundaries of the fence around their big beautiful garden, the landslide had wiped it out, dumping it in the river below. In its place was a large gaping hole in the mountainside which to this day reminds them of the power of our God. As they recite the story, they snap their fingers against their gourds or chest cavity, the gesture of overwhelming awe and disbelief at that which happened. God was making Himself credible to these people."

Chapter 10:
The bird and the snake

—〰—

A nd now you must hear the story of the small *pirigobit* bird and the snake, which I feel very much shaped the Dani worldview and certainly is the heart of that extraordinary yearning after eternal life which we noted upon our arrival.

"Real life for the Dani people," they say, "began when two men came up out of a hole in the ground at a place called 'Taakobak.'" Taakobak is an actual geographical spot several miles outside the city of Wamena in the interior of Papua. These two men carried with them a stone axe and the bow and arrow! Arriving at the top of this hole, they tried to step out on the ground but sank in mud and water. The brother carrying the stone axe buried it in the mud, whereupon the ground immediately solidified, enabling them to walk about on it. With the bow and arrow, they were able to survive, eating raw meat (fire had not yet been discovered) and leaves which they found in abundance. But alas, there were no women with whom they could cohabit to reproduce themselves.

In the process of time, this also took care of itself; two women came up out of the same hole. The women carried the sweet potato shoot, as well as the banana shoot. With the women—so the story goes—a dog squirmed its way up and in its ear were found lodged a gourd seed and a cucumber seed which were taken and planted.

Life took its natural course. The older brother took one of the women for his wife, but alas, the closer he got to her, the more he itched, until he had to refuse her. Coincidently, the younger brother was having the same problem. The other woman, whom he took, set forth in him an allergic reaction in which he, too, broke out in a rash and incredible itching and had to flee from her. After some disappointment they decided to switch women, which they did, and to their utter surprise and incredible pleasure, both brothers ended up with women whom they could tolerate physically and who therefore became their wives.

Allow me to digress just a moment to clarify several matters. Note there was some form of life prior to them coming out of the hole in the ground. Any questions directed to them about the information gaps in their story, at best, will receive only their famous *"Eekwak!"* answer, which means, "We know nothing more than that!"

Note too, that the ground on which they tried to step was only mud and water. Does this not remind my reader of Genesis 1:2(KJV), "...the ground was without form and void..."? The solution was to bury their stone axe, undoubtedly their answer to the bedrock beneath the soil.

And finally, the shoots the women brought up with them were planted and provided the necessary diet for the Danis' survival. These were the basic foods found in the tribe when the missionaries arrived in the mid1950's.

The story of the mismatch of the women may make us smile but it also takes us to the very root of their marriage taboos. Not being able to physically tolerate the first women they tried to take led the two brothers to deduce that undoubtedly they had tried to take their own clan sisters. Therefore they decided they were never to marry within their own clan. This would be considered incest, and serious harm would come upon the clan: all the sweet potatoes in their gardens would rot on the vines causing an area-wide famine.

So they married and began to reproduce upon the face of the earth. Death had not yet made its advent. Life was good; they were happy. Unaware were they that out of the distant past a bird and a snake were racing toward them. The bird was bringing mortality; the snake, immortality. And, as the story would have it, the bird being faster, reached them first, bringing mortality. If the snake had reached them first, man would live forever because the snake, they believe, was bringing immortality. This is affirmed by its shed skin seen in the rocks and brambles. It continues to live on, periodically shedding its old skin and taking on a new one.

That little sparrow-like bird called the *"pirigobit"* brought them death. After the body is cremated, that bird will come, they say, and perch on the tip of the "tombstone," the pole stuck into the ashes of the cremation on which is hung all the possessions of the deceased, and cry, "Ha, ha, you missed it! Ha, ha, you missed it!" In their anger, they give pursuit with their bows and arrows; in their grief they weep and wail, pulling out their hair and tossing it up onto the grass roofs of their houses; and in their feeling of hopelessness and helplessness, they sever the knuckles from their fingers. Such is their deep grief in the death of their loved ones.

Grieving the loss of their dead by severing the knuckles
of their fingers

It may be interesting to my reader to know that the word we use to translate "eternal life" in Dani, harks back to this story and uses the term *"nabelan-kabelan"* "my skin in exchange for your skin." When we accept God's gift of salvation through His Son, He gives us *"nabelan-kabelan"* "His (eternal) skin in exchange for our (mortal) skin." And this is the word you will find in our Dani translation of John 3:16: "...that whosoever believes...will not perish but be given God's (immortal) skin to replace his (mortal) one!"

Chapter 11:
Shaping a new worldview

—⟋⟍—

The event of the burning of fetishes forever changed the way the Dani lived. He had courageously destroyed his gods—gods responsible to produce food in his garden; gods which protected his pigs and guaranteed them healthy litters; gods which protected his person from sickness, from the enemy, and from those dark malevolent spirits; gods which moved alongside him when he hunted; gods on whom he depended for rain, for marriage, for posterity, for victory in war—everything in which he had trusted for centuries he had destroyed in his acceptance of the message of the Gospel brought by us foreigners. "We want now to learn the way of this God revealed in that Big Book," they pressed on us.

In ridding themselves of these fetishes through which they communicated with their gods (read, spirits), the Danis had ripped away the foundations of their thinking and living. It was now our awesome responsibility to help them formulate a new worldview based upon principles from the Word of God. These principles would then become the stabilizers in the change they would now experience.

Several significant changes we noticed immediately. Walking along the paths, often we would come upon a shell (their money) or a string of beads dangling from the tip of a stick stuck in the ground. Upon inquiring, we were told that the item had been found along the trail and someone had tied it to the tip of that stick so it could more easily be seen by the owner when he came looking for it. Stealing was literally a thing of the past.

Since they had not seen us or the pilots smoking or chewing betel nut, they assumed these two habits were a forbidden part of the total package of receiving the gospel message in its purest form. Smoking and chewing of betel nut disappeared nearly overnight. Tobacco plants were pulled up out of their gardens and burned, tobacco leaves drying in their houses were destroyed, and betel nut trees growing around the villages and in the forests were chopped down.

Some months later this matter was discussed in the context of whether rejection of these habits should become a condition for baptism. Though we strongly urged them NOT to make it such, one of the men preparing to be baptized put the matter to us like this. "Tuan," he said. "Smoking and chewing of betel nut to us is like a flea on a pig. It is not the pig; it is just something undesirable on and irritating to the pig. We, as a people, have agreed that we do not want these habits to move with us into the new lives we are developing for our future." That was pretty good reasoning, we felt, and certainly an apt illustration. Smoking and betel nut chewing were discarded as they moved to build a new society based on the principles of the Word of God.

Fear of the darkness, when the spirits were known to attack or harass, also became a thing of the past. Normally, when the cicada bug sounded as night fell, or upon hearing the sound of the Kuguruwo spirit in the late afternoon—which to us sounded every bit to be the call of the tender-eyed dove—all would rush to the warmth and protection of the fire in the nearest hut. From that safe place they kept their ears open to detect the movement of that call. Now, at night we would see lines of fire sticks (handfuls of grass) waved back and forth to shed light on their paths as the people moved from one village to the next, or as they came to speak with us about some matter. The darkness was no longer their enemy.

The service on Sunday, though well-attended by our standards, increased significantly in numbers after the burning.

They still would come singing and dancing out of the paths and up the airstrip, but since they had burned their bows and arrows, these things were missing as they came to worship. Prior to the burning of their fetishes, quite often the Sunday morning worship service would break up over the application of a point of truth.

When we would preach against stealing, or adultery, the worship service would dissolve into two fighting parties, as the owner of the stolen pig would rise to his feet shouting: "That's right. It is a sin to steal another person's pig, and that person is going to experience the judgment of God, isn't he! May this God put a curse upon him and his family"—all in third person! Hearing this, the accused would jump to his feet, shouting out his answer to the accusation. In a matter of seconds the group would take sides, race to their weapons leaning against the rock fence around the airstrip, and arrows would begin to fly as we grabbed our Bibles and notes and raced for the shelter of our homes!

After burning their bows, arrows and long spears, these incidents grew less frequent and less intense. But they still had their moments when an argument erupted, sending the group into two factions who, no longer having access to bows and arrows, would pick up rocks and clumps of dirt to hurl back and forth at each other before racing down the paths to their homes. Eventually, the moment would pass and they would gather again the next week to hear those "living words" from the Big Book.

I recall this happening at a big feast we were enjoying together. What triggered the intensity of the moment I have forgotten, but rocks, sticks, chunks of meat and clods of earth were all flying back and forth as they shouted at one another. Somewhat close to where we were gathering up our things to get out of the fray, one such flying object struck a young man on the side of his face. I'll never forget the big beautiful smile as he absorbed the "hit" and, with blood running down his face, sank into the grass near us. I figured he was probably saying, "Wow! At last a fight! We haven't had such fun in a long time!" In a matter of moments it was all over, and the older men gathered around us, grieving their hot tempers and apologizing.

We realized the danger of leaving them in a vacuum. They had rejected their gods in which they had trusted for centuries. We now had to find ways to fill that vacuum with the words of the God of the Big Book but also with acceptable, positive health and societal-building activities.

Since most of them gave evidence of disease and poor nutrition, we began there, concentrating on the simple things first: bathing; building simple toilets; making fish ponds; building better houses with reed floors in them; moving the pigs out of the women's houses by fencing them outside the village area which radically influenced the cleanliness and tidiness of the village; diverting a small stream of water through the village, making it more available for washing of hands and food preparation. We also initiated a road building effort, making it easier and faster for them and for us to travel, and to further break down and negate any hostilities between the areas.

In the small airplane we flew in all types of animals: chickens, ducks, rabbits, cows, sheep, goats, better pigs, horses, and even deer; we introduced all types of vegetables and fruit trees which would grow there. Eventually these efforts moved into skills development such as soap-making, sewing of clothes and knitting of warm sweaters for the children using the wool from the sheep. We brought in pit saws and taught them how to saw boards using the "pit saw" method; we taught them building and carpentry skills. We worked to teach them intensive farming methods, bringing in seeds such as crotalaria and other legumes to enrich their soil. You name it, we probably tried it—all to fill the vacuum created by the rejection of their past and to build a better society in which they could enjoy better health.

We already understood that the simple truths of salvation reduced to our formulas—that God had a Son whom He sent to die for man's sin, and if man trusted Him as his Savior, he could enjoy eternal life—were all very vague notions and a bit of nonsense to their ears in that there was absolutely no background on which to build.

Their questions had been, "Who is this God? Tell us about Him!" Then, "Why would he send His Son to die for my badness? Wasn't that sort of a foolish thing to do?" Basically we had to start right from the very beginning, and teach who God is: His creatorship, His attributes, and what He was like as drawn from the Old Testament stories. This had a very sobering effect on them, answering a lot of their questions about the reality of life around them.

The story of creation was very foundational and important. One of the first Dani chants we heard over and over again was as follows:

Who made the sky?	God did!
Who made the clouds?	God did!
Who made the earth?	God did!
Who made the rocks?	God did!
Who made the trees?	God did!
Who made the people?	God did!

And the chant would go on and on with the leader using his creativity to lead them in naming the things God had made. Then the group would respond with the refrain, "God did!"

We taught them about sin and why God could not tolerate it in our lives. Interestingly and in accordance with Romans 1, the Dani did have practices within his culture which he perceived to be unacceptable. Whether he perceived them as only socially unacceptable or whether his feeling went further and he understood them to be morally wrong, I cannot say. But he knew lying was not right; he knew stealing another's possessions was wrong; he knew adultery and fornication were wrong; he knew killing was wrong. The law of God was indeed embedded in his conscience even to the point where certain men in the society were known as the *"aap mage-mili"* "the men prophesying doom and judgment if taboos were violated," and who publicly protested such actions.

My first encounter with this was early in our career before the fetish burning when the warriors gathered to organize an attack on their enemies down valley. I recall at least one older man within several of the groups who stood and passionately spoke against them going to war. One in particular, his counsel disregarded when the warriors jumped to their feet and ran down the path in the direction of the enemy, very slowly and soberly shuffled over to sit down on a nearby large rock, shaking his head and muttering to himself.

And yes, at first, we did use our name for God. In the process of transliterating it into Dani however, it came out with the same pronunciation as the word "goat!" Lest we give the impression that our God related to us through the totemic physical form of the "goat," and since we were moving in the direction of eventually relating more closely to Indonesia, we felt it proper to teach them the term for God which the Indonesian believers use, which is "Allah," but transliterates into Dani as *"Ala."*

The Dani had been animists, believing the invisible part of their world to be inhabited by spirits which governed every aspect of their daily lives. These spirits were malevolent unless placated with sacrifices of food and given respect by keeping the taboos governing their relationships.

In vain we had searched the world of their spirits if perchance we could find one around whom we could build a proper concept of the God of our Scriptures, or at least a spirit being whom they respected and to whom they attributed the creation of the world. The only one coming close was one by the name of "Mbok," but their concept of him was very vague. This particular spirit being did not place the land masses but merely walked through this world, giving the continents and islands their current shape and terrain.

There are three words the Dani uses when he refers to the different activities bringing about the existence of the material world in its present form. The first is *"wakkoorak"* meaning "to make something out of nothing," and the Dani has no problem with the concept of making something out of nothing. That is what God did when He made the world; it is the term we used in the creation story out of which they composed the above chant.

The second word is *"ogobakkigiriyak"* meaning "to make/create something out of something." This word is most accurately used in the act of God creating man "out of the dust" and "woman out of man." It is more an everyday term used for making something a bit unique, such as a piece of furniture or some special innovative object.

And the third word is *"nenaariyak"* meaning "to carve out." Basically, and practically, the Dani concept of the origin of their world begins with a situation like that of Genesis 1:2(KJV): "Now the earth was without form and void and darkness was upon the face of the deep." They have no answer as to how it got to be what it currently is. All they perceived was a huge, unstructured "cosmos" through which strode this powerful spirit being called "Mbok," "carving out" the valleys as it moved along. Where it came from and where it went, was a mystery to them.

As it walked through Papua, carving out the mountains and valleys, they say it left its footprints at various places. One such print is found in the Mulia valley where we served; another about three days walk to the southeast; and another about five days walk to the west. These footprints are basically huge indentations in large rocks which, if one allows his imagination to run wild, can be seen as huge footprints.

However, since there was not enough positive knowledge of this spirit about which we could wrap a biblical concept of our God, we felt it best to use the term for God used by the church in the greater Indonesia.

Chapter 12:
The "Witness School"

—ɯ—

With the foundations of their worldview destroyed, the Dani needed more consistent teaching; they needed the training of leaders; and eventually they would need translation. So the "witness school" concept seemed a good one. Each village would pick a younger but responsible couple to come to school three days a week, Tuesday through Thursday. Here they would learn the stories of Scripture, simple doctrinal studies arising out of those stories, and how a believer lived out his new life in Christ within the community. Then, on the weekends, they would return to their villages to "give witness" to the teaching we had given them that week.

The bigger picture was that in this way we would be developing future pastors and church/community leaders right from ground zero. We would be bringing an entire population under the hearing of the Word of God, and filling that vacuum left by the burning of their fetishes. Granted, the risk was high that some of the teaching would be distorted, but the desire to hear the Word, coupled with their yearning to again possess and enjoy the eternal life promised by that teaching minimized this possibility.

Each village took the responsibility to bring in the materials necessary to build the small round house where their couple would live during those three days each week while attending school. In addition, with building materials which they also brought in, we helped them build a large round school building—a replica of their normal small family round house though much larger. It measured about 25 feet in diameter with a peak rising 20 feet in the air, rectangular holes for windows, and a roof of the local grass they used for roofing their own houses.

The "witness school" with the men in training

Those nearly 50 small round houses, with the large round school building, made quite an impressive site off to the side of the airstrip. And what was really great was that they built these simple buildings themselves, at no cost to us, to learn the message of that Big Book we wanted to share with them. They were ready for school to start. And so were we!

They came that first week, both husband and wife, bearing on their heads and backs sweet potatoes to eat and firewood with which they would cook those potatoes. Some 120 bodies crunched themselves into that school building, sitting on pieces of bark laid on the ground and around a table we had placed there on which to put our lesson materials. When they heard the sound of the "bell," a piece of iron we had picked up from somewhere being hit with a rock or an axe, they would come pouring out of their houses, bodies freshly bathed, and ready for the lessons.

Being a mile high in the interior, some mornings were pretty cold, so we would build a fire in the middle of the school building around which they would huddle, warming themselves while listening and learning the stories we would give to them. Afternoons and evenings they would gather in smaller groups and review the lesson material given them that day so as to minimize transference error. Come Thursday noon, following the lessons of the day, they would board up the openings (doors) of their houses and head back down the trails and over the mountains to take the words we had given them to their home villages.

And their kinsfolk would be waiting for their coming, with the cooking-rocks being heated for a small feast of sweet potatoes and sweet potato vines. Every Friday afternoon the smoke of dozens of fires throughout those valleys could be seen drifting heavenward, with the people gathered to hear the words of God.

While the food cooked in the pits, led by these men, their Bible School students, the people in the villages would learn the new chants composed and sung in the school; they would memorize the verses of Scripture we had given them; and they would listen to the Bible Stories we had taught their "students" during the school session. That afternoon and on into the evening around the fires, this teaching went forth. And it was repeated the next day.

Each Sunday morning, the men from the "witness school" would have a service with their kinsfolk in each village. In the afternoon, or, depending on the distance they had to travel the next day, on Monday, they would head back to the school with their food and firewood to begin another week. In this manner we reached a population of over ten thousand people in our area, and about the same at Ilu, another UFM area upriver. At the same time, we informally trained future leaders and unconsciously pushed the population to be dependent on their own people for the leadership in learning this new message.

These men with their wives, and often a young child, would walk up to eight hours to get back to school. It was this routine of the "witness school" which formalized the names of the days of the week, of which they had none, nor could they speak of years. Terms such as "yesterday," "today," "tomorrow," and even "day after tomorrow," were common expressions in this language, but after that they would indicate time by counting on their fingers how many "sleeps" it had been since the action had taken place, or how many moons had risen. With the routine of the "witness school," we began to hear names for the days of the week, depending on the activity in which we engaged on that particular day.

Sunday was "the day we meet to pray." Monday was "the day we purchase vegetables" from them. Rather than having them bring food from their gardens to us any day of the week, we had picked Monday as the day for them to come with their sweet potatoes, cucumbers, bananas, a type of bean, corn, and other vegetables for which we had given them the seed. These we would purchase as needed with our white salt, matches, soap, shells and other items which were far more valuable than any actual money in whatever currency we could give them.

Tuesday was called "the day we come to the school"; Wednesday was "the middle day we learn"; Thursday was "the day we leave school" because they would return home in the afternoon; Friday was "the day we unravel (recite) the living words" given to them in school to share with their kinsfolk in the villages; Saturday was "the day we gather food" so they would not have to desecrate the Sabbath by going to their gardens on Sunday to find food. Did not the Big Book say, "Thou shalt not pluck any green thing on Sunday?" This was their paraphrase of the commandment,

"Remember the Sabbath to keep it holy!" So Saturday was the day they would dig the potatoes and pick the potato vines to cook and eat on Sunday. And those names are still used today in speaking of the various days of the week, although the Indonesian names are becoming more widely known and used, especially among the younger generation.

By the middle of 1961 another UFM family, Leon and Lorraine Dillinger had located at Mulia with us. They had preceded us to the field but had been helping at another mission station. The Dillingers' gifting and burden for ministry was to teach the Word, training men to become spiritual leaders of the church and community. Eventually, this "witness school" was replaced with a more formal Bible School which Leon and Lorraine founded. They took the lead in building the facilities, in planning then writing up the curriculum, in managing the affairs of the school, in consistent long-term teaching, then in tutoring select men to replace them in that ministry, making the Bible School truly indigenous.

Due to efficient administration over these many years, the school has graduated hundreds of pastors, missionaries, and community leaders, making a lasting, impressive impact on the total Dani church scene in Papua. The Dani Bible School still functions with national leadership prepared by Leon and Lorraine who, in these latter years, have moved into the area of producing helps for Dani pastors and men in church leadership positions. Such helps include a Dani Bible concordance and commentaries which, with other publications, are greatly appreciated by these men and women in their ongoing spiritual development and leadership roles within the church/community.

But training men in the Scriptures eventually required the translation of those Scriptures into their own tongue, and learning to read that translation necessitated teaching them how to read and write. A literacy program was mandatory.

Chapter 13:
Introducing literacy

—⟋ɯ⟍—

W e were now moving into 1962. The Dillingers had relocated to Mulia; the simple "witness school" training program was producing leaders, while at the same time it was grounding the masses in basic doctrines of the Word along with the pragmatics of living the Christian life. There was a level of excitement and momentum of positive progress throughout the entire area which was very satisfying.

While continuing that program, with the Dillingers, we began to brainstorm the basics of a literacy program. We were dealing with an incredible number of highly motivated people; literally thousands of men and women wanted to learn to read and write.

Dani language analysis by the linguists in each of the four missions working in the Dani area was progressing favorably. We shared our findings and language analysis with our sister missions through letters and meetings, motivated by the requests from the Dani in each of the areas to learn how to read. Without that skill, they would never have access to those secret words of the Big Book out of which the missionary produced his lessons. Thus, work on formalizing the Dani orthography was our priority so that literacy programs could be implemented in each area.

Both we and the Dillingers had heard of and had some basic materials on Frank C. Laubach's "Each One Teach One" principles of developing a literacy program among illiterate peoples such as the Dani, and we felt this was the way we should move with our program. Though very much feeling our inadequacies and limited knowledge in this area, we had to make a move. There was no one else to step forward to initiate and implement a program to teach these thousands of eager Danis to read and write. So, with much prayer and much paper, we sat down and outlined a program of 11 primers, eventually to be enhanced with several readers, to bring them to a satisfactory level of comprehension and fluency in reading.

These we produced ourselves, often at night by the light of our kerosene pressure lantern, as cockroaches and every other conceivable bug flew about the room. When our arms got tired of turning the handle of the mimeograph machine, we would ask some of the men working with us to take a turn. This at times was both hilarious and frustrating!

While in their culture they had an up-and-down as well as a back-and-forth motion, they did not have a circular motion. Thus, turning the hand crank on a small grindstone (we started on that!), then moving to the mimeograph machine, was a real challenge to them. The first few deliberate revolutions they could handle, but when they moved up to speed, more often than not they would end up in the back-and-forth or the up-and-down motion with the disastrous effect on the mimeograph machine of having torn stencils and ink all over. And in the case of the grinder—with it torn off my work bench!

But we did it! That little room in our upstairs, that mimeograph machine, that kerosene pressure lamp, and all those flying bugs were witnesses to the hundreds of primers we ran off. But then the problem moved to the field. To whom should we give the books? We knew the youth would be our best target group, for they would learn more quickly than the adult population. But the youth were not the keepers of the secret words of the society. This was the responsibility of the older men, the elders of the people, the least likely to understand what reading was all about! Would we not be undermining their respect, influence and position in the community if we were to bypass them and give the first primers to their youth? So after teaching the basics of reading, we gave those first hundreds of books to the men in the "witness school" and to the elders of the people. And what excitement we created!

After teaching a handful of younger adults to be helpers to those in the community who were learning to read, and since these primers were planned so that one could basically teach oneself to read by way of the simple pictures introducing each letter of their alphabet, the learning process moved to their own villages and men's houses. Then, once a week on the designated day, if they had mastered the material in their primers, they would come in and we would check them out on the sounds and syllables in the particular primer which each carried. If he had mastered the material, we would take the primer which he had learned, give it to another and give him the next primer in the series to take home to learn.

Some would be back the next week for the next primer while others took longer, sometimes up to a month, to work their way through the material in their specific primer. But in this way, they could learn at their own speed. And they did! The interest and excitement of learning to read swept through the community. Out along the paths, in their village yards, by the light of the small fires in their houses, they pored over those strange marks on the "banana leaves." This was the path to those secret words promising immortality, was it not? And how they studied!

Using this method of learning resulted in several positive things. First, it released us from a heavy schedule of teaching literacy so we could continue with the development of and teaching in the "witness school." Second, the youth and younger adults quickly moved to the top of the class, and would then help the older men and women in their villages to master their books. Third, and after trying for some time, many of the older men realized this was something which they just could not learn! Sometimes it was poor eyesight. Other times they perceived it to be just too revolutionary a concept. Still other times their level of sharpness at that age could not handle something so radically different.

When after the third or fourth time they would come for us to check their progress and we saw that they were just not going to make it, we would encourage them to bring one of their younger brothers or sons with them the next time they came, and we would give him their book.

The next week, leaning on their walking sticks and with big smiles, they would shuffle down to the reading line, each with a bright young man, their reading representative, at their sides. To him we would give their book with the admonition that he was to learn to read quickly so as to be able to share the written word of God, which we were translating, with his clan fathers. In this way, we retained the respect and dignity of the older men, but were able to key in on some of the sharpest minds in the community without traumatizing the leadership structure.

At its height, we had some 2,000 men, women, and youth participating in the literacy program throughout the area. It was working so well that one missionary, professionally trained in the skills necessary to pioneer such a program in his mission, flew over to Mulia to see our program in action. After evaluating our primer series, then sitting with me, seeing and hearing what was taking place, he shook his head in utter amazement and said, "Dave, according to what I have been taught, this cannot work, but obviously it does!"

The Danis' high level of motivation kept us busy working ahead of them to prepare the next primer, or reader, and kept them moving toward the goal of comprehension and fluency. In addition to a simple booklet on the miracles of Christ, we recorded some of their own cultural stories on hunting, building and other everyday activities which we made into simple readers for them. Later on, we had them write their own stories for us. This again proved delightful for them as well as incredibly educational for us.

Learning to read from our primers

One day, as we were working our way through the reader series, one of our best young readers came to me with concern written all over his face. "Tuan," he said, "these stories about the things we do in our culture are all right as we learn to read, but how many more of these readers must we learn before we have in our hands portions of the real *'ki wone'* 'living words?'" That comment turned on a small light within my own heart; it became an indicator of their deep desire to learn the Word of God so as to be able to not only hold it, but to taste it and to apply it in their own lives.

The young man who asked the question, with his beautiful young wife, eventually became one of the first national missionary families sent out by the church. Over the past 30 years, Nggerenok has built airstrips, learned languages, evangelized and planted churches among several other unreached tribes in the eastern highlands of Papua. His is an amazing story of faithfulness and passion to reach tribes that have not yet heard the Good News. "There was a man sent from God whose name was…(Nggerenok)!"

That basic literacy program initiated back in the early 1960's is still producing readers. Over the years, it has been revised and made more relevant for today's youth by several of our colleagues, particularly Jim and Carolyn Hively. While the program is totally self-propagating, Jim and Carolyn continue to give oversight, encouragement, and refresher courses to dozens of teachers who teach literacy to hundreds of youth in literacy schools throughout the Dani area. And their point is well taken: without literacy, the church will die because the people cannot read their Scriptures.

Chapter 14:
The impact of medicine

—⟆⟆—

A highly influential tool in building credibility among the Danis in those early days was our medical work. They wanted to live; introducing them to the marvels of modern medicine made quite an impact on them.

Lack of natural iodine in the soil and water resulted in thyroid malfunction of the women causing early abortions, stillbirths, and the birth of many cretins and retarded children in the area. Many women and some men had goiters up to the size of a football hanging under their chins. This lack of iodine also resulted in a very high rate of infant mortality. Both conditions required long-range solutions. Eventually, a medical team from Holland developed a simple injection of iodine in oil which fed iodine into the body over a four-year period and was extremely successful. Small goiters disappeared; large goiters drastically shrunk, allowing unrestricted breathing; and rarely did mothers any longer give birth to retarded children. This had quite an impact upon the community.

It was common knowledge that the tropical ulcer, as well as the ulcer caused by yaws, was contagious. The Dani culture had developed its own system of caring for the worst patients whose bodies were covered with these huge sores, or whose stench was impossible to live with in the village. Small, crudely-built huts up in the forest, away from the village and isolated from the people, were built to restrict contact with them, and thus any contagion. At times such a patient would build his own garden there in the forest, but usually such activity was beyond his physical strength. Rather, he was to exist until death released him from his suffering, with the family bringing him food which they would leave in designated spots. Then the family would retire to the comfort of the village and the diseased would take the food and other things left for him.

A typical goiter due to lack of iodine in the soil

Thus, it was glorious news which circulated in the valley that a *liiru* "injection" would bring healing to those who for years had suffered from these huge putrefying ulcers. They came and they were brought — some being led; others carried on a pole; still others on the shoulders of their relatives, piggyback style; or stuffed in large net bags — to get the shot of penicillin which in just a few weeks brought miraculous relief and healing.

Many yet are the eyes that tear up when they remember the injection they or their relatives received which brought relief and social acceptability back again to them. In this the missionary not only showed compassion, but he awakened a sense of gratitude and indebtedness, initiating a relationship which was to grow stronger in the years that followed.

UFM nurse and midwife, Rie Dedecker, having arrived shortly before us, took her responsibility seriously. Everything from long-term putrid sores, to arrow wounds, to broken bones, to delivery of babies, to health education and hygiene, kept her busy.

Infant mortality was very high, yet before help could be given in this area, the value of the woman in the culture, as well as her fear of breaking the many taboos which controlled all the activity of childbirth, had to be overcome.

Many were the babies lost due to improper technique and irrational taboos. Among these taboos, they believed that no one could assist the mother in delivering her child, for if anyone, either deliberately or otherwise, looked upon the blood of that delivery, that person would lose his or her eyesight. Thus, though mothers were assisted by local midwives who would wrap their arms around them and squeeze during the contractions, when the baby came those women were forced to flee from the house, leaving the actual delivery and the cleanup of the child, the cutting of the cord after the afterbirth had come, and the disposal of the afterbirth with all the leaves on which she lay during delivery, to the mother.

Into this arena of fear, failure and often death, the missionary nurse and midwife came with her medicine and medical knowledge.

Prenatal care brought us smiles as the women began to trust the nurses' help given in the clinic. It was not uncommon for labor pains to remind the woman that, as she had been told, to minimize risk of complications, she should give birth to the baby at the clinic. So when the contractions began, she would grab her newly-made net bag and come hurrying down to the clinic. And often she would not make it.

Contractions would force her into the grass along the side of the path where her baby would be born. Wiping the newborn off with clean leaves and grass, cord still attached, the mother would slip the newborn crying infant into the soft leaves of her bag and keep right on running down to the clinic, proudly proclaiming the news of her new baby!

The medical work grew over the years to eventually include a hospital founded and operated by Dr. and Mrs. Jerry Powell. The Powells' ministry, along with several nurses, made its mark upon the church and community as a worthy vehicle of evangelism and development of the church. The staff's sacrificial service, along with Jerry's incredible energy and contagious vision, was deeply appreciated within the total ministries of UFM. All of us felt bereaved when his death, orchestrated by a Sovereign God, snatched him from us.

According to the clinic records, the infant mortality rate of over 85 percent was reduced to 15 percent due to the medical program. This was very apparent, for in later years, moving through the villages, we literally would be swarmed by dozens of children who would race out to warmly greet us, with their parents proudly and teary-eyed proclaiming, *"Ninapuri iinggen paga ndarak ti aret o."* "Those are our children born of the pill (medicine)!" The Mulia medical program is still in operation under the direction of Dr. Buce Tahalele and his wife, Janet.

Chapter 15:
Contextualizing the message

—∿∿—

It is impossible for me to place the following illustrations on the contextualizing of the Gospel message among the Dani people on a chronological timeline. The event of the burning of fetishes to the initial baptism of 13 men and women whom we believed clearly understood and personalized the message of the Gospel, spanned nearly two years during which time most of the scenes mentioned in this chapter took place. I include this brief sketch of the first baptism at Mulia in this section because it so clearly reveals the mind set of the people regarding this strange practice.

First baptisms:

Sunday, the 14th of July 1963 was another great day at Mulia for both missionary and national. On that day some five thousand Danis gathered on the banks of a nearby stream to witness the event of the first baptism in the area.

For months we had been teaching against many false rumors circulating in the community regarding baptism: if sick pigs are baptized they will live; if someone has an infirmity, they will be cured; if a woman is barren, she can conceive; if she has given birth only to stillborn children, she will be able to deliver a living child. If one wants eternal life, this is the way to get it!

In spite of the stories, during the two years of teaching prior to that first baptism, we had watched a group of men and women come out of the darkness of animism to embrace the message of the Gospel and to become a part of the Body of Christ. Such was evidenced by their own personal testimonies, by their obvious spiritual hunger, and by the witness of others within their own community.

Several weeks before the event, we had spent time examining, questioning, and teaching regarding this step, and we felt that there were at least 13 men and women mature enough to be included in that initial baptism. Our strategy was to baptize these first 13, and then they could assist us in examining and evaluating the personal lives and testimonies of hundreds of others who wanted to be baptized.

The questions were very basic: "When did you become a child of God? After God gives you a new heart, does He also give you a new skin? Is it possible for you to become sick after you have been baptized? And what about your pigs, will they become sick?" These and other questions on doctrine as well as their own personal experience with the Lord, we asked of those preparing to be baptized.

That Sunday morning, after a word of instruction to the candidates, we walked down to the stream which they had dammed up for the baptismal ceremony. We were not the first to arrive. Since daybreak, the paths about Mulia had been crowded with people making their way toward the baptismal site to witness their kinsmen taking this step.

After explaining what was to happen, (we had heard that morning that the Holy Spirit was returning to alight upon these men as at Pentecost!), Ralph and I walked into the water. Before we baptized them, each candidate gave a personal word of testimony before the crowd of some five thousand people gathered there.

From the water, we came up to the large grass-roofed church building to enjoy the Lord's Table together. This was their first communion. All sat cross-legged in a circle on pieces of tree bark. After they had chanted hymns of their own, we partook together of those sacred elements. A roasted sweet potato served as the bread and wild raspberry juice, the wine. There was no rattling of glasses; each of us held a leaf in our hands. And the wine, wild raspberry juice prepared by the people, was poured into that leaf from one of their hollowed-out drinking gourds. There was no beautiful organ music, no cathedral-like atmosphere, and no nice white linen clothe on the table. However, the Lord's presence was there with us in that simple building and He gave meaning to that sacred moment.

The first baptisms

After a word of prayer, we, with the group of 13 new believers, solemnly yet joyfully, left for our homes. These were brethren with us about the cup; brethren with us around the broken body and, more, they were brethren with us within the Body of whom Christ is the Head.

It was months later that I heard one of the church leaders use a strange term to identify the baptized ones—*"aap nggumun."* On questioning them, I learned this was the term used for those initiated into the spirit world—those to whom the secrets of the spirits were revealed. Having thought about it, I said to myself: *Why not? These, too, had been initiated into the (Holy) Spirit world: They had believed. They had been mentored in the teaching from the Scriptures; they had participated in the proper ritual (the public ceremony of baptism and communion). Spiritually they were now able to enjoy a personal relationship with the Holy Spirit and the God of the universe; to them the secrets of His Word and of walking with Him in the daily routines of their lives were revealed.* And I thought no more about it.

Chanting:

One of my first disappointments in our teaching role occurred during those initial weeks of the "witness school" schedule. All had gathered when the "bell" rang, and as usual, one of the men would stand and lead us in a chant or two before we had prayer to begin the lesson. This particular morning, a short older man named Timbombi was leading the group in their chants, with everyone enthusiastically joining in on the particular refrains he would call out to them. They chanted on and on for several minutes and I, sitting on the desk, began to get rather impatient to begin my lesson and, indeed, tried unsuccessfully to bring a close to the chant.

On and on he led the group, disregarding my fidgeting, mounting impatience and disappointment that one of our promising men would hijack the lesson time just to sing his "homemade" chant. *This was a new week; we had lesson material that we wanted to work through with them that hour; and he was eating into my time. The very idea! Remembering our pedagogy classes in Bible School, I had hoped to review the lesson given the previous week before beginning the new one. Alas, that seemed to be impossible, the way things were going.*

Then, I started to listen to the words he was chanting. To my utter astonishment, I heard him chanting through the main points of the lessons we had taught them the previous week. He had learned his lessons well and, being a natural and known chant producer in the community, had put the stories and main points of those lessons into chant form, and HE was reviewing the previous week's lessons. I shook my head in disbelief. This was what we wanted; they were putting the stories and Bible verses into chant form to recite around the fires at night. Extremely pleased, and a bit wiser, I waited until his chant ended to begin my lesson for the week.

To this day, they sing these truths in chant form. We have not felt it necessary to teach them our tunes. They are a chanting people. On the trail, while working in their gardens, or while sitting around the fire at night, chants fill the air as old and young join in. We have encouraged them to continue to use their chants in their worship.

The Old Testament, now translated into Dani, has become a virtual hymnbook to them. Many of the Psalms and Proverbs they now sing as well as read. As the children of Israel chanted (sang) the Psalms in their worship, in their celebrations, and in their trips up to Jerusalem so the Danis sing their chants. We want them to preserve this cultural form of expressing their emotions.

Confession of sin

We were several weeks into the lessons outlined to give to these men when we encountered another mind-jarring experience. That particular week we were teaching them about sin. Confessing one's sin to God was not a problem, but when we taught that confession of one's sins to God included making restitution with one's kinsfolk if they had been affected by that badness, they were horrified! The school exploded with men and women all talking at once; I could tell by their shaking heads, the snapping of the gourds, and the concern on their faces, that this lesson was just not being accepted. And I soon learned why.

When I had quieted them down, several men who were emerging as voices for the class began to speak. "Tuan," they said, "if we were to make restitution for the past secret sins we have committed one with the other, we would have a major war on our hands. There are people here who have had adulterous relationships with other men's wives. There are some of us who have stolen pigs. We have placed curses on our own people to bring about their deaths, using the fetishes we have burned. We have killed in war; we have raped women. Surely, there is a better way to handle these matters so that we can continue to enjoy peace in our valley and the eternal life which that Big Book offers to us."

I had to agree with them. Thus, after lengthy discussion, together we arbitrarily drew the line at the burning of their fetishes. Anything that had happened prior to the burning was history, and having confessed it to God, would not be allowed to surface within the church/community. That past action which would normally have brought about fighting, raping of women, killing of one another, burning of houses, stealing and butchering of pigs, and all sorts of undesirable repercussions, died with the burning of the fetishes. They wanted to bury the past with all its trauma and step out into newness of life. This indeed was to be *nabelan-kabelan* "my (mortal) skin being exchanged for His (immortal) one." This was eternal life!

A second episode regarding confession of sin created quite a stir in the school. During one of our teaching sessions on this matter, one of the men in training stood to his feet and, in the hearing of all, spontaneously began to recite the names of his personal spirits, numbering them on his fingers as he spoke. That simple classroom exploded. I looked up from my notes to see people running out the door, others were jumping out the windows, others were sitting as far away as they could get from this man with their fingers in their ears blocking out what he was saying, and still others with their fingers in their ears were shouting at him to "shut up and sit down."

Totally astonished, when order was restored in that classroom, I asked what had happened. I was informed that the spirits which he had worshipped and to whom he had sacrificed were "his affair." In addition to the general spirits, there were the individual, personal, ancestral spirits which had been a part of their religious forms and to whom they offered sacrifices, but each person had to deal with them individually with God. "We do not want to know the names of his spirits," they said. "These are 'his affair' and must be confessed, but not in our hearing." They feared the possible consequences of publicly confessing those spirits. We went on with the teaching that day, but were made aware of another area of truth upon which we would need to focus.

Cutting their hair

On another occasion during those first days of seeing this new message take root in this culture, I looked out the clear plastic in our living-room window to see a man stealthily work his way through the long grass in a small meadow below our house. I ducked out of the way so that he could not see me, and watched him make his way slowly through the grass, look carefully around him, then slip down into the grass, lost to my sight. Several moments later another man did the same thing, then another, and I wondered, *"What is going on here?"* So I slipped out the door of our home, sneaked down along a small stream behind our house, and then worked my way upstream and into the small meadow toward the tall grass where these men seemed to be disappearing.

As I drew closer, I heard voices but could not determine what was being said or done there in the tall grass. Moving cautiously closer, undetected, I came upon this group of men sitting in a little circle, chatting away while each one was cutting the long hair of the man in front of him.

You need to be reminded that the men had the long hair, not the women. This was the glory of the man, and if he could not grow it naturally, when his father or uncle passed away he would cut the hair off his dead kinsman's head and tie it onto his own hair to make it longer. The goal was to have hair at least down to the level of the string around the waist which held the gourd in place, and further, if possible. On the very end, the man would then tie a string with pretty feathers—or sometimes colorful leaves—which would bounce against his ankles as he walked.

Normally the man's hair was kept up in a net bag on his head and let down only for special occasions of celebration when he would be seen by the young ladies and women. During those times, he would come dancing up the trail and around the gathering site, tossing his head from side to side, flipping those long heavy locks, dripping with pig fat and soot, back and forth, often chanting, and always rattling his bow and arrows. It was quite a thing of pride. But also it was filled with all types of filth and a perfect environment in which their head lice could reproduce. I had often seen them sitting behind one another, picking out each other's head lice and crunching them in their teeth before spitting them out. But this was different. With their bamboo knives, each was cutting away those long heavy-with-dirt-and-lice locks of the man in front of him, then placing them in neat little bundles before the owner.

When I gave that little "I'm here" cough, they all looked up startled as I stepped out of the grass exclaiming, "What are you doing?"

It was a moment or two before they could organize who would tell me the story, but one of them finally ventured forth. "Tuan Kobo," he said, "we are cutting away these old dirty locks of our hair. Look," he said, showing me a handful loaded with dirt and crawling with lice. "We don't want to live this way any longer. It is not consistent with the teaching you are giving us from that Big Book. If we are going to be clean on the inside, we must also be clean on the outside. This is something we do not need to preserve!"

"Fine," I said, "but don't go around telling people that we missionaries told you to cut your hair. If this is your decision, I can accept that, but what about the other men out there?" "Oh," they exclaimed, "they will be cutting theirs as well."

And this haircutting movement swept through our area, ridding the men of their long, dirty, lice-filled locks and, in the process, some of their pride. In its place the comb industry flourished. They made hardwood combs with which they would comb their hair, then, they would leave the comb sticking out of the shorter locks on their heads. This became a sign that they had accepted the teachings of that Big Book and was symbolic of other changes being made, such as cleaner, better-made houses with floors in them, fences around the village yards to keep the pigs out of their houses, and the making of paths and planting of flowers along the paths into their villages.

Cleaning up their villages

On our frequent treks out into the community we had encountered all kinds of filth on the trails occasioned by the feces of their many pigs and the places where they would wallow. Their villages also were a mess with pigs running hither and yon. Sleeping with them in their houses, often in the middle of the night I would be awakened by a cold snout on my face, or legs, to find that a pig had somehow escaped from its pen at the back of the small house. It was nosing around during the night for discarded skins of sweet potatoes left near the fire, or cold sweet potato vines the people could not finish off before drowsiness, caused by the warm fire and a full stomach, took control and they would find their places, feet near the fire in the middle of the house and heads pointing outward toward the outer wall, to spend the night.

The villages were made up of at least one *kunume* located near the center of the village and out of bounds to the women. Here the men and boys of 4 to 5 years of age and above would gather to sleep, while the houses of the wives of the men would be further out at the periphery of the village yard. Many of the men had at least two wives, with a house for each. These could be in the same village but, more often, in different villages, depending on the disposition of the wives and their kinship ties.

And the wives were the keepers of the pigs! The men made the gardens; the women planted and then weeded them. The idea was to produce enough potatoes to feed the family as well as the many pigs they would raise for themselves and for their husbands. And while there was the occasional house outside the village area where the pigs could be kept, at the back part of the woman's small round house would be several little hutches or pens in which the woman would feed, then lock up the pigs, keeping them warm during the night with the heat of her fire. She would lie down between the pig hutch and the fire, spending the night on the ground, with her smaller children by her side or suckling at her breast.

This is probably why the woman was called the *"wam ore"* the "friend of the pig" because the pigs were largely cared for by the women. And happy the man who had a wife with an *eenggi ki* "a green hand"; everything she touched would turn to material gain for her husband. The woman's position around the fire with her baby resting on her thighs was also the reason for many burns, because she would fall asleep leaning over into the fire, with the child rolling off her thighs into the hot coals.

With the people and the pigs living together causing the paths and village yards to be cluttered with pig wallows and feces, the normal traffic tracked this filth and clutter into the houses. It was not a healthy situation. So we encouraged them to pen up the pigs like we did in America, to make for cleaner yards and healthier people.

To give some motivation toward that goal, we felt that we could increase both the number in the litter and the size of the pig by mating their smaller pigs with larger ones such as were being raised on the coast. So, in the small MAF Cessna, we flew a pair of the larger Yorkshire pig stock in from the coast, keeping them in pens, and hand-feeding them with food containing what we felt were the right amounts of nutrients. This created quite a stir in the community. First of all, they could not believe the size of those pigs, even though not yet fully grown, but penning them up was just unthinkable and irresponsible.

Often the men came pleading with us to turn the pigs loose, so they could root in the ground like their pigs, finding the nutrients they needed to grow and reproduce properly. "No," we told them, "we raise pigs like this in our villages in America. They will be O.K. You need to be able to live in cleaner villages."

This went on for several months, until finally a local delegation came pressuring me to give them the pigs so they would not die. "If you leave them penned up, it will be only a matter of several Sundays (weeks) before they will die." Again I resisted, and sure enough, several weeks later the female died. And though I immediately gave the male to one of the villages to care for, it was not long until he too succumbed to the inevitable and died. And did I get a tongue-lashing from those "natives" about the way I handled pigs!

In the end, we flew in another pair of pigs which we gave directly to them to care for, and this did have the desired effect within the community. The litters increased in number and the pigs in size, making quite an impression.

At the same time, the people took our concern to heart. Instead of penning up the pigs to keep the village area clean, they penned up the people, i.e., they put a nice wooden fence around the village. This included all the houses in the village, but left the pigs outside in other smaller huts closer to the gardens. In this way, we were able to incite them toward a healthier living environment.

In addition to the fence around the village to keep the pigs out, they saw our yards with paths and flowers along the paths. So they did the same, making paths, and planting flowers and colored bushes making their yards very attractive. This again was a part of their desire to release themselves from the unhealthy environment in which they had lived for centuries, and to look ahead to a better, healthier future.

A typical village after their conversion experience

Bathing Dani-style

Of bathing and birth control

Regular bathing in the morning before they moved out upon the day, the cutting of the men's long locks, cleaning up their villages and putting the pigs outside the village yard—these became the signs that this people was driven to make major changes in their way of life. Whether this was due to their desire to become a part of the world of which they knew little, or due to their yearning to regain the eternal life they had lost in their distant past, or both, I am not sure. But major change, at their insistence, was seen everywhere.

One day I was busy building our first home out of round poles and tree bark. The floor plan included various rooms such as kitchen, sitting room, bathroom, and two bedrooms. As I was working, a man by the name of Pondogo, a friend in a nearby village, came by to see how the "white man" built his house. So I invited him to step inside, and went around the house showing him the various rooms we were working on. "This is where we will cook; this is where we will eat; this is where we will bathe; this is where our daughter, Dawn, will sleep; and this is where I will sleep with my wife," I told him, indicating the rooms.

When I mentioned the room where I would sleep with my wife, he looked up with a question, "Oh, do you sleep every night with your wife?" And when I responded positively, he said in all sincerity, "Well, I think that is what we should do, too." And the word went out. From now on men had to sleep with their wives every night. And that worked O.K. —for the first few months.

Then word began to drift in that some of the women were getting pregnant while still nursing their infants. This was taboo to be sure, with the consequences that not only the mother's milk would dry up starving the nursing infant, but the sweet potatoes in their gardens would rot on the vines. So a delegation came to speak with us about it.

This they could not handle, they said; they must rebuild their men's houses and go back to sleeping in them. We reminded them that it was not our idea in the first place, and encouraged them to do so.

Killing of the sorceress

In the process of developing spiritual leaders for the church/community, another interesting event occurred during those early months of teaching in the "witness school." We had already begun the schedule for the week when I noticed that two of my best Bible School students were not present. Interrupting the normal flow of the class material, I asked the men present where these other two were. No response! All was quiet! I asked again, and again I noted the same we-don't-know look on their faces. Pressing them further,

I learned that one of their kinsmen had died the evening before, and these two men were out trying to discover the reason for his death.

Quickly, my mind kicked into gear: "...trying to find the reason for his death." That was a general statement hiding the particulars. I knew something strange was going on—something they were reluctant to share with me. Only upon further questioning did I learn that following the cremation of the body the day before, they had followed the trail of the florescent-like white clay, which led them to the house of the woman suspected of committing the crime. Sometime during the night they had caught a pig of the suspect, a sorceress noted for her murderous *magagirak* "poisoning" activity and, having killed the pig, they had milked the intestines of the pig looking for evidence. It had been found in the form of a tuft of hair recently cut from the head of the deceased. There was no need to look further. This was the evidence they needed; a search for the woman had begun.

When found, if she did not confess to the deed, they would strip her and force her to stand in the hot sun on a pole with her feet not touching the ground. Should she manage that, her innocence would be established. If not, when she finally slipped off the pole and her feet hit the ground, the crowd would descend on her and literally shred her to bits with their feet. I knew that this was the fate of the woman should the men find her. We had to act quickly.

From those present, I learned that my two promising Bible School students had left to search for the woman in her home valley, about a five hour trek away. Quickly, I sent two runners on their way to intercept their plan to kill the woman and for all of them, including the woman, to return, and we would discuss what should be done. They took off running down the trail, and we resumed our teaching.

The following morning, when the men gathered for their lessons, the two runners I had sent, along with the two searching for the woman, were present. "Where is the woman?" I asked. Silence! Again, I pressed, "Would she not come?" Not a word! And only after further questioning did I learn that the two men searching for the woman had accosted her on a large bridge built high above the main river on the way to her village. Having shown her the evidence found in the intestines of her pig, they had stepped back and filled her body with arrows, letting her drop into the river below. "A woman like this does not deserve a decent burial," they had murmured as they released the tension on their bow strings and tied up their remaining arrows. Mission accomplished, they were returning to continue their pastoral studies when they met the two runners I had sent. The four of them had returned!

Sick at heart, I sat with my head down, tears forming in my eyes as I pondered how to handle this. These were my Bible School students, the future pastors of the church, who had just murdered, probably unjustly, a woman accused of black magic. Would they never learn? My voice breaking up, partly due to anger, partly due to their heinous act, I tried to get my point across. "You men have just committed murder and you know this God about whom we are telling you, hates murder. Man is God's creature, made to love Him, having an immense value attached to him. You have broken God's commandment by taking the life of one of your people! God will punish you for this!"

It was deathly quiet in that little round grass-roofed classroom. All heads were bowed; many were flicking tears from their eyes; still others were sniffling in sincere remorse. Finally, one of the men participating in the killing of the woman stood to his feet. "Tuan Kobo," he said humbly, "why are we being rebuked for getting rid of this woman? She is a sorceress, guilty of many deaths. Does God want her to continue to kill at will throughout our community? We felt we were doing God a favor and obeying his laws to curb this evil. Now we are the ones being reproved for what we have done!" And he slipped down to squat on his haunches in a burst of wailing! We had something else to work through in the formation of a new worldview which would be relevant to their living situation.

Weakness of the Gospel

As the Gospel took root within their culture, the Danis saw it as amazingly powerful in the changes which they felt within themselves and saw in their community; they also saw it disappointingly impotent in other areas.

How was it that we could get on the talking box, the single sideband radio, and, in a matter of minutes, could tell them almost exactly when a plane would be landing on the airstrip, but we could not use it to help them find their lost pig? Often a concerned tribesman would come to us saying, "I've looked for days for my brood sow without finding it. Could you call that man on the radio, asking him where my pig is?" Or, "My wife has left me. Could you find out where she is hiding from me, or if she has run off with another man?"

The Dani had several rituals called the *"tili pagangge"* "revealing the unknown." If a pig was stolen, the owner could take a net bag and, holding it in front of him with hands about 12 to 15 inches apart allowing it room to swing freely, could say the name of a suspect. If the bag did not move, he would say the name of another, and another, until the mention of the right man's name was confirmed by the net bag of itself beginning to move back and forth. Then, armed with this evidence, he would confront the man whose name was affirmed by that ritual.

Another ritual was to cook a pit of sweet potato vines, naming each section of the pit according to the direction he thought his pig had gone, or perhaps speaking the name of the man whom he suspected had run off with his wife. When opening the pit, the uncooked section of it was the confirmation and thus the answer. The Danis were disappointed to learn that prayer could not be depended on to reveal such unknowns.

One day, walking in from another valley, we had ascended to the pass where we had stopped to have a rest up in the forest near a small grove of one of our men's pandanus nut trees. Having had our drink and quick rest, we were ready to move on except that the owner of the grove of pandanus trees was having a look to see if any of the nuts on his trees were ready to pluck. He wanted to share them with us.

All of a sudden we heard him exclaim and then call out, *"Wologwe! Pekka woraanip,"* "Hey friends! Come and see this!" We quickly gathered around the tree where he was standing. He was holding a branch which had once boasted a large nut. Using an axe, someone had slipped in and stolen several of the ripening nuts. He was crestfallen and very angry!

Grabbing several pieces of dry foliage, he was in the process of pushing it into the crotch of one of the lower limbs of the tree to put a curse on the man who had done this evil act, when he remembered. He looked at us, then, realizing that what he was doing was not in accordance with the teaching from that Big Book, he grabbed that handful of dry twigs and leaves, threw it disgustedly into the forest, sat down on the ground, and literally began pounding the ground with his fist, wiping the tears from his eyes—and this from a normally quite mild-mannered man!

These nuts were a specialty and were used for planned occasions within the family unit or, if there were enough of them, the owner would send word around the community that he was having a special "nut cook" and the people would gather, work all day for him, then in the afternoon he would serve them the normal sweet potato with cooked potato vines, along with this special nut. I do not recall for what he had planned to use the nuts but it was obvious he was very disappointed.

In their former way of life, that little bundle of leaves and twigs placed in the crotch of the tree over which a curse had been spoken would bring sickness or misfortune on the man who had stolen. And in this way, his act would be avenged. But that was contrary to the teachings of the Big Book! The Gospel said, "Love your enemies; do good to those who despitefully use you."

Must those who follow God's way always suffer the loss of all things? Was this the price of obedience? Was there no ritual or recourse within the Christian faith to avenge such activity? Would only a prayer to God prompt Him to act on the believer's behalf?

In this case it did. We gathered around our friend, and, having reminded God of this man's rejection of his past way of life and desire to follow Him, we prayed that God would take the action necessary to right the flagrant wrong done to him. Then we picked up our bags and descended to our valley, and to our home where a warm shower and a good supper awaited us.

Later that week the man came to me with the story. Several days after we had prayed with him there on the mountaintop, early in the morning a man brought him a large chicken in payment for the nuts he had stolen. His comment was, "God does hear us when we pray."

On that occasion, in grace, God had righted the wrong, but it was not always so to be, and this was a problem to these believers moving on toward maturity in their faith.

Harsh punishment for stealing

Both Ralph and I tried to get out and visit various villages where Sunday services were being held by our "witness school" men. Often I would go either on a Friday or Saturday afternoon, overnight in the village then return home after the Sunday morning service.

On this particular Saturday morning, I wanted to go to one of the churches in the valley over the mountain behind us, so I set out with several of the men. We climbed to the top of the mountain and were looking over the beautiful valley below, estimating the time it would take us to get to the church across the river, when we noticed smoke billowing out of several houses in a closer village below us. Then, we watched other houses begin to flame up as men ran from house to house, igniting the grass roof of each house. We quickly realized that something was not right about the situation so we grabbed our bags and took off on a run down the mountain path toward that village.

Apparently the entire village was being burned to the ground by men with bunches of flaming grass in their hands. Even then, smoke was billowing up into the heavens, darkening the sky overhead. As we approached the fence around the village, we had to cross a small stream. In that stream sat an older man cupping water from the stream with his hands and splashing it onto his eyes. "Help me, please help me! My eyes! My eyes! Help me," he cried out to us as we passed by him. He appeared to be blind and, with our focus on the burning houses just a few hundred feet away, we could not stop. Telling him we would be back after stopping the men who were burning down the houses, we quickly stepped up the ladder leading into the village square. Perched on top of the fence, a cursory glance told me what I did not want to see. The men setting the houses on fire were my Bible School students. Astonished, I stepped down the ladder where they were waiting for me.

They spoke first. "Tuan," they said, "please sit down; we need to talk with you!" Holding back my fury, I very impatiently sat down, while they found places to sit around me. "Tuan," they said, "this is the village of our clan father. We helped him build these houses; we helped him build the fence around the village; we helped him make his gardens outside the fence. We can rightly claim it. The man you saw sitting in the stream begging you for help is our father.

"Over the past several weeks, he has secretly been killing and eating pigs from our former enemies across the river. We are his kinsmen; we pled with him to leave those old ways. Such actions are stirring up contention and leading us back into the killings of our former way of life. Disregarding those pleas, last night he killed another one of their pigs, so this morning we have come to discipline him. We have burned down his houses, killed some of his pigs, and have taken ashes from his fireplace and rubbed it in his eyes."

I was horrified and numb with anger. "You are Bible School students," I cried. "You are the men who are studying God's Word, the future leaders of the church. How could you even think to do something like that? You have burned out his eyes, making healing and regaining of his sight impossible."

"Yes," they answered, "we know that but we had to discipline him. Several times we have pled with him to stop lest our former enemies make new bows and arrows and come to burn his village, rape his wives, kill his pigs, and bring about his death. He is our father, and we will carry him up and down the mountainside to the place God's Word is being taught so he can straighten out his heart (repent) before he dies, but at least he can't see any more to steal pigs!"

And they did. I saw them often with their father on their shoulders, bringing him to the services where God's Word was being spoken, and I knew they were fulfilling their commitment to him. But how does one handle that? This is another illustration of the problems experienced as the message took root within the Dani culture.

Discipline for a disobedient teenager

His name was Kiginggwe; he was another charismatic, very likeable, friendly, and helpful Dani. This particular morning the airplane had just taken off and he and I stood chatting amicably at the top of the airstrip. In his hand he held his bow with string taut and the normal handful of arrows.

While we chatted, I noticed he was watching several people who were making their way slowly up the path at the side of the airstrip. The closer they got, the more agitated he became. At about 50 yards away, he turned his wrath upon the group coming up the path, screaming something which I could not understand. In a flash, he had drawn his bow and shot an arrow in their direction.

Friendly chatter turned to horror as I saw the young lady sink into the grass, apparently wounded by the arrow. When I turned to ask him what was going on, he was already a good distance up the path, moving quickly in the direction of his village.

I ran down to where I had seen the young lady sink into the grass and watched fascinated as the man accompanying her, her uncle, pulled out a bamboo knife, made several incisions in the flesh of her forearm where the arrow had embedded itself, and with a bone needle gently worked out the minute pieces of string intentionally wrapped around the point of the arrow to stay embedded in the flesh, causing infection after the arrow was pulled out. He then wrapped the incisions with a type of healing leaf and helped her sit up. The young lady had silently endured all this with only the occasional tear forcing its way through her tightly-closed eyelids.

I was full of questions which the uncle was happy to answer. This was basically a case of discipline by the father for a disobedient teenager! Without permission she had slipped off the afternoon of the day before to spend the evening in her uncle's village. During the evening hours, she had been coaxed aside to attend a courtship ceremony being carried on in the village and, being of courting age and a beautiful girl, had accepted the attention of one of the young men attending.

The courtship ceremony is a culturally acceptable orgy between sexes, normally enjoyed by the young people and married men with single girls, but is open also to married women and occurs after a crisis within the community such as a death, war or disaster of some kind which leaves the community grieving. By consensus the protective bars of morality are temporarily suspended and the community is free to engage in unrestricted sexual encounters with whomever they please.

The participants arrive dressed in their most provocative clothing, with faces and bodies painted attractively. They congregate in one of the men's houses with the men on one side of the fire and the women on the other. Then, the chanting of appropriate love songs begins as the men seek to woo a female partner through advances made to her across the fire with gifts such as bracelets, pretty feathers or leaves and other trinkets which he passes to her. If she dislikes the source of the gift, the item is returned; if accepted, the wooing continues.

The fire in the little round house burns brightly at first, but as the night wears on and the fire burns ever lower, some of the men will slip over to the women's side to sit next to their partners or coax their partners to come to their side to sit next to them as the lovemaking continues with more physical advances. At a given signal, the fire is extinguished and intimate relations occur both in the house and outside, where the man takes his partner to engage in sexual pleasure with her.

And that was the problem with the young lady shot with her father's arrow. She had attended such an event the previous evening. Though her virginity was still intact, she had accepted a gift from a young man and her father's anger was white hot. That she had not come home but had been duped into attending the ceremony was unacceptable. That she had accepted a gift was the height of irresponsibility, so he had waited for her at the top of the airstrip to discipline her with the bow and arrow! He also threatened the young man, who was trying to get to the daughter to help her, and would have shot to kill if the fellow had come closer. This young lady did grow up to be a fine lady of faith and good works within the church/community, but the lesson was painful!

Spiritual renewal in Daniland: altar calls or fetish burnings

I could not believe it! The gentle murmuring of some 3,000 happy people enjoying a Dani feast suddenly turned raucous and angry. I looked around, stunned! Rocks, sticks, and even pieces of half-cooked pork were being hurled through the air. I turned to shout but the words were lost in the din of angry voices.

A stick landed at my feet. Picking it up, I chopped at the hands of those around me holding rocks and clubs. A young man limped past me with a foot torn open and bleeding, yet on his face was one of the biggest most beautiful smiles I have ever seen on a Dani face. Another slumped in the grass with a gash on the side of his head; still another walked past clutching his bleeding hand. Just as suddenly as it had begun, it had stopped and a community and church, with its pastors and leaders, sat humiliated, ashamed and weeping!

The occasion was the "welcome back" feast for us and the Powell family from our furloughs. In true Dani fashion, a pig feast was planned. To highlight the occasion, two cows which we had given to several of the leaders in the area had been butchered. Unfortunately, in the ceremonial distribution of the meat, one group was unintentionally overlooked.

Feeling this slight, that group had stood and had begun to chant their feelings to the others. Then it happened—a hothead threw the first club and the valley erupted!

The frustrations of old and new worldviews jarring together, of aggressive personalities with no direction into creative community change, of youth promised the world in educational opportunities only to realize their inability to absorb that education and, if they did make it through the system, to find those doors of opportunity closed to them—these sparked the fires of unreleased tension. Quickly the flame ignited; hotly it burned; then, energy spent, it died a humiliating death sliding into the past, begging to be forgotten.

That afternoon they came; the next morning they came; we wept together. "What's happening to us," they asked. "Where is the happiness that motivated us to forget our past, to build new villages, to settle our disputes graciously? Maybe we need to burn our fetishes again."

The question touched the area of greatest concern to us: how to realize a renewal movement among these who had so dramatically come to Christ a decade ago! But wait! My mind spun into gear.

Altar calls, dedication services, hitting the sawdust trail, hands raised—that was the western way of saying, "I want a new thing from God." The focal point of the Dani acceptance of Christianity was their fetish burning. Was a fetish only a polished stone used in contacting the dead? Was it just a pair of dried bird claws hanging on one's neck or an exotic piece of wood used in animistic ritual? Or a shell dipped in pig's blood? Was not anything taking the place of our love and obedience to the Lord, in a sense, a fetish?

Seizing the opportunity, I slipped into the group of grieving men. Awed into silence were they as I built upon their statement about the need for another fetish burning. "Love for money and for education, compromise of your faith for government jobs, an upsurge in stealing and immorality, the desire to take second and third wives, anger and threatened revenge with the bow and arrow or sorcery and black magic—these are your current fetishes that have dissipated your love for the Lord and the happiness you first experienced. Sins must be confessed, then a public acknowledgment of that re-commitment to Jesus Christ in a symbolic fetish burning would be very much in order," I encouraged them.

The thought planted matured then triggered new and more exciting aspects as to how their broken-down relationships with the Lord could be mended. Around the fires at night sins were confessed; retribution was made with one another for stolen possessions. Men used the opportunity to encourage their sons and daughters to make a total life commitment to Jesus Christ; a cleansing Spirit settled down on the community.

One church felt ready for the public demonstration of what God had been doing in their hearts. Bringing the firewood and brush, they sat each in their village group behind their elder. One by one, these men in true Dani fashion arose, gave testimony of God's renewed working in their hearts, then they, with their families, came and put on that fire their symbolic fetishes: a piece of paper, a board on which was written (they could write by that time!) the particular sin which had severed their fellowship with God, or an artifact which symbolized the point of their departure from following the Lord.

A pastor stood with a piece of paper in his hand. Weeping he turned to his own people saying, "I've searched my heart to know at what point I lost my love for the Lord. One night several months ago, a root of bitterness sprang up in my heart as I thought of all my younger kinsfolk getting an education to ultimately receive a 'wage' for their services. Here I was, only a poor pastor, with no guarantee of any funds to purchase a bar of soap, or a pair of pants for myself. At that point, my happiness and desire to serve the church left me. I turned cold in my relationship to the Lord. That sin I have written on this paper; I have confessed it and today it goes on the fire."

Another man, breaking a bow and handful of arrows across his thigh, stood to tell how his bow and arrows had been the tool Satan used to lead him away from God. Legitimately made to hunt small tree possum in the forest to give meat to his family, his bow with accompanying arrows had often taken him away to the forest on Sunday rather than to church. More recently in a small village dispute, it had occurred to him to use it to settle the issue. Now broken it lay on the pile of firewood to be burned—a symbolic fetish, a way of life rejected for a life rededicated to the Lord.

Young men and women realized they had never come to grips with the issue of their own personal salvation; they had been depending on their parents' past fetish burning to save them. Now, having confessed their sins to God and having written the names of their sins on pieces of paper, they came publicly acknowledging their decision to follow Christ, identifying with their elders in the things held dear to the Danis' initial acceptance of the Gospel.

From heartaches to happiness! From fights to fetish burnings! Altar calls are meaningless; raised hands misunderstood. Personal evangelism is suspect. A public fetish burning was the Dani way of saying, "Thanks for the opportunity to meaningfully express what I am feeling in my heart."

This movement swept through several of the churches in our area and, I wish I could say, has continued. But changes taking place in the church/community and the emergence of a new generation of believers, has pulled the pastors and church leaders toward the methods used in the more traditional protestant churches in Indonesia—hand-raising and altar calls rather than symbolic fetish burnings—as the proper way to publicly express their new steps of commitment to Christ. Perhaps it will surface again sometime in the future.

Sharing the Word with a typical crowd

Chapter 16:
The urgency of translation

—◦◦◦—

I t was the expressed persistent motivation of the people to learn to read that catapulted us into the first steps of translating the Word of God into the Dani language. We began with a booklet on the Miracles of Christ. We also included in our reader set a series of five booklets—paraphrases of the main Old Testament stories from Genesis through Kings.

Seeing that motivation, we moved on to translate and publish the Gospel of Luke during our first term on the field. Though the Dillingers were seriously moving ahead with plans for the Dani Bible School, they had no Scriptures from which to teach. Thus, after our first furlough when we returned to Mulia, while assisting the Dillingers in a teaching role, translation of the New Testament into the Dani language became our priority. This was the fulfillment of my lifelong dream: to translate the Word of God into the language of a tribal people.

We, with colleagues from three other missions also working with the Western Dani tribe, produced, published, and, in 1982, distributed the translation of the New Testament in Western Dani. Great was the excitement on that day. Let me relate a portion of the story of that celebration about which I wrote at that time.

God's Word has come!

The year was 1982. The month was March. The day was Good Friday! The moment of a lifetime had arrived.

We were in flight to one of the many mission stations located in the center of the Western Dani tribe, the largest in Irian Jaya, numbering about 150,000, for the official dedication of the New Testament. I, with a colleague from the Christian and Missionary Alliance, had had the major part in its translation into the Western Dani language.

The seed of this moment had been planted not during the years of my academic career, but in my heart as a teenager by the impressions made upon my life as I read missionary biographies. While following the horses in the field, or doing the chores on the farm, the question had often come to me, "Can I ever be used of the Lord to give His Word to a people who have never heard of Him?" That seed question aroused the possibility, "Why can't I?"

This goal was nurtured during my years in Bible School. Linguistic training confirmed the ability and equipped me with the tools.

I had begun translating in 1963 during our first term on the field, working on the Gospel of Luke since a colleague from the Christian and Missionary Alliance had begun work on the Gospel of Mark. Constantly there was the discipline of self, of time, of strength, and of keeping to priorities. Days stretched into weeks, weeks into months, and months into years.

Always there were the struggles to know really what God was saying in my own language, and then how to say it in the Dani language. One example was just the fact of so few animals known to the Dani: pigs, dogs and a variety of possums in the forest. Would it be right to render the verse, "All we like wild pigs (for sheep) have gone astray..."? The sense was not too far off, but, "Behold the piglet (for lamb) of God..." certainly did not ring right.

The Dani concept of God was a little known spirit being called Mbok who was said to have walked through the mountains, carving out the valleys and leaving an occasional footprint on a hillside or rock formation. "Could we use the name Mbok for God?"

Then, there was the syntax: verbs were always at the end of the sentence; relationship and dependent clauses came first. So, some passages had to be restructured which made verse 1 become verse 6, and verse 2 become verse 4, and so on!

Geographical directions in Dani are determined by the flow of the rivers: Christ went up to Galilee, but down to Jerusalem because the Jordan flowed south toward the sea. In narratives, all movement is expressed in terms of moving away from or toward the speaker. Where was Paul when he wrote his letters? At times our informants would become exhausted with the tension of trying to convey to us the correct Dani method of thinking and would slump into the corner and fall asleep.

Then came endless typing, revising, then retyping, then stenciling, printing, revising—enough to take the joy out of any translator's task! Yet, the persistent church was constantly asking, "When can we have just a few pages of those Living Words?"

They had it now! 12,000 copies of our order of 17,000 had arrived. MAF flew all 11 tons of this New Testament into various interior Dani mission stations in just a few days.

Now as I looked out the window of that small MAF aircraft I spotted the airstrip, our destination, in the distance. It was not the normal fog which obscured the visibility of that moment, but clouds of smoke, billowing up from the firewood ignited to heat the rocks for the large feast in progress on this special day.

Masses of dark bodies—some 10,000 would eventually gather to enjoy this occasion—obediently parted to allow our plane to land, then closed again as they continued feast preparations.

The formal ceremony began with proper recognition to government officials, salutations to some of us who had worked for several years in the preparation of this translation, and presentation of copies to the church leaders and informants who had helped.

Then, as if sensing the inadequacy of all foreign pomp and ceremony, several men in local festive Dani dress of colorful feathers, blackened bodies, and long new gourds, jumped to their feet inviting a proper Dani response to this historic moment. Loudly they called out, "Hear my fathers and mothers; hear my brothers and sisters! It has come. God's Word has at last come to us. Thank Him with us."

10,000 voices representing a church of nearly 75,000 believers within the entire tribe of 150,000 people lifted their voices in a mighty shout of praise which echoed back and forth across the valleys.

I had dreamed of it. I had labored for it. My heart throbbed with excitement. This was my moment and it was strangely satisfying!

Not only did we have a translation, but we had a believing constituency of over 75,000 who were waiting to use it. This was the fruit of that seed desire planted in my heart during my youth. I savored it just for a moment, then turned and walked back toward the small airplane to return home. I was not sure whether the drops on my face came from the rain that was beginning to fall, or from the tears of gratitude to God for making this moment in my life a reality!

During the next 20 years, the circulation of the Western Dani New Testament would reach a distribution of over 60,000 copies, so great was the desire of these new believers to read the Word of God.

It was in 1991 that we remembered the request of the church which had been officially communicated to us, the translation team, roughly 12 years earlier. At the close of a large feast in our honor for completing the translation of the New Testament, in typical Dani style, they had fed us. Then, represented by one of the leading pastors of the area, they had thanked us profusely and in tears for our tireless efforts to produce the New Testament in their language. At the very end of this little speech, this pastor had said to us, "You have given us the New Testament and we are grateful. But don't forget that is only part of the words of God. We will wait for the other half!" And all of us knew he was meaning the Old Testament!

Recalling that desire, and encouraged by more specific official overtures by several Dani church leaders, we were confident of God's gentle push for us to begin the translation of the Old Testament into their language.

The translation checking committee at work

By this time we had located in Jakarta, where we had been asked to move to better represent our mission and the national church in the offices which granted us visas and proper work permits. There, in 1993, we began work on the Old Testament with our national translators who had moved to Java with their families to work with us on this tedious task.

The translation team, consisting of two national translators and me, would work three to four days each week during the year, preparing the translation. Then, once a year, Christian and Missionary Alliance retired pioneer missionary-linguist and fluent Dani speaker, Gordon Larson, would fly in from the States, and Wesley Dale of WorldTeam, also very capable in the Dani language, would come up from Australia. These two men, with several other experienced national Dani translators from Papua, would gather as the checking committee, working with the three of us who had produced the translation to fine-tune it for eventual publication.

After 10 long years—in the year 2002—the translation of the Old Testament in Western Dani was ready; 22,000 bound copies were printed by the Indonesian Bible Society in Bogor outside Jakarta, shipped to Papua then flown into Dani church centers in the interior. From these centers, they are currently being distributed and used by the churches.

In addition, since the translation of the Dani New Testament is nearly 25 years old, during our annual trips to Papua in 2003-2006, we completed revision of it. At this writing the Indonesian Bible Society is printing 26,000 copies for the believers in Daniland. We are thrilled beyond words to realize this is our final legacy to the amazing Dani church. To God be the glory!

****

I want to end this section by recalling for my reader, the heartwarming testimony of a young Dani who joined our checking committee on the Old Testament translation for several days. This young man's name is Indep; he came up through the public school system where he learned Indonesia well. From the interior he went out to the coast to the main university in Papua where he did so well that one of the missions, seeing the potential in this young man, sent him to Australia to take his Bible training in English.

It was vacation time in Australia, so Indep had come back to Papua to enjoy his own culture, language, and kinsfolk for several weeks. Since his mother tongue was Dani, and since he was sharp in both Indonesian and English, we asked him to join our Old Testament translation checking team for a few days. This he was very happy to do.

About the third morning working together, we noticed that suddenly he had grown very quiet and, with head down, had begun flicking tears from his eyes. Wondering if we had somehow offended him, or if he was sick, we had stopped our discussion on the text under observation to ask. Lifting his head and struggling to control his emotions, he had answered, "My spiritual fathers (All of us were older than he.). I'm O.K. I just cannot believe that God is speaking to me through my own language. I have spoken Indonesian since I was in grade school. I am currently in Australia learning and speaking English, your language. I read my Bible in Indonesian and I read my Bible in English, but I have never felt the moving of God's Spirit in my heart like I have felt it the last several days reading and pondering His Word in my own Dani language. Thank you, my fathers, for making it available to us."

It was a long moment before anyone could comment. My mind raced to the fatigue of working day after day in our struggle to have God's Word speak Dani to the Dani; to the frustrations of personality conflicts occasionally surfacing on the translation team, of computer break-downs and glitches, of sicknesses which often thwarted us in our work; it raced to the fear of driving up to our translation center every week at 10 or 11 o'clock at night and to the phenomenal funds we were spending on seeing this project completed. Here was a young man who had said it all! He was giving us, the translators, the supreme compliment: "God's Word, in my own tongue, speaks louder to me than any of the other languages I have learned."

He had said enough. With renewed dedication, we went back to the task. There was a church in Daniland of over 150,000 believers waiting for that Word!

Chapter 17:
Enemies reconciled

—⚬⚬—

In those early years of our missionary experience we noted that bows and arrows, long 8- to 10-foot spears, and wars were very much a part of the Western Dani's existence. He was never far from his weapons. Sleeping, eating, working, walking—his weapons were either in his hands or nearby where he could grab them if needed. Often several hundred men would be working on the airstrip when a call would echo through the valley. In a matter of moments, the men working would rush to their weapons hidden nearby and would run whooping down the trail to join their kinsmen in a fracas that was either already in motion, or soon would be, or to organize because the enemy had been sighted and a battle was imminent.

Normally intravillage battles were caused by problems with pigs or women. A pig had been stolen, or a woman raped, or run off with, and arrows would fly. In such a case, the person accused would scream to prove his innocence in a duel with the accuser, or the accuser would dare him into a duel. If in the duel he was able to dodge the arrows shot at him, or if he was able to pull off a shot that would wound his accuser, he would be exonerated. Unfortunately, a fatal arrow to either would lead into a battle. If in the battle a shot should prove fatal, then that fatality had to be answered by a further battle to "even the score." And since that was difficult to do, a confrontation over a stolen pig or woman could produce long-term wars in which the entire area would be involved, with warriors picking sides according to their participating kinsmen. This could lead into a major *yewam* "exchange of wealth" ceremony between the war parties during which hundreds of pigs would be exchanged along with stone axes, shell (money) bands, and other less valuable items, to pacify the parties who had lost relatives in the war.

Ambi'kunik was a man we estimated to be in his mid twenties. He was without a steel axe, and very badly wanted one. So he arrived one day on our doorstep requesting to bring in the bark with which we paneled our houses. At that time, I was building a house for our nurse and needed that bark to finish it. So I was glad to ask him for 40 pieces of this tree bark, approximately nine feet long, for which I would pay him a steel axe, the rate we had established as the value for such a "hot" item.

He was a keen, macho, handsome Dani man. Though not arrogant, he carried himself with a confidence that bespoke of a warrior courageous in battle but also responsible in the normal activities of his village. He had a full bushy black beard, with bright feathers tied to the tail of the net bag holding his long hair; when he walked, these would bounce off his heels in true Dani fashion.

He worked hard bringing me that bark and was, at times, helped by his brothers. The day soon came for me to pay him his axe, which I was glad to do. He had received it with a big smile and a sincere, *"Wa!"* "Thank you!" as we snapped fingers in true Dani style. Then, after looking at it and fondly fingering that smooth piece of steel with its sharp edge, he had reached into his net bag and pulled out a round 30-inch piece of wood from which he had crafted a beautiful round handle, which he slipped through the tapered hole of the axe head. Of course it fit perfectly, and I could see he was pleased as could be. Hooking it over his shoulder, he said, "Tuan Kobo, you won't see me for a few days because I am going down valley to bring my other wife into this area. I'll see you upon my return."

It took a moment for me to realize what he was saying, so I responded, "Where does she live?" "Oh," he said, "she is visiting one of her kinsmen on the fringe of the enemy group about a day and a half walk from here."

"Is that not dangerous for her?" I asked, knowing that the tension of war still hung heavy in the conversation of the people. "No," he responded, "she is free to travel between both areas because of her family relationships."

"What about you?" I asked. He replied with a bit of a laugh, "Oh, I'll be fine because the source of the war between our two areas is not in me, and I have a wife that I am bringing back with me."

Satisfied that all would be well, I turned to lock up the shed where we kept these trade items for which the people worked, and he slipped off down the trail in the direction of the enemy group two full days walk away to get his wife. It never occurred to me that this would be the last time I would see Ambi'kunik.

Life went on as usual for the next few days, and I nearly forgot about his trip until late one evening when one of the leaders of a nearby village, in the darkness, knocked on our door: "Tuan Kobo," he said, "I need to speak with you. Things are very bad." I invited him in and as he sat on the floor in front of our woodstove, wrapping his arms about himself to get warm, he said, "Have you heard the rumors?"

"About what?" I asked. "About Ambi'kunik," he said. "The word that has drifted up to us here is that he was found and killed by the enemy with the axe you gave him."

"Oh, no," I exclaimed, and hung my head as tears filled my eyes. "This could not be. Perhaps this was just a rumor," I suggested. Shaking his head sadly, he confirmed that the information was reliable. Ambi'kunik had been killed with the axe I had given him.

It was a sad day for all of us. The following day was Sunday and, as the people gathered to worship, there were many new faces in the group. The young men especially, I noted, were all painted and dressed up in their war finery. Then it dawned on me that they were not coming to hear the message of the Big Book on this day; they were coming to hear the plan for revenge to be announced by Ambi'kunik's older brother. They were ready for war! A killing like this had to be avenged. Justice had to be given. Tension hung heavy in the air.

Thus, we shortened the Bible lesson that morning and, after the closing prayer, waited for the people to stand, stretch, and begin to huddle in their small groups to chat as they normally did. But this morning after the closing prayer, all was quiet. Not a soul moved; even the babies were silent—the air pregnant with anticipation. Several minutes later, I heard a voice from the middle of that large gathering. It was Ambi'kunik's older brother, who had stood to his feet requesting permission to address the group. This being granted, we turned to listen more carefully.

His spindly legs shook under the responsibility upon him to convey to the group his decision regarding his brother's death; he spoke softly—tears running down his cheeks: "My fellow kinsmen and friends," he said. "You have heard the news of my younger brother's tragic death. He was killed with the very axe Tuan Kobo gave him for bringing in bark for the house he was building. This is not a rumor; it is the truth. Secretly, we have sent messengers down valley to the place where he was killed. They have returned verifying his horrific death. I know that you have come to hear my decision regarding avenging his death.

"During the night I struggled to know what to do. In the past this would have been no problem for us; we would have organized and gone to war, but we have received the message of that Big Book. That Big Book admonishes us to love our enemies. As a people we have burned our weapons, putting revenge killings behind our backs as we reach out to a new way of life. As the one responsible for my brother's death, my decision to you this morning is that we continue to gather to hear God's Word and allow this God to avenge the killing of my brother."

Wailing audibly, he sank to his haunches, flicking away the tears from his eyes and with a small stick wiped away the mucous running down from his nose.

Across the large group could be heard the sniffles of many others who keenly felt this loss of life. One could also feel the anger of those who desperately wanted to avenge this death, Dani style, but who knew it was contrary to the teachings of God's Word and who were willing to forego the past to follow this new teaching. Wordlessly, the crowd slipped away down the paths to their various villages, leaving only this older brother with several older grieving relatives. We slipped over to them, expressing our own felt grief over the loss of their brother, and our friend, but also our gratefulness to the brother for his decision. We promised that we would do all we could to bring about reconciliation with the enemy group so that such a thing would not occur in the future.

Several weeks later, feeling strangely obligated by that promise to this older brother, with a few trusted men, Ralph and I headed down valley to the enemy group. The three-or-four-day trip would take us the back way to a small valley on the periphery of the enemy group's area where Ambi'kunik had been killed. We had spoken with men who knew the geography, and were fairly sure that the route we had chosen to take, though much longer, minimized any possible danger to us. We trekked all that first day. Rising early in the morning, we climbed the mountain which would lead us into the small valley where Ambi'kunik's death had occurred.

It was early afternoon when we slipped out of the forest into a small grassy meadow which once had boasted several huts. Several local men led us over to a small clearing in the grass and told us the story: Ambi'kunik had arrived from

Mulia and was sitting with some friends from the village where his second wife was waiting for him. His long hair he had let down out of the net bag in which the men wrapped their hair and these friends, after admiring his new axe, were sitting behind him, picking the lice out of that magnificent head of hair and chatting about life in general.

Suddenly, the tall grass nearby exploded as several men rushed out, grabbed that new axe lying on the ground near him, and with it slashed his knees so that he could not run, then used it to sever his head from his body, leaving as suddenly as they had appeared—with the axe. His friends had cremated his body there on the site. We gathered around those ashes, the proof of his death, prayed that God would somehow bring peace between the two areas, and left, using the shortest route to get out of the area and to get home.

Several months later, after much discussion with the elders and the war leader of the community referred to as the *"ndugure"* "the one in whom rests the responsibility of the war" and prayer among ourselves, we decided that a trip down to speak with the *"ndugure"* in that area was necessary. On this trip, we planned to go right to the village where this "war chief" whom they had referred to as Eeri'mban "the man who just does it," lived, to speak directly with him, if perchance to find a way to bring about peace between the two areas.

I left early in the morning and was walking down the airstrip at a good pace when I heard the sound of running feet behind me. Turning around, I was surprised to see the war chief of our area running toward me. Quickly he caught up, strode out in front of me, then swung around and, walking backwards in front of me, said, "Look at me!"

I did, pausing for a moment on the trail, wondering what he meant. "Look carefully at me," he said again, motioning with his hands to his eyes, and the word he used was not just "to look at." It was the word "to scrutinize," "to perceive fully."

The man's name was Wogoriya'mban, a man whom God had used in those early months to explain the message we had brought. He had had no little influence in the change coming into the community, or in the history of the wars of that area. He was, in fact, the *"ndugure"* "the man in whom rested the responsibility of the war" in our area, and the man for whom the enemy was looking. His command to me to look at him was his attempt to ascertain if I had had a special word from my Deity that indicated whether or not he should go, and in going would be guaranteed protection. I told him that I could not guarantee his safety, and that perhaps for this, the first visit, it would be best that I go without him. "If there is a problem, they probably would not kill me as soon as they would you," I replied.

"No," he countered. "This morning when I slipped down through the little hole in the loft of my hut to sit at my fire wondering what I should do, I sensed that God wanted me to go, and that's why I'm here." I could not argue with that but assured him I would be delighted to have him come if he felt it was the right thing to do. If there was any threat to him, he could always flee, following the tops of the mountain range, from where he could find his way back to his home. He grabbed one of our packs and took the lead down the trail.

We trekked up and down those steep ravines, crossed several rivers, and late in the afternoon arrived on the periphery of the enemy area where we put up a small brush shack in which we spent the night. My men were alert through the night, at intervals taking a cautious walk around the area to ascertain if there were any visitors. We were fairly sure we were alone, however, since we had kept the exact time of our departure a secret.

The next morning, bright and early, we were on our way. This was the day! Would we survive? We had prayed earnestly that morning for safety as we trekked into the heart of the enemy territory. Since we were on the direct route past the place where Ambi'kunik had been axed, we stopped for just a moment to view his ashes and to pay him our respect then moved on. Shortly I noticed that Wogoriya'mban began drifting back to walk just ahead of me. I knew he was anxious and I could not blame him.

We had walked on for several minutes when he pulled in under some trees and motioned for me to stop. He wanted to speak with me. I could see the anxiety on his face, and his voice quivered as he asked, "What should I do? I'm confused. Do you feel it is safe for me to go on with you?"

I pressed him to return if he felt inclined to do so, but he dismissed that idea then said, "Tuan. If I am killed, promise me that you will cremate my body and take word to my family. I do not want to fall into the hands of my enemy and to have my body mutilated or desecrated in any way."

That matter settled, we walked on for another half-hour, approaching a garden fence. Suddenly, Wogoriya'mban stopped, retraced his steps for several yards and, slipping behind some of the larger red pandanus fruit trees, informed us that we were close and requested that we have a moment of prayer. He knew and sensed the danger that we were in and the possible consequences of his visit. All of us squatted down on our haunches, as they do, and in prayer reached out to the God who had directed us to come that way. Then, picking up our bags, we walked briskly up to the wooden fence. Within its enclosure we could see several round houses. We climbed up the several notches made for our feet on the log which was the ladder over the fence, then stepped down on the inside. We were standing at the outer edge of the war chief's village there along the mountainside.

Around and in back of the huts was a sweet potato garden with some women digging sweet potatoes for the evening meal. They came forward to greet us with strained smiles and the cautious yet courteous typical Dani handshake of snapping fingers. Quietly, we asked them where the men were and they pointed over to another ridge where we could hear the men singing as they worked, slashing the brush and pulverizing the dried grass and branches with their bare feet, preparing a new garden site. A couple of the older children with the women took off running to take word that we had come; we waited there on the outskirts of the village, wondering what our next move would be.

I was standing, leaning against the wood fence with Wogoriya'mban sitting at my feet. With his long fingernails, he was digging the rot out of a small piece of wood. All of a sudden we heard the swish of the long grass which opened onto the trail, and out came Eeri'mban decked out in all his chieftain finery. His face and muscular body, blackened with the normal mixture of pig grease and soot, glistened in the sunlight. The red clay streaks running down his nose and across his forehead created a mask-like effect to hide his true identity. His bushy black beard and his long hair bundled up in the normal net bag with the trailer of red bird of paradise feathers running down to and bouncing off his heels, created quite an unusual effect! In his hand he held his bow with several arrows. I remember thinking, *"Wow! This is a man's man."* He carried himself with an air of confidence and regality.

Immediately he came up to us, greeting me first in Dani fashion, *"Wa! Kawonak,"* but instead of the normal snapping of fingers, he grabbed my forearm, giving me several quick squeezes, and moved down to my hand, then my finger, which I extended to him for the greeting. All the while, he kept saying, *"Wa! Wa! Wa!"* meaning, "Hello, hello, hello," but in this context the greeting meant, "My happiness, my happiness, my happiness."

I could see that he was emotionally affected, and when he grasped my forearm for a second time, working down to my hand and finger, I saw tears forming in his eyes as he then went on to say, "Thank you for coming to my village. We have heard that the people at Mulia have burned their weapons and fetishes to embrace the words which you brought to them. We, too, want to join them in the rejection of our former way of life. We, too, want to experience and enjoy the message of *'nabelan-kabelan'* 'eternal life' which you have brought."

All the time Eeri'mban was speaking to me, Wogoriya'mban was seated at my feet digging at that rotten stick. At the mention of the burning and yearning for eternal life, Wogoriya'mban stood to his feet and, facing him, extended his hand in greeting. Eeri'mban's eyes went from the extended hand to the face, and he immediately recognized whose fingers he was snapping.

For an infinitesimal moment, their eyes locked. That look of recognition which moved across Eeri'mban's face as he looked into the eyes of his archenemy made me fearful. Then I heard him say, "I know you. You are Wogoriya'mban from Mulia, my enemy, a man for whom I have waited to kill to even the score of deaths between our two areas. By right, we should duel on sight, but you heard what I just said to Tuan Kobo. We, too, want to hear the words of eternal life which he has shared with you. Let us forget the past. You spend the night in my house; eat my potatoes; and we will listen as you share those words with us around the fire."

And that is what we did. We slept in his house; we ate his food—something rarely done since that food could have been poisoned; and we talked long into the night hours of this new message being received by the Dani people. The next morning, with net bags full of roasted sweet potato and hearts wildly exuberant at what God had done in the hut that evening, we headed back toward Mulia and home.

Several weeks later, long after dark when I was preparing for bed, I heard a strange noise at our door and then my name being called, *"Tuan wae. Tuan wae. An nogo aret wagi o."* "Sir. Sir. Concerning me, I have come."

I rushed to the door, swung it open, and there stood Eeri'mban glancing cautiously about, wondering if he had been seen, and asking to come in. He immediately slipped in through the opened door and sat down in front of our wood-stove which was yet warm. He was still very cautious. This was the first time since the reconciliation that he had come to Mulia, and he did not know if Mulia would receive him.

We sat chatting for a few moments; then, since it was late at night, I stoked the fire, and gave him a blanket with which he wrapped himself as he slipped down onto the floor to spend the night hours. Early the next morning I found Wogoriya'mban, who came and took him to his village. All was well, and in the following months Eeri'mban would often be seen in the valley. God had worked a miracle between the two groups, and to this day peace reigns in those valleys.

No longer enemies

Chapter 18:
Pondogo and the airplane

—⚏—

It was a normal day in the Mulia valley. I had rigged up a couple drums under the eaves to catch rainwater, then, piped it into the kitchen for dishwashing as well as into the bathroom for our needs there. Esther was going about her tasks of washing the clothes in the motorized Maytag washing machine we had brought with us, and preparing the noonday meal on the woodstove, keeping it stoked at just the right time and temperature. Occasionally she would slip outside to spend time chatting with the women who would drop by to see her about their health, their babies, or their husbands.

She was enjoying the spacious skies and timbered mountains around her as well as the people who would come with their needs. The pig fat and soot mixed with the pungent, at times repulsive, smell of unwashed bodies she could take as long as there were people—real people, loving people, hurting people—beneath that grease and under those net bags draped over the heads and shoulders of the women.

We were still in our small, single-bedroom bark mansion and enjoying all that was going on around us. This was REAL living. God was good; life was good; and missions was fun!

Following devotions and personal Bible study in the morning, my normal day was spent working with the language: analyzing the phrases we had heard and jotted down, writing up a description of the grammar, memorizing words from the previous day's notes, asking questions of my informant, checking those subtle clues he would give, and loving every moment of it.

In the midst of this normalcy that particular day came a voice through the walls of that little bark house. *"Tuan Kobo wae!"* "Hey, Mr. Scovill, are you there?" I answered back, *"Wonage agarik o. Nonggop?"* "Yes, I'm here; what's up?" And the voice responded, "May I come in?" The answer was, "Yes," so Pondogo came in and, standing in front of our woodstove, indicated that he wanted to speak with me. "Fine," I said, "sit down, let's talk."

"Oh," he said, "we can't speak here; there are too many ears. Let's find a place outside away from the people." *"Op aret o."* "That's fine," I said and opened the door for him to slip out with me right behind him. With the door still open, he swung around and asked, "Do you have your pointed stick (pencil) and your piece of banana leaf?" "No," I replied, as he continued, "Better get it. I want you to do some writing for me."

This was going to be interesting, so I got my pencil and paper, and followed him as he led me across a small stream running past the side of Ralph's house, then up on a small plateau, taking me deep into the tall shoulder-high grass which grew there in that small meadow. Finding a suitable place, he trampled the grass down with his feet, making a clean place in the grass for both of us to sit.

After getting comfortable on the grass he said, "The words you have been giving us from God's Book are good. They have touched my heart. I do not want to continue in this way of death. I want to become a child of God to enjoy *'nabelan-kabelan'* 'eternal life' which God has prepared and wants to give us. In order to enjoy this, I know I must confess my sins. And I want to do that to you now." And he proceeded to confess the names of his ancestral as well as other spirits to whom he had given allegiance over the years, pushing me to write down the names of those spirits along with the functions of each as he gave them to me.

I was indeed interested in documenting this information, so I wrote as he would explain them to me. This went on for some 30 minutes, with me taking notes, but also pondering what was behind this action which seemed so important to him. Plus, it was past dinnertime, and I was hungry. We had already documented the names of some 14 or 15 of his spirits, and it did not seem that he was anywhere near finished, so I said to him, "Brother Pondogo. I can't forgive your sins, only God can do that; you must confess those sins to God. Just talk to Him as you are talking to me. God will hear you and give you the forgiveness you desire, then, He will make you His child."

"Oh, no, Tuan Kobo," he said. "You don't understand. I want you to write them all down on that piece of paper, then, when the pilot comes in, I want you to give him the list of my sins." Bells and whistles started going off in my mind! *"Give the pilot a list of my sins...why the pilot?"* and the picture snapped into focus.

Where did that little MAF airplane come from? One could first hear the noise which soon became an airplane landing on our airstrip. After taking off, they would watch it again become a speck in the distance. Where was it going? The obvious answer was that it came from and returned to heaven where God was. They were not aware of an outside world and civilization a mere hour's flying-time away from their spot there in the interior. They had never seen the cars, the big airplanes, the stores packed full of clothes, soap, and steel axes.

Understanding our message through the grids of their worldview led them to the obvious concept that the airplane came and went back to heaven where God was. Therefore, Pondogo wanted me to write down his sins, give that list to the pilot; the pilot would take it up to God (Had not they seen us give the pilot our letters to be mailed?). God would read off the confession of the list of his spirits whom he had worshipped and to whom he had sacrificed, cross off each name (like we crossed off their names on that sheet of paper having paid them with the axe, knife, or clothes they had worked for) and bring back that piece of paper with all the names crossed out. Transaction was completed; forgiveness was granted; he was now God's child!

I immediately tied this to another phenomenon we had experienced. When we initially taught them about life after death, and the coming of Christ, we noticed that the space around the airstrip began to fill up with small round huts which the people were enthusiastically building, "…to hear more of the words of that Big Book…" they would tell us, but now I understood.

If one believed and became a child of God, he could go to heaven when he died. How was he to get there? In the airplane, of course! When your friend or loved one died, all you had to do was to bring the corpse to the airstrip, load it on the airplane, and send it up to heaven where he would receive eternal life and live happily ever after. Had not they seen their deceased loved ones in some of our movies, which we would play for them during an evening of entertainment? Though deceased, in those pictures, their loved ones were quite alive—moving around, speaking and laughing with one another! How was that possible, apart from such reasoning?

Christ was coming again some day to take his children, those who had believed on Him, to heaven. How were they to go? In the airplane, of course! The houses they were building about the airstrip was their effort to assure themselves that when Christ came, they would be on hand to be among those who would be taken with Him on that flight! Not bad reasoning!

Well, there in the grass I had to disappoint Pondogo with some explanations: about faith, about confession of sin, about death, and about the return of Christ. He understood, and made the decision to move past the concepts his worldview dictated to him, to receive forgiveness of sins through grace, and to become a child of God. He believed, and became an active pastor in the community the rest of his life.

We, too, understood better the complexity of the grid through which our teaching had to penetrate to bring a soul into faith in Jesus Christ. Perhaps this is why the Apostle Paul, overwhelmed by the change the Gospel wrought in the hearts of those who embraced it, could declare in Romans 1:16(NIV), "I am not ashamed of the Gospel, because it is the power of God for the salvation of everyone who believes. . ."

Part II:

Faith in Action

Chapter 19:
A taste of Dani culture
and religion

—ᵚᵚ—

Lest we think lightly of that world out of which the Dani
came when he embraced Christianity, or feel the things
he rejected to follow the teachings of that Big Book were
just a bunch of garbage he called "gods," allow me to break
the flow of my story and take you on a brief trip into the
animist's mind as he perceives, then seeks to control, his
universe. And while this is not a class in animism or anthro-
pology, it can increase our understanding of and appreciation
for the worldview of the peoples we serve.

Animism is a religion because it is a system of beliefs
which link a man with his culture and, within the context of
nature, to the supernatural. Very simply stated, an animist is
one who believes in spirits whose activity affects his universe
and whom he seeks to control to his advantage through ritual
and ceremony. The Christian faith proposes one God who
alone controls the universe. He is sovereign, doing as He
wills within that universe. In contrast, an animist, especially
in the context of Papua, is one who believes in multiple gods
(spirits) and feels that he can and must control his universe.
Thus, through ritual and ceremony he seeks to placate, manip-
ulate, coerce, or whatever to achieve his best interests.

Animism proposes that the right ritual guarantees the
right result, so the animist seeks by all means possible via
his ritual to rise to the controller position. His gardening, pig
breeding, warfare, marrying, hunting—these all flow out of

the religious concept that if he properly links himself with his everyday activities in his material world to the invisible, supernatural world around him, all will be favorable to him.

As I alluded to earlier in this book, the Dani knows no years, only seasons, months and day and night. The months he counts by full moons which shine upon his fair land; the days and nights are attributed to the sun's trip about his universe. Seasons are explained by the sun's north-south movement from its "home," far to the southeast, back behind the mountains. When it goes into its home, the weather turns cold and rainy. As it moves out in a south-to-north direction, the weather begins to turn warm and sunny with only the occasional cold, damp day experienced in the valley caused, they explain, because the sun goes behind an imaginary range of mountains in its route to its farthest northern position when it "sits out on the hip" of the universe. In that position, there will be several weeks of clear, sunny weather with little or no rain. This is the time when all move out to make their gardens for the next year, because shortly the sun will move back towards its "home" and the weather will deteriorate.

Whereas we view our universe as being made up of two distinct parts which we refer to as the natural (that visible material world in which we exist) and the supernatural (that invisible nonmaterial world which is "out there" or perhaps more normally viewed as being "up there" somewhere and, to one degree or another—depending on our rationale— influences our lives), the Dani draw no lines of separation. The natural material world and the supernatural spirit world coexist, with events in the visible material world being determined by what happens in the invisible nonmaterial world. Therefore, if the animist can interact properly with his invisible nonmaterial world, his visible material world will be more beneficially responsive to his needs.

The Dani conceptualizes the invisible nonmaterial part of his universe much as he does the visible material part in which he lives. This invisible world around him is densely inhabited by several races of spiritlike creatures and spirit beings (notice the two different terms) interacting with and greatly influencing his behavior, often determining the normal activities of his life. We can further identify these spiritlike creatures and spirit beings as those who are nonhuman-in-origin, and those who are human-in-origin.

Nonhuman-in-origin spiritlike creatures and spirit beings

The spiritlike creatures and spirit beings of these nonhuman-in-origin races seem to have always existed in the Danis' world. They vary in number and are normally structured into hierarchies of the original being, referred to as the "elder" or "big man," then, varying numbers of subordinates who work for this "elder." I will write first of the spiritlike creatures.

Very clearly the Dani conceptualizes a race of spiritlike creatures living out on the roof of his world, which I am calling *creatures in the heavens*; at least two distinct races of these creatures living underneath his world, which I am calling *creatures beneath the ground*; and a host of other spirit beings cohabiting his visible material world, which I am categorizing as *spiritlike creatures in the forests, and spirit beings in the Dani universe*. As you will note, it is to the interrelationships within these categories that the Dani must fine-tune his entire way of life.

Spiritlike creatures in the heavens

The Kumbuloma-Abeloma were a species of inhabitants within the Dani universe which he concedes existed in the heavens, but of which there was little linkage of relationship. They were a race of spiritlike creatures originally inhabiting the forested areas of the Dani world, interacting with them by making clothes (probably net bags, grass skirts, and gourds) which they would hang about in the forest. When in need of such items, the people would move deep into the forests to places where these articles were left, taking what they needed.

This race of spiritlike creatures did no gardening. In their daily tasks of making clothes, when hungry they would come out of the forest and steal potatoes from the Dani gardens. In time, this incensed the Dani to the point where they rose up against these creatures, driving them with all their clothes out of the forests.

Now they exist out on the roof of the Dani world. Certain cloud formations in the heavens indicate that they have learned to garden and rain is felt to be those creatures urinating on the earth below. They were not worshipped and were little respected, having no direct relationship to the Dani, and no involvement in his universe. The Kumbulome-Abeloma existed somewhat like our fairies in a "wonder world" of their own.

Spiritlike creatures beneath the ground

The Dani believed that there were several races of spiritlike creatures living beneath the ground; one of them was called the "Liimbu." Creatures of this race were described as being disgusted-looking, dwarflike, and heavily-bearded. They dressed in the pretty net bags taken by this spiritlike creature from the poles driven into the ground at the cremation site on which were hung the remaining possessions of the deceased. They were the "pests" of the Dani world; they existed in large numbers, inhabiting the deep, dark holes in rock formations and the damp, unseen spaces underneath tree stumps deep in the forest. When one of the taboos governing a relationship had been broken, the offender had to make a sacrifice to appease the Liimbu, or he would become sick and eventually die.

Spiritlike creatures in the forest

Another category of spiritlike creatures of which the Dani speaks inhabited the forested areas of his world. One such race of these creatures within this category was called the Mbanunggwok. The Mbanunggwok loved to steal pigs and eat children. They bore many similarities to our "boogeyman."

The Dani pictured them as huge, but dull, grotesque, apelike beings living in caves and other suitable spots in the forests. There are two areas regarding the Mbanunggwok about which the Dani had difficulty finding enough superlatives to describe him.

The first is that he had *zillions* of children. Every shelf and board, every nook and cranny in his "house" had a baby Mbanunggwok. Mbanunggwok's wife, Ligiwakwi, "the one who kills with the vine," had a mania for bearing children; she also had an influence on pregnant women.

Pregnant women were forbidden to go into the forests for fear this grotesque female spiritlike creature would abort the child in the womb by tying an imaginary vine to it, then pulling it out of the mother's body. Mbanunggwok gave birth to sons only: light-skinned, strong, and dressed in all their finery from the womb.

The second area the Dani finds difficult to describe is the size of the Mbanunggwok. He was *huge* in size, carried a *mammoth* stone axe and a *large, heavy* stone knife. His net bags were *incredibly* big; in them he carried human bodies upon which he fed. His mouth was *unimaginably* large. Both the size and length of his genitalia was *staggering*. Whenever he went into the forest, that part of his anatomy preceded him by several hundred feet.

He chased and ate both people and pigs, and at times even his own beautiful children, because his appetite could not be assuaged. Yet pigs were not given to him because he did not respond to overtures of appeasement. Mbanunggwok was both feared and enjoyed; stories abound of his interaction with human beings who always tried to outsmart him.

Such tales about this race of spiritlike creatures appeared to be the vehicle within the society to teach cultural themes and values in an interesting fashion to the children. The children begged their aunties and grandmothers to repeat them around the fire at night. Each story concluded when the "auntie" gave an appropriate application and spat into the fire. Whereupon all the children did the same so as to escape the consequence of waking up in the morning with disjointed backs!

Enjoy with me: **A Myth from Daniland**

Several friends went out to hunt birds and possums in the forest. Moving through the trees in search of wild game, they caught the smell of smoke, then of meat being cooked. Cautiously, they went on and were startled to come upon Mbanunggwok, who with his wife, Ligiwakwi, was sitting in the shelter of a large tree, opening up their cooking pit. This Mbanunggwok and his wife were both blind, so, as quietly as possible, the fellows slipped up close to the meat that Mbanunggwok was cutting up and dividing for him and his wife.

Mbanunggwok would cut a piece of meat, placing it between them within his wife's reach; then, Ligiwakwi would place a roasted sweet potato from the pit within the reach of her husband. Without a word, the boys took that food, eating it as it was placed there by Mbanunggwok and his wife. This continued for some time until alas, the boys forgot that while Mbanunggwok was blind, he was not deaf, nor dumb. Enjoying every morsel of that delicious food, the boys forgot to chew quietly and Mbanunggwok heard them. Reaching for his huge bush knife, he jumped to his feet screaming, "Who is stealing my pork?" and the chase began.

Though blind, Mbanunggwok was fast in the forest and kept gaining on the boys, whose flight took them to the edge of a large river. They thought themselves cornered until one of them shinnied up a tree on the bank of that river, to be followed by the rest of the boys. Mbanunggwok was too clumsy to climb the tree, plus he had a better idea. He started chopping at the tree, where the boys were hiding in a large hole in its trunk.

Within minutes the tree, with the boys inside, fell into the river, where the strong current carried it far downstream. There it washed up onto the bank of the river in a part of the country where there was a race of women only. In spite of their need to build their own gardens and houses, and to carry in the firewood and hunt in the forests, these were beautiful lasses longing for the pleasure of a man's love and for children whom they could beget and nurse.

One day as they were gathering firewood, they came upon this large tree, wherein the boys were hiding, washed up onto the bank of the river. The girls laid their stone axes to the tree, and soon it was neatly stored in their house in the firewood rack above the fire to dry out; eventually it would be used to heat their hut and to cook their food.

As is the custom, after the evening meal in the house, prior to climbing upstairs to sleep, the girls put their leftover sweet potatoes and potato vines in a net bag, hanging it next to the wall boards out of reach of the rats, to be warmed and eaten in the morning for breakfast. During the night, while all the girls were sleeping, the boys would slip out of their log, distribute the sweet potatoes and potato vines, then, crawl back into their log as the dawn began to break. This continued for some time, with the girls utterly frustrated that there was no food in their net bags in the morning.

Finally, the firewood was dry. One rainy morning the first girl to wake up took her axe to split a splinter off the log to place on the fire. As she raised her axe to the log, out jumped one of the boys. Startled but pleased, she dropped her axe and grabbed him saying, "At last my husband!" and together they took off into the forest.

This went on each morning, with each of the girls getting her husband, until at last only a very tiny piece of the log was left, and only the quietest, most reserved but most beautiful of the girls was yet without her mate. Feeling a tinge of self-pity that all her sisters had found their husbands but she, she

*picked up the axe and, in a mighty swing of frustra-
tion, directed its blow onto the remaining piece of
wood. Just before impact, out jumped the tallest,
most handsome, light-skinned muscular macho male
of them all. She immediately claimed him as her
husband, and all lived happily ever after.*

(Don't forget to spit into your fire!)

Spirit beings in the Dani universe

We have just described for you the nonhuman-in-origin
spiritlike creatures whom the Danis feared; we now want
to describe several of the nonhuman-in-origin spirit beings
whom the Danis believe cohabited his world.

—Aap-Endak—

Within this category of spirit beings living in the Dani's
world was a race of beings known as the "Aap-Endak" "just
like men." As there are good and bad people so there were
good and bad spirit beings of this order.

Their homes were in various secluded spots in the mountains or nearby forests which the people knew and respected.
Such places of dwelling were lined with the brightest of the
bird of paradise feathers; these birds, the Danis claimed,
belonged to them.

Though benevolent to humans, this race of beings was
hot on pigs. Dead, swollen pigs found in the forests were
said to be caused by this spirit because the pig got too close
to the spirit's home. Such a pig was cremated on that spot and
ritually given to the Aap-Endak who inhabited that area.

Their function was decidedly in the area of warfare. They
carried weapons of war, and were clothed with the same

paraphernalia worn by the men who went off to war. They were considered to be the epitome of an *"aap abe"* "a real Dani man." Their dress was THE finest in Dani garb; their bows were made of THE hardest wood; their arrows were THE straightest; their skin, THE lightest; and their nature, THE bravest!

In times of crisis the Aap-Endak would affirm their assistance to the local war leaders with a force of invisible warriors equal in number to their human counterparts. They would present themselves dressed in all their war finery. Such a "sighting" would be considered a good omen and battle plans would then proceed. The Aap-Endak would also warn of an impending attack by appearing to a respected community leader with the news that within several days a war would ensue. Sure enough, within that time frame, some wife would be stolen, or a pig killed, and a battle would erupt.

In times of war, spirit beings of the Aap-Endak race preceded the real warriors to battle and were often "sighted" walking ahead of the Dani warriors, again dressed in all their war finery and carrying long spears and bows and arrows, with faces greased with pig fat, and with pigs' teeth decorating their nets. The human warriors then would dress according to how they perceived their spirit counterparts.

These spirit warriors would not actually engage in battle, but by their presence assured the human warriors of victory. They stood by to witness what took place during the battle — the bravery of the men, the keenest of the arrows and so on. These were the "cheer-leaders" of the real warriors.

When wounded in battle, the warrior was brought home. Anticipating his death, the other spirits would gather around to indicate the parts of the wounded warrior over which they were responsible. A pig would then be killed, cooked, and cut up, with each part offered to the spirit who claimed responsibility for that part of the warrior's body. This spirit would then protect the wounded warrior and bring healing. Should an arrow have embedded itself in the warrior's body, a pig was sacrificed to this Aap-Endak spirit who then became active in working the arrow to the surface where it could then be removed by a friend.

If after a war the Aap-Endak were not properly thanked with pigs sacrificed to them, they would visit the negligent chief or war leader with sickness in the lungs—coughing up blood as well as bleeding through the nose—or with the death of his finest warriors.

—Tile—

Another race of nonhuman-in-origin spirit beings cohabiting the Dani world is called the "Tile." This order of spirits was very much involved in the lives of the people. They were a household name, but of a very complicated, though common, function. They seem to have been the foulest of all their spirit forces. It was this Tile race of beings to whom the Dani compared our Biblical Satan and the structure of demons and demoniac activity under his jurisdiction. They appear to be sexless, having long heavy eyelashes. Their name was frequently used in placing a curse, and repeating of the name is the closest thing to a swear word that I know in Dani.

It is difficult to put a finger on the specific function of this spirit. It was a very sinister—obviously malevolent— force, operating in the community much like a disobedient and rebellious child. It was most active in maintaining the multitude of taboos in Daniland, instilling fear, possessing pigs and people, and raising general havoc in the community. To the Tile were attributed all the common social sins of the community: lying, stealing, hating, adultery, murdering, and so on. Let me cite several illustrations.

A pig breaking into a garden where it trampled the sugarcane to build its resting area had to be taken out and killed by the owner then disposed of by one of the non-immediate family members. If eaten by the owner or one of the immediate family members, that member would either die or shortly be killed. The pig had desecrated the sugarcane having a special relationship to the Tile spirit and had to be sacrificed.

In turn, those who ate the pig had to be certain that on the way home they did not touch certain trees or bushes, or any sugarcane, along the trail. All such trees had to be circumvented for several days or until it was certain that the remains of the feast had been eliminated from the body!

Hard rain, a thunder storm, or lightning during fair weather were signs again attributed to a pig in the sugarcane patch. Should such occur, a man's pigs were immediately brought and counted. If one turned up missing, the owner would head for the sugarcane patch to find it. It was then killed and cooked in the manner described above.

A pig giving birth to its litter in a place where these Tile spirits were said to reside brought foul weather. A search was made for the offending pig, which was then killed, and the weather again turned fair.

People having sexual encounters in these spirit-inhabited areas immediately became ill. Upon confession by the offender, a pig was taken and placed in the exact position of the woman as she lay during intercourse. The owner then killed it, allowing its blood to fall on the place where the semen was said to have fallen. The pig was then cooked on the spot where the woman's head lay. The meat was eaten but the carcass with its bones had to be burned on the site. This placated the spirit which caused the offender's illness; and the illness immediately subsided.

This Tile spirit was such a common yet foul force in the community that sacrifices to it were frequent, yet very secret, and made only by special men. In rituals placating other types of spirit beings, meat of the sacrificed pig was cooked and eaten by "special" people. However, sacrifices to the Tile spirit were burned in their entirety at the base of certain trees deep in the forest, after which a fence was built around the sacrifice site and bows and arrows were placed within the enclosure. The Tile spirit beings were felt to be the source of all evil; the Dani's world was burdened by frequent ritual to placate them. The liberating Good News changed all that!

—Kwewa'nakwe—

Another race of spirit beings inhabiting the physical material world of the Dani was the Kwewa'nakwe. She was a female spirit, very stubborn and fierce. Surrounded was she by her children though nothing was known of her husband.

She was believed to be the source of any abnormal or mentally retarded child—the normal healthy one having been stolen and traded for the retarded one while the new mother was searching in the forest for the fibrous stalk of the *ligi* bush. From this she would make the string to weave into a new decorative net bag in which she would place her newborn infant. Evidently the stealing/trading act occurred while the child was still in the womb. Thus, retarded children born to the Dani were called the children of the Kwewa'nakwe.

Normal paths known to be traveled by this female spirit were closed by a fence built of certain wood of which she was afraid. The fence was built with upright poles, and painted with pig's blood, after which the meat of the pig was cooked on the people's side of the fence. A fernlike plant, called the *"ngguum,"* was then planted in the pit where the pig was cooked. The meat was eaten only by older men: absolutely no women, uninitiated youth, or children.

Symptoms of being affected by this spirit, the Kwewa'nakwe, were headaches, fever, and losing one's mind, leading one—both crying and laughing incoherently and uncontrollably—into the forests. She could be controlled and appeased only through sacrifice.

These are several examples of the nonhuman-in-origin but very common, powerful spirits interacting with the Dani within his universe. There are many others.

The human-in-origin spirits

In contrast to these more malevolent nonhuman-in-origin races of spirit beings inhabiting the Dani world, were the benevolent human-in-origin or ancestral spirits. When speaking of the human-in-origin spirit beings, the Dani refers to two main categories: the "close" or "yard" spirits, more commonly called his "navel" spirits, and his "grandfather/grandmother" or ancestral spirits.

The "navel" spirits

The Danis believed that when a male child was born, his spirit counterpart, was also born, or at least became distinguishable. The placenta was the visible evidence of the spirit counterpart to the child being born, and thus its name, the *"amulok"* "navel" or "umbilical cord" spirit. When the placenta was disposed of through burning, the spirit lived on as the male child's invisible counterpart and moved with him through life as his friend and close helper. Thus, the name "close" or "yard" spirits since they provided personal protective care for the male child.

This spirit counterpart belonged only to the men; it was personal and secret. Only the owner knew the name of his "navel" counterpart, and it was definitely benevolent. The evidence of this spirit was one's personal reflection in the water. When one brought his index finger down to his reflection in the water, the reflection finger, which he believed to be the finger of this spirit, came up to meet his finger. This was proof of its existence.

Probably this accounts for the episode which occurred in our "witness school," which, in a matter of seconds, emptied itself of all our students when one of the men felt it necessary to confess publicly his protector spirits, that is, his "navel" spirits. It was right that he transfer responsibility and dependence on those spirits to his new Protector in the person of a personal God about whom we were teaching him. Perhaps this was the reason why mirrors were so much in demand in those early days. He could carry his personal protector with him in that little mirror; each look into the mirror affirmed that his spirit protector was present with him. Replays of movie film, in which their deceased relatives were seen speaking or moving about, only confirmed the living presence of these spirit beings.

These "navel" spirits were intricately woven into the life and movement of the Dani, confirming his personal identity, guaranteeing reproduction, and affording protection to its human counterpart to secure his health and longevity. This spirit made certain his human counterpart did not get sick, did not fall down a cliff, was not slain by an enemy, did not go hungry, and so on. Proper respect to this spirit allowed the owner to feel "safe" from the possible threats of other spirits, which were referred to as the "further away" more impersonal spirits. Thus, there were always pigs set apart to this spirit; these were the pigs killed during the night prior to the burning of the fetishes. The Danis were cutting themselves loose from their spirit protectors and helpers. And friend, that could produce a lot of fear as he looked into his future.

These, his helping spirits, ensured that the pigs set aside for them grew faster than the other ones in the litter; they went hunting with their human counterpart into the forests advising him where to find the possums, where the wild pigs were "hiding out," and where there was water to drink and shelter from the rain and cold. When proper respect was lacking, a spirit from this category of his "navel" spirits would react by causing temporary paralysis and withering of the right arm, the symbol of the Dani male strength. Only a ceremony utilizing a special string called the *"nggiru"* string could restore that limb to health again. These "navel" spirits were intricately involved in all the mundane activity of the Danis' lives.

There was another spirit of this category of protector, or helping, spirits which was most active in guaranteeing the virility of the human counterpart. In the rite of passage from boyhood to manhood, care had to be taken to properly introduce the male youth to this spirit prior to any contact with a woman. Should conception and pregnancy result from an intimate relationship with a woman prior to the secrets of this spirit being communicated to the youth, the pregnancy would result in a stillborn. The soul or personality could not be transmitted to the infant in the womb without the assistance of this spirit.

The nature and function of these spirits was revealed to the young male when he became of age, or when something a bit extraordinary happened to him, such as the killing of a wild pig, becoming critically ill, or taking a wife, which experience seemed to indicate that the spirit had manifested an exceptional interest in the lad and it was time for his introduction into the family's spirit world.

During the lengthy and frightening ceremony which introduced the boy to these, his "navel" or "personal" spirits, his pig, set aside for this occasion by the family, was taken, killed and cooked, after which the pig's teeth, ears, tail, and bladder—together with a seed from the red *wandin* bush and a small curved white shell called the *meeli* which they wore hanging from their necks—were given to the boy. These normally became a part of his dress, symbols he carried on his body indicating his respect for the spirit.

When the live pig set aside for this helping spirit was needed to fulfill the family's obligation to it, a younger pig was ceremonially presented to that spirit assuring continuity of its help and protection. In such a case, the large pig was brought together with the smaller one. The family was asked to sit down beside that large pig. Whereupon, the smaller pig was taken and passed over the family AND the large pig as these words were spoken to the spirit: "Here is your pig. Leave my children and wife alone. I have respected you and exchanged this little pig for the larger." And continuity of health and longevity was assured the family through this ritual.

Many of the pigs killed the night before the fetish burning were pigs which had been ceremoniously set aside to these "navel" spirits. The fetish burning was no "dumb decision" on the Danis' part. Though fully awareness of the consequences, they were literally stripping themselves of all the fetishes through which contact was made with the spirits to protect the worshippers' health and to guarantee their longevity.

It is nearly incredible that the words of God given to the Dani were so deeply embraced that they felt it right to turn from their dependence upon and the protection of those spirits to transfer their allegiance to their Creator God and to embrace Christianity. It is truly awesome!

The ancestral spirits

The second main stream of human-in-origin spirits is referred to as the *"ombomini"* "grandfather" and *"owogelo-mini"* "grandmother" spirits, or, in a wider sense, their ancestral spirits, the living spirits of their deceased relatives.

There is no question in the Dani mind that this category of spirits was extremely important and obviously active in their lives, to the point where they were referred to as the "real" spirits. These, like the "navel" spirits, were allied with the Dani in his struggle for survival in his universe, and thus benevolent in nature. In contrast, the nonhuman-in-origin spirits were more feared and far more threatening to him.

Names of these ancestral spirits were not made known to the children until the father felt his strength ebbing away. Calling his sons to him, he would release the names of these spirits to them, and die soon afterward. It was clearly believed that these spirits gave the daily strength necessary to live and to maintain one's role in the community.

The ancestral spirits seemed to be benevolent and were active in providing for and protecting their kinsfolk; they operated in a man-woman combination. Thus, the *ombomini* "grandfather," and the *owogelomini* "grandmother" spirits functioned in all the defined male-female role patterns of the society:

In war: The female ancestral spirit bound the enemy with an imaginary vine; the male spirit empowered the male descendant who would come upon the enemy to make the kill and find him totally paralyzed, immobilized by fear.

214

In feasting: The female ancestral spirit symbol was a large, heavy, but short, special stone wrapped in the cooking leaf and placed in the very bottom of the pit as her name was repeated. She was responsible for the thoroughness of the cooking process, as well as for the sufficiency of the food to feed all who attended the feast. The male ancestor was responsible for the total pig-cutting-up ceremony, along with ensuring that the meat would be properly and adequately distributed so all would return happily to their homes.

In reproduction: This male-female ancestral combination was active in guaranteeing the birth of male children to its descendants. If a man's ancestral spirit was not properly worshipped and eulogized, there would be no male children born into the family. This spelled disaster in the Dani patriarchal system.

In gardening: A special ritual was performed when a small rectangular-like piece of land in the garden was consecrated to this ancestor. Prior to planting, men, initiated into the world of the spirits, would gather in that designated place with pigs and potatoes. There the pigs were slaughtered, cooked, and given to this spirit, then ritually eaten.

After the feast, in the cooking pit permeated by the juices of the meat, the shaman would plant only the original food which sustained their ancestors in the beginning of time, and invoke the assistance and blessing of the ancestral spirits on the garden area. Following this ceremony the garden could be planted.

Though normally the women planted then weeded the garden, this special area of the garden, dedicated to the spirits was planted, weeded and finally harvested only by the man who had invoked the blessing of the ancestors. It was always harvested prior to harvesting the other parts of the garden. The "first-fruits" of the garden were given to the shaman who represented the ancestors in performing the ritual which prepared the garden for planting. The growth and quantity of the potatoes was now the responsibility of the female ancestral spirit.

Anyone not honoring his ancestors in this way could not expect to have sons born to him and, in the end, he would die of some strange sickness or catastrophe. It is interesting to note that many pigs were set aside for these ancestors. When a pig was killed, the buttocks half of the carcass was given to the *ombo* "grandfather" and the head half of the carcass was given to the *owogelo* "grandmother."

I could go on but I will not. My point was to take you on this little trip into the invisible supernatural world of the Dani in the hope that it would give you a wider knowledge of their spirit world to which they related in every aspect of their lives. I also wanted to give you an appreciation for the decision which was made to loose themselves from that authority to enjoy the freedom of belonging to the Lord.

I close this section by giving you a taste of the taboos associated with their worship of the spirits.

It was forbidden to take your axe into the woods to make a garden for a period of three days after having had intimate relations with your wife. Disregard of this taboo would cause the axe to be chipped while working, which in turn would cause the potatoes and other food in the garden to become uneatable mush.

It was forbidden to go into one's garden after eating possum, rats, or wild pig. Disregard of this taboo guaranteed that these animals would sneak into one's garden, root up, and eat all the food.

It was forbidden for any male, young or old, to see the afterbirth of a child being born. To see one would cause immediate blindness.

It was forbidden for either the younger men or the women to eat the liver and spleen of the cassowary bird. To eat such would cause blindness because these parts were reserved for the older men only, since they were believed to ensure longevity. In addition to eating these parts, the older men would pull out, cook, and eat the vein and nerve structures of this bird, believing this would make them strong and able to live longer; the women were given the legs of the bird so they would not age too rapidly.

It was forbidden for young men or boys to eat the liver of the pig; that part was reserved for the men and women only. Disregard of this taboo caused one's voice to go bad. Probably this becomes the explanation as to why the voice of young men changes during puberty.

It was forbidden for women, younger men and boys to eat the meat of the *kaneta* possum. Disregard of this taboo would cause baldness. The older men do not have any hair; therefore they can eat it. Presumably this is a bald-headed possum!

It was forbidden to eat the meat of the *wuundu* bird, which was reserved for the older men only. Disregard of this taboo resulted in infected arrow wounds which would swell to the size of the large egg this bird lays.

It was forbidden for men to eat the meat of the *ndindin* bird because it is blind to the daylight; anyone can catch or kill it. If a man ate of its meat, he would take on the nature of the bird and become a very passive, naïve man, easily vulnerable in time of attack.

That is a small sampling of the many taboos which assisted the Dani in making the right choices in life to ensure his well-being and in building positive relationships necessary for his successful survival in his universe. You can see how bound he was by the rituals and taboos surrounding his every move. Of this bondage he wanted to be free. That freedom was found in his acceptance of the Gospel!

Chapter 20:
Tales of fun and fulfillment

—ɯ—

A recent guest in our home asked a question which many have asked us over the years—a question we have found difficult to answer: "What are some of the most difficult challenges you have had to face in your 45 plus years of ministry to a primitive tribal people?"

My mind raced back over the years to try to find those difficult experiences, such as being chased by a native with a long spear, or a severe illness with which we had to cope, or an earthquake or a landslide out of which we had to dig ourselves. However, the more I searched the more I could only remember the many smaller activities which brought laughter and amazement to enliven our days. This chapter will include some of these incidents; I'll write as I remember them.

The "noise saw"

We had just returned from our first furlough during which we were able to purchase necessary items we had not thought to bring the first time to the field. One of these was a chain saw, a gift given to us by some friends in our small sending-church in California who knew we could well use it after seeing our pictures and hearing our stories. This we disassembled and put in one of the 55-gallon drums in which we packed our things to bring back to the field.

These drums finally had been flown in to Mulia. One afternoon I had unpacked this chain saw, re-assembled it, mixed some gas, and pulled the cord to start it. There were always people standing about wondering what other amazing, incredible thing the white foreigner would come up with. And this day was no different.

When I pulled the starter cord, and that brand-new chain saw fired, caught, and began to run, the group backed off a few feet (they were getting used to seeing and hearing these strange things), but when I hit the throttle and made for an old post laying there in the yard, they literally fell over one another trying to get away from the noisy little machine. From a short distance away they watched in utter amazement as, in just a few seconds, I sawed through that post roughly 10 inches in diameter.

The steel axes we had brought for them were an incredible advantage over the old stone axes which they had used. Now this! They cautiously gathered around to see it. With one hand each felt the sawdust thrown out from the cut I had made; with the other hand, he clicked his gourd, their gesture of total astonishment.

Several weeks later, a large village at the base of the mountain close to us announced that they were making a new garden. Kinsfolk and friends gathered for that occasion. There would be pork and sweet potato in abundance for the workers. Since it was high up on the mountain near us, we could hear them singing and dancing as they pulverized the dead brush and grass with their feet. They were working their way toward a large wooded area along that steep mountainside which they wanted to include in their garden effort.

About midmorning, I suddenly noticed that all activity had ceased and a pervasive silence had fallen upon the valley. Looking up from my work, I saw a small group of men making their way down the mountain path toward our house. *Has someone been injured? Perhaps they are coming to have me sharpen their axes on my small hand grinder?* I wondered.

Having arrived, they stood around for a few moments waiting for me to finish what I was working on so I could give them my attention. Finally one of them spoke. "Tuan Kobo," he said. "Several days ago we saw you cut that post with your 'noise saw'. Would you be willing to come up with it to the garden site we are clearing to cut down some big trees? These will take a long time for us to fell even with our steel axes."

I figured this would be another interesting language learning experience, so I said, "Certainly, as long as you don't mind carrying the saw and the gas up to the site." So we took off up the mountainside with them in the lead, proudly carrying my new chain saw, with the cans of gas and oil on their shoulders.

As we moved into the large area full of virgin timber which they wanted to include in their garden site, I noticed that some of the trees were already notched waiting to be felled. My guess was that we would start on the lower side, then, work our way up the mountain. But when I suggested this, they were adamant that we move further up the mountainside to work on the big ones which they found tiring to fell with their axes. So we kept climbing until they stopped at a big gnarly old tree about three feet in diameter at its base, its huge branches spreading out over the smaller trees around it. *"Wait a minute,"* I thought. *"I am not a pro at this. Let me start with the smaller stuff."* But they were pushing me to go for the "big one," and with my ego at stake, I could not back out now.

I cleared the brush away from the base of the tree, planted my feet firmly, and pulled the cord. The "noise saw" came to life immediately, and so did I. I took a big notch out of the down side of the tree, and then put the bar to the upper side for the cut which would make it fall. About me stood several dozen workers, thumbs clicking their gourds, their mouths wide open in awe, and their feet positioned in such a way as to sprint from the scene if necessary.

Seconds later that big tree groaned, shuddered and began to fall. As those naked natives jumped and yelled in glee, I straightened up to watch. I was totally astonished to see all the trees in its path fall with it, leaving a wide swath of felled trees all the way down the side of the mountain. *"How can this be?"* I mused, as I looked about me.

It was then I noticed that all the smaller trees which had fallen with the larger one had been notched on the down side. They had brought me with my "noise saw" to fell the big one so that when it fell, it would create a domino effect by pushing all the smaller trees in front of it, leaving the site clear for their garden—which is exactly what happened, with only a lone sapling or two having escaped the effect!

Now it was I clicking my chest with my thumb (the alternative if one did not wear a gourd) at their incredible strategy! "These amazing Dani," I muttered, shaking my head in total disbelief as they led me a short distance away to another "big one" that awaited its fate.

The pregnant airplane:

Since there was no other way into the interior except with the small Missionary Aviation Fellowship (MAF) aircraft, planes and pilots were very much a part of our missionary experience. To be more efficient in their trips in and out without bulking out (filling up the cargo space but not reaching the allowable weight limit as determined by distance, airstrip condition, and pilot weariness), MAF had designed a pod which was molded around and attached to the underbelly of the airplane. In it they could carry smaller boxes and dirtier things like pigs and chickens! It made the plane look every bit like it was pregnant!

This particular day a plane was due to arrive with food stuffs and with the first livestock which we were to fly into the interior—some chickens to keep us in a supply of eggs. And it was not long in coming. We heard the drone of the motor, then the small plane dipped and swooped over our little airstrip, racing down valley to a wider area where it made its normal 360-degree turn, and came in for a landing. The airplane was still a super phenomenon in the interior. When the plane was heard, all closer houses and villages disgorged themselves of their occupants, who rushed down to the airstrip to see what new thing was happening that day in the arrival of the airplane.

And this day was no exception. The pilot stepped out of that little plane with a knowing look and a big smile on his face, giving us the sign to keep back. Then, he squatted down, twisted the wing nuts which opened the door of the pod, and stepped back. There was just a moment of felt silence; then, suddenly, with all eyes watching, out from the pod flew a couple of dozen wild chickens that scurried away into hiding. "Catch them! Help us catch them," we cried to those standing about, which they finally did, but the story began circulating in the community that the pregnant airplane had finally given birth to its babies right there on the Mulia airstrip.

We flew in not only chickens, but eventually fish, ducks, goats, sheep, calves, horses, deer and even bigger, better pigs to mate with their smaller breed. This was in an attempt to provide the nutrition they lacked, as seen by the red bleached-out hair of their children and their large potbellies. But it was the big black billy goat which created the most excitement in the community on his arrival.

He was full-size and wild—a big one whose feet we had firmly secured, immobilizing him so he could not thrash about or kick his way out of the plane in midflight. When the plane arrived at Mulia with the goats, we pulled the smaller, tamer female goats out of the pod, then lifted the big billy out of the fuselage of the plane, placed him on the ground near the airplane, untied the ropes with which we had laced his feet to his body, and stood back. We expected him to rise elegantly to claim his freedom, but alas, having loosed him, he just lay there on the ground, probably exhausted from his struggles during flight.

Wondering if he might be sick, we gathered around. Of course the nationals had never seen an animal of this size, so they too crowded in to see what we had brought, exclaiming their amazement and clicking their gourds. Then, I saw it: a slight quiver of his thigh muscles and a twitch of his legs. I stepped back expecting an explosion, and I was not long in waiting.

With all the nationals crowding around, suddenly that big billy knew he was free and in an unusual burst of strength he leaped into the air, right into that large group of people who were standing around watching him. People ran everywhere, tripping and falling over one another to get away from this big black devil who then took off running full flight down the airstrip.

We, at first, laughed ourselves silly, but then realized we had a loose billy goat, so we pled with the people to help us catch him to bring him back to the pen we had made. "Oh, no, Tuan! We won't have anything to do with that wicked beast. You brought him in; you catch him." And while some of them did return to their villages, after the plane left we were able to get a number of the young men who, with long clubs and bows and arrows to protect themselves from him, went in search of this black demon and herded him back to his new pen.

The peeping tom

While our houses were not shabbily built using those local materials, one did have to be careful of the cracks in the walls and, at times, even the floor, especially since the bark, with which we lined it, would dry and shrink.

On this particular night all was quiet at Mulia. Ralph and Mel Maynard, our longtime colleagues there, were having a restful evening. Ralph was probably sitting in front of his homemade fireplace reading C. S. Lewis or J. B. Phillips when Mel slipped into the bathroom to have her usual bucket shower.

Not long afterward she called out to Ralph that there were some strange noises underneath the floor of the shower. She wondered if there might be something there. Ralph answered that it was probably one of the local dogs nosing around. But when Mel persisted, Ralph tied up the belt of his bathrobe, found his flashlight and slippers, quietly opened the door of their home and slipped out.

We built our houses on posts, or on rocks which we placed every four to five feet under the foundational bearers, and Ralph's house was no exception. Under the bathroom, since such posts could conceivably contact water, Ralph had used stones for that purpose. And when he shined his flashlight under the bathroom, the beam of his light fell upon a large muscular black national who, upon seeing the beam of the flashlight, had hidden his head behind the rocks, but could not hide his entire body. "Aha," said Ralph, as he reached for some smaller rocks to motivate his intruder to scat.

His peeping tom got the point. He headed out from underneath the house on the opposite side and took off running. With flashlight and rocks in hand, Ralph scurried around to meet him on the other side, but he was too slow. The man dashed down the path ahead of Ralph and made for the open airstrip. "The very idea…," muttered Ralph as he emptied his hands of the rocks at his running target—missing, of course, which only fueled his mounting anger. "I'll get you, you…" and Ralph started after him full flight, slippers sliding in the airstrip turf, bathrobe tails flying. "If I get my hands on you,

I'll wring your neck!" And what happened next is in the secret files of the mission.

The eyeball in the knothole

It was a dark, drizzly night and past bedtime for Dave Cole who, very promptly, guest present or not, closed down at about 8:30 in the evening to make his way to his bedroom. On this particular evening the noise from the hot, hissing pressurized kerosene lantern only accentuated that trait.

As he reached to turn off the gas lantern, he thought he heard a sound outside the door. "Who could be out on a night like this?" he muttered to himself as he glanced in the direction of the door. In the rough boards of which the door was made, he noticed that a knot had fallen out, leaving a hole about an inch in diameter, and his fun-loving nature (for he was always playing jokes) kicked into gear.

Quickly he found his camera, focused on that hole, and pressed the button. There was a blinding flash of light from the camera and the sound of running feet outside. Several weeks later when the film, which had to be sent out to the coast to be developed, was returned with the pictures, a big, beautiful, black eyeball, fully framed in the knothole, could be clearly seen. Someone peeping through the knothole had enjoyed an evening of entertainment at the expense of Dave and Dina Cole!

Resetting a shoulder the hard way

He was short and stocky; every muscle in his body bulged and was hard as nails, betraying the strength of the man standing on our small porch. His mouth and gums were bright red and his teeth coated with the pale stain of the betel nut which he regularly chewed. But what caught my attention was his right shoulder which drooped unnaturally with his hand turned outward—all evidence of a dislocated shoulder. When he spoke he used the dialect of a small group of Dani-related villages out on the fringe of Daniland, and I knew he had walked at least two days to come to us.

Upon questioning him, I learned that he had taken a bad fall in the forest several days prior to that time. Since he had not healed to the point where he could use the shoulder again, he had made his way to Mulia to ascertain whether or not we could help him.

Getting out our medical books and diagrams and following the directions indicated, we tried several times to reset it, but without success. Since we had mission doctors standing by on the single sideband radio, we called Dr. Leng asking for his advice.

Having heard our story, Dr. Leng informed us that it would be nigh impossible to reset the shoulder without anesthesia since it had been several days since the dislocation had occurred, and the man's muscles would have tightened around that dislocation. But he said to give it a try by having him lie flat on the ground with his left arm around something solid like a post or tree. Then, I was to lie parallel alongside him on the dislocated right shoulder side but with my head at his feet, putting my foot in his armpit and pulling the arm outward while using my pushing foot as the fulcrum to bring the arm around and back in a parallel position to his body. "Perhaps this will snap the shoulder back into place," Dr. Leng had said, "but be careful that you don't force it and break the ball on the upper arm. You can feel it slip back into its socket. If that does not work, he will have to be flown over here to the hospital where we can reset it under anesthesia." "O.K," we said. "We'll have a go!" and turned off the radio.

Outside, we explained to him what we were going to do, and looked around for a solid post or tree which he could grab onto while I did my pushing-pulling act!

All this time a crowd was gathering to see what on earth was going on, especially once we had found a nice flat area in our yard with a tree about 10 inches in diameter that he could hold onto. And we were both lying on the ground end-to-end practicing that technique.

After a few trial runs we got the hang of it, so I said to him, "O.K. This is the real thing now, grab that tree in a life and death hug," which he did. And I grabbed his dislocated right arm. With a mighty sustained pull with my hands, and a powerful sustained push with my foot into his armpit, I slowly brought that arm out, then around, and back to his side while he screamed as if he were being butchered alive. Nothing happened!

So, we agreed to try it again even though the yard was fast filling up with curious onlookers because of his screams. Again, a gorilla-like hug with his left arm around the tree; again my mighty pull on his arm with a more powerful sustained push with my foot. And the scream! I can still hear it—but with a smile because after each try we would both lie there on the ground, panting from exhaustion while laughing hilariously, waiting for the energy and will power to try it again. We were now surrounded by a large group of local Danis totally bewildered about what was going on in this missionary's yard.

In the end we were unsuccessful, so we told him to stick around the station to wait for a flight which would take him the 20 minutes flying time to the mission hospital and Dr. Leng with his staff to serve him.

He hung around for a few days, and then we lost contact with him. About a week later, Dr. Leng radioed telling us that the man had arrived at the hospital, having walked three days over the trail; that the shoulder had been reset and the man was happily on his way back.

The saga of our surprised psychologist

Two days trek upriver from the mission airstrip and the Mulia station is another station with an airstrip called, Ilu, also among the Dani tribe.

During our first term on the field, the late Reverend Ralph Odman, General Director of the Unevangelized Fields Mission along with the well-known mission psychologist and author, Dr Henry Brandt, made a special visit to Irian Jaya. Dr. Brandt enjoyed walking and dreamed of trekking in the mountains of Irian Jaya. So, we helped make that happen.

They flew into Ilu and after spending several days there with Stan and Barbara Sadlier, the plane flew Rev. Odman on to Mulia as Stan and Dr. Brandt began the two days trek following the Yamo River down to Mulia.

They overnighted in a Dani village the first evening, and then proceeded on their way to Mulia the following day. Trekking up to the pass which led them into the Mulia valley, they walked into one of our typical torrential afternoon showers and were drenched and cold to the bone by the time they arrived at the summit. There, in an old gardening shelter complete with bark roof, their carriers, also cold and shivering, had already gathered and, to Dr. Brandt's astonishment, the Dani men were in the process of building a fire with wet wood and with rain dripping on them.

Having arrived at Mulia, that evening we sat around Ralph's homemade fireplace as Dr. Brandt, totally astonished at what he had witnessed, gave us the following account:

The scene was incredible. Rain still pouring from the heavens, and dripping over our cold, wet bodies huddled there in that small shack, I watched with amazement as one of the men slipped the cap off the tip of his long gourd, and withdrew a small tuft of very fine, dry grass which he placed in the crotch of a short stick about 10 inches long taken from the net bag over his shoulder. Placing it on the ground, he held it firmly under one foot as he drew a short length of vine back and forth with ever increasing speed and tautness at the precise point of the dry grass in the crotch of that stick. Shortly the vine broke from the friction created by the vine being pulled back and forth, but not before depositing a small bit of ash on that tuft of grass which produced a tiny thread of smoke. Immediately he picked it up and began to blow on that bit of smoking ash which became a tiny live coal and which shortly burst into flame in his hands. Soon there was a roaring fire around which the men gathered to warm themselves and, mission accomplished, the man carefully deposited the remaining tuft of grass back into the tip of his gourd to be used when another occasion demanded.

The following day, for our guests' observation, we had planned to put a grass roof on a large literacy school building which measured 30 feet wide and 100 feet long. I had informed our guests to be ready with their cameras to watch this feat.

Looking at the size of the building, Dr. Brandt had asked, "How many days will it take to finish the job?" To his utter astonishment I had answered, "Oh, they will be finished by early afternoon after which there will be a feast before they return home."

The day dawned bright and clear. Dr. Brandt was out early taking pictures and waiting for the event to take place. With still no activity about the scene by 8 o'clock, Dr. Brandt came rushing up to me asking, "Dave, has it been called off? If they are going to finish that roof today, hadn't they better get started?"

Tying the grass roof on the large school building

I answered by pointing toward the tops of the mountain ridges around us. Gathering there were masses of dark bodies silhouetted against the green of the forest. Moments later the call went out. More than a thousand black bodies glistening in the bright sunlight, with bundles of the long roofing-grass on their heads, and bundles of small saplings on their shoulders, could be seen snaking down the mountain paths around us. It was quite a scene.

In just a few moments the area around the building was full of busy men. Some had climbed up on the round pole rafters and were tying on the small saplings running horizontally to the rafters; some could be seen splitting those saplings and spearing them up to the men on the rafters; others could be seen making small bundles of grass from the larger bundles brought in; still others were observed tossing those smaller bundles up to the men who were tying them on. It was quite a sight!

In the middle of this activity Dr. Brandt came running up to me, "Dave," he said, "take me to the man who has organized this; I've just got to shake his hand and compliment him on his ability to organize such a vast group."

Puzzled, I looked at him and said, "There is no one man who has organized this; everyone is just doing what he sees needs to be done." And he walked away, shaking his head at the incredible scene he was witnessing.

While some were tying the grass to the horizontal saplings fastened to those roof rafters, other groups of men and women, who had brought in firewood and food, were preparing the feast for the workers. By early afternoon, having finished putting the grass on that large roof, the men sat with us around the cooking pits enjoying sweet potatoes, sweet potato vines, corn and cooked cucumbers. It had taken less than four hours to finish the task and by 3 o'clock in the afternoon, rested and with renewed strength, they were on the way home, some of them, to villages three hours walk away.

Several days later, Rev. Odman and Dr. Brandt were on their way back to the States with sensational stories, yes, but also with a deep appreciation for those amazing Danis!

The ground is close; step out

"Daddy, Daddy! He jumped out!" shouted our son, David, as he beat on the partition separating the cab, were I was, and the back of the small pickup box, where he was.

As mission stations go, Mulia was growing, both in ministries and in missionaries to expedite those ministries. In addition to the normal church-related activities, Mulia boasted medical services complete with hospital facilities, and the Dani Bible School which was located about 10 minutes fast walk upvalley from the top of the airstrip.

To enhance communication, to more effectively use our time and energy, and to haul supplies brought in on the airplane, we had imported two small three-wheel vehicles from Japan—both having pickup-like boxes on the back in which one could transport people or haul supplies. And the Danis were always waiting for their chance to have a ride!

This particular day, I had to make a quick trip from our home up at the Bible School location down to the airstrip to pick up something left by the airplane. Son David, about 8 years old and home during a school break, had climbed into the back along with a Dani man who helped us in the yard work.

The vehicle was made for the level city streets of Japan and thus underpowered for the interior situation. Going up from the airstrip in the three-wheeler was always in first gear, and slow, whereas going down was downhill, so we sort of opened it up to feel the wind in our sails. And this day was no different. We were pushing some schedule—I have forgotten what it was—so I had raced down for a fast pick up.

About halfway down and going at a good clip, David started pounding on the partition separating the cab from the box and shouting, "Daddy! Daddy! He jumped out!" I slowed down to stop, then, since I would be coming right back up the road, I went on, picked up the item I was after, and started up the grade to our house wondering where our Dani friend was. About halfway up the grade, we found him sitting at the side of the road, his clothes in tatters; the skin of his arms and legs torn and bleeding; his body scraped and bruised. He was in extreme pain.

"What did you do?" I asked after stopping. Wincing in pain, he answered as he brushed the flies off his wounds, "I wanted to get off here to see a friend. Rather than make you stop, I saw that the ground was close, so I stepped out! Now look!" he said as he showed me his wounds.

He had really taken a spill and was near crying. Stiff and sore, he got back into the three-wheeler and we took him down to the clinic to be cared for. It was a hard lesson, but how would he know that one never steps out of a moving vehicle?

Chapter 21:
Some mundane of missions

—〰—

Our homemade hydroelectric plant!

Missionaries need to be creative not only in ministry, but also in surviving in places of ministry. We were in the mountains of Irian Jaya, an hour and 20 minutes flying time in a small 185 Cessna airplane from the coast to a place where people from the outside modern world had never been. These Danis were locked into their own little community, never having seen paper or pencils, cars or motorcycles, stores and clothing. There were no telephones, no mail service, and no electricity. We worked at night by the light of a small kerosene lamp, or by the light of the more modern kerosene pressure lantern which we either took with us in our outfit, or purchased at the coast where European models could be found. And the cost of flying in that fuel in the small airplane was considerable. It was so expensive, in fact, that one of our colleagues from UFM Australia, Wal Turner, had a better idea.

The humiliating defeat and eventual retreat of the Japanese forces occupying New Guinea was accomplished by the United States forces under the leadership of General MacArthur. This forced retreat left the beautiful tropical white sandy beaches of the coast and surrounding islands littered with relics of World War II. Amidst this rubble were wrecked and abandoned airplanes. On these Wal had found small turbochargers made of cast aluminum, designed to kick in at high altitudes, converting the exhaust of the airplane into extra power for maneuvering at high altitudes. Feeling this could be adapted to provide electricity by utilizing the abundance of water in the interior, he put his creativity and technical knowledge to work; he designed a simple system using water to turn the turbocharger, which he then belted to a 110-volt, or 220-volt electric alternator. And it worked, though it needed further fine-tuning which he was not able to give before he left the field.

After we got settled at Mulia, my colleague, Ralph, continued to brainstorm the serious possibility of setting up the same type of system at Mulia in a stream which ran right by his house; he hoped it would provide some electricity for the houses on the station. Discussion turned the possibility into feasibility; we began to look around for the supplies. Ralph already had his hands on a turbocharger and a small 3 KVA alternator was on the way from the States. So we ordered the 6-inch-diameter galvanized pipe needed to guide the water into the unit and began to prepare on the local scene.

There was a good elevation drop in the streambed running past Ralph's house. With a lot of national help, we built a small dam across that stream with large boulders and several long, large logs, filling in the gaps with gravel from the creek-bed and sod from the banks of the stream. This allowed us a small reservoir of water which we then diverted into a 55-gallon drum. From there it plunged down through that 6-inch pipe roughly 120 feet to turn the turbo unit below.

That evening as we sat near Ralph's homemade fireplace enjoying our first electricity and patting ourselves on the back at the product of our creativity, it began to rain. The more it rained, the greater the volume of water which came cascading down that small stream behind his house and the greater the rumble of boulders being carried along by the strong current.

Minutes later the bright white lights of our electric venture turned to a dull red and, shortly, we were sitting in darkness. And then we heard it: the rumble of boulders, the splintering of logs, the sound of metal barrels and pipe being driven downstream. We grabbed our flashlights and ran out to see our dam. There was nothing, literally nothing there but an enlarged gap in the streambed where the dam had been.

The next morning, though the turbocharger and alternator, being set back away from the stream, were still intact, we found pieces of the pipe strewn along the streambed each looking like a straw from a McDonald's milk shake which someone had wrapped around his finger before tossing it in the trash.

Gone was all our hard work; gone was the new pipe; gone were the large boulders and logs we had carefully placed; and gone was our enthusiasm—but not for long. We let it rest for a few weeks; then we began to re-think, to revise our design and to re-order materials.

As I recall, this venture failed twice before we pioneered a design which channeled a smaller stream of water into a man-made pool. There we placed a 55-gallon drum complete with a gate connected to a cable. This cable we could pull from the house to open or close the gate allowing the water to plunge down through one hundred plus feet of pipe into the turbocharger.

The pool also acted as a sediment controller. If the stream rose too high, it would push rocks and other debris into the mouth of the small channel feeding the pool and automatically cut off the water, saving the pool. The following day a couple of men, in just a few minutes, could clear the debris in the mouth of the channel and the pool would fill again for electricity that evening.

A rain causing moderate flooding of the stream would bring mud, small gravel and some debris into the pool. However, the pool, acting as a giant sediment bulb, allowed the sediment brought in by the current to settle to the bottom before the water reached the drum. From the drum, the water plunged through the pipe to spin the turbocharger, which turned the alternator, which produced the electricity, which made life much easier for the missionaries!

Eventually we had two such units at Mulia, fine-tuned to run efficiently by Leon Dillinger; they provided inexpensive electricity for our needs for many years. Granted, we had to work within the limits of the watts produced; we divided the total watts among the households served. The load (number of lights on) controlled the revolutions per minute (rpm) of the alternator. When family A needed to wash clothes and needed more wattage to run the washing machine, family B would turn off some of their lights. Or, when family B needed more wattage to iron, family A would turn off some of their lights. It worked well for the normal electricity needs of the households: lights, laundry, ironing, and use of simple electrical tools. We were most grateful for it and the thousands of dollars of mission money we saved over the years.

The school bus with wings

Another unique feature of living in the interior of Irian Jaya (now Papua) was that twice a year our children had to climb into the small airplane to fly to the coast where they attended the mission school administered by the Christian and Missionary Alliance. They would come home for a long Christmas break, then again for the summer break. Midsemester we would try to fly out to the coast where our children went to school to spend a couple of weeks with them.

When the plane came in, we would always look first for the mail bag brought in by the pilot, which we hoped would bring us a letter or a cassette message from our children. Always, we would send out a note keeping them informed on what was happening in the valley. With the note we would include some special thing which they enjoyed—fudge, sugarcane, popcorn or cookies—just to let them know they were not forgotten, that mom and dad, somewhere in the interior, loved them, missed them and sought to keep the relationship warm and caring even though distance kept us apart.

One day as we waved goodbye to our son, David, overcome with emotion, I slipped off to my office and penned the following few lines which seemed to wrap up my feeling each time our children climbed into that plane to fly off to school. We tried so very hard to make those departures happy times. And it was only when the fading sounds of the motor were lost in the echoes bouncing back and forth against those mountainsides, and only when the last speck of that airplane was lost in the clouds, that we would quietly turn away with tears in our eyes to move back into the routines of our work. The following captures that emotion:

> *There is a time to laugh and there is a time to cry. It was clearly the latter!*

> *There was a little boy who went for a last walk with his dog.*
> *There were those few moments sitting on that big rock out in the yard with hand cupping the chin, and the far away look in his eye. Unconscious was he of his daddy who was watching.*

> *There was the daddy who watched and who, feeling that lump rise in his throat, quickly wiped his greasy hands and, leaving the motorcycle parts strewn over the workbench, went to that little boy on the rock, and took his hand without a word— he couldn't.*

> *Together they walked through the yard making small talk—when possible.*

Then, there were the few sweet potatoes given to his little horse, Smokey; its final pat on the nose, and his comment, "Smokey's a nice horse, isn't he, daddy."

There was the last meal—a little something special for the kids, but different because it was somehow hard to talk those last few minutes together.

Then, there was the sound of the airplane. His time and yours...had come.

There was the bundle of arms and legs that somehow managed to wrap themselves around you in a good-bye hug,
The withdrawn but brave little face of a 6-year-old who didn't really know what it was all about,
And the pilot who fastened the seat belt...adjusted for "big people."

Then, there was the final wave of the hand as the plane's engine caught, and roared to life;
There was the rev of the motor; and a mommy and daddy looking off into space, blinking hard...
As the plane roared down the airstrip heading for Sentani with your son and daughter on board.

And that's what it is like to see your kids off to school in Irian Jaya.

Of burning buildings and forging friendships

We were enjoying the fellowship and strategy discussions of our annual UFM missionary conference when I was called out of the room. The voice on the single sideband radio, our only means of communication in the interior, was a bit garbled, so I asked for a repeat. The strange message came again from a voice that was hardly audible and broken up with sniffling and the occasional sob. "Tuan Kobo," he said. "Your workshop/laundry building burned to the ground this morning and everything is lost." Sobbing!

After processing what he said, I asked, "Were you able to save anything?" Back came the response: "Yes, we pulled out your big motorcycle and the washing machine, but could not save anything else." I did not hear much after that because of the thousands of questions which negated any sane conversation. "I'll try to get a flight over as soon as possible," I said, and released the mike button.

My workshop was gone! My tools were gone! The chain saw, gone! All supplies of building materials along with the small supply of rough lumber underneath the shed, gone! Our supply of firewood, gone! The black waterpipe to link us to a small spring upstream and hundreds of other accumulated odds an' ends, gone! Wow! I said to myself, and contacted MAF to fly me over to see what had happened!

The next plane in to our conference site took me across to Mulia, a flight of about 20 minutes. I could see the remains of the building from the air as we flew over. Sure enough, my workshop/laundry room, about 25 feet wide and 45 feet long, which I had built of round poles and hand-hewn boards, and had roofed it with grass, was now reduced to a pile of ashes. Stepping out of the plane, I saw the young man whom I had asked to watch over my place. He was seated on a rock at the edge of the airstrip in tears.

Along with many other projects I was introducing to assist the Dani toward a better way of life, I had a nice bunch of little chicks which had just hatched in a borrowed incubator. I had taught him how to care for them by giving them the proper food and water, and also how to fill the tank with kerosene which fueled the flame to keep them warm at night. In the filling of the tank that morning, unknowingly, he had dribbled some kerosene too near the flame. Then he had grabbed his towel and had gone down to the river for his normal morning bath. When he returned, the place was in flames.

I walked the short distance up to the site past a group of people seated on the ground near the burned-out remains. Quickly, since the plane was waiting to take me back to our conference site, I sifted through the charred ruins: the chain saw, all my wrenches, a case of nails, some axes and a host of other things. As I brooded over what had happened and wondered how quickly I could rebuild, this group of men had risen to their feet and were now standing around me, many of them with axes on their shoulders, heads down, flicking away the tears. I immediately recognized them as the young lad's kinsfolk from the valley of Kiyage, three good days trek to the north from Mulia over incredible terrain. They had heard about their clan son's misfortune and had come to speak with me.

The young man's father pushed himself through the group and positioned himself to speak: "Our father, Tuan Kobo," he said. "These are my people," then, motioning with his hand toward those standing with him, he went on, "and my people are your people. You found us on the backside of this large mountain range. You have walked our trails, climbed our mountains, crossed our bridges, and slept in our houses. We cannot forget your visit into our valleys to share with us the Living Words. We have come to help you. By the time your conference is finished, we will have all the materials here, ready for you to rebuild your workplace. I have said it; we will do it." I thanked them profusely and, making my way back down to the waiting airplane, I remembered.

I remembered those first men, the Wanos speaking a fringe dialect of the Dani language, who had come from their valley, three full days trek away, to meet with us. They had come requesting to be included in our ministry. I remembered the father who, months before, had brought his older teenage son, this lad who was caring for my place when it caught fire. He had begged us to allow his son into the "witness school" to learn to read. "We are old," he had said, "and cannot make the trip back and forth from our valley to learn about these Living Words, but he can. He is young; he will learn quickly and eventually will become our pastor."

I remembered our first trek out to his area: the climb over that 12,000-foot-high mountain range which taxed our strength to the limit. I remembered our fires under those large overhanging rocks which shielded us from the cold and wind, and around which we spoke of other unreached peoples in that vast lowland area, drawing simple maps in the ashes of our fire.

I remembered our journey the next day, following the river. We had passed alongside this incredibly high waterfall cascading down the mountainside which, when I tried to follow its fall to glimpse its source, I found a good portion of it was hidden behind low-hanging clouds with only the source visible high above us.

I remembered the fatigue we had experienced as we walked that afternoon, fatigue which turned to superstrength when we reached a promontory along the trail overlooking the valley and looked down upon a group of about 300 people waiting for us in a village yet 20 minutes away.

We had raced down the mountain toward that village. Still embedded in my memory was the overwhelming sense of God's goodness when, after arriving and being welcomed, this young lad's father had stood up, flicked the tears from his eyes and said: "Tuan Kobo. These are my people of the Kiyage Valley. I surrender them to you. Teach us the message of *'nabelan-kabelan'* 'eternal life' from that Big Book."

I remembered that a month later, accompanied by several of our faithful men, I had made a second trip into the area, determined to visit the people living in the lower region of that valley. The first day, at dusk, we had found a large over-hanging rock. Around three large fires we had cooked our food, chatted and slept. The next morning we had crossed the range and went down into the upper end of the valley.

Still an hour trek away from the first village, one of our men had stopped me and said, "Tuan Kobo, look here!" as he pointed to tracks on the trail. "A large group, with their pigs, was climbing up this trail but on hearing of our coming has gone back to the nearest village to wait for us."

The men had made this deduction from the footprints on the trampled path. Shortly, we had met the entire group of about 30 people under a crude temporary shelter, waiting for us. How glad they had been to see us! Over and over we were to hear the same expression during the next four days: "We are going to Mulia to get the Words of Life; we are going to Mulia to hear the Living Words."

I remembered that one dear old father, blind but with a smile on his face, would not release my hand—he was so happy. His sons were carrying him on their shoulders to the Mulia valley since he could not walk, blind, up that almost impassable trail.

I remembered another old man excitedly crying out as we had entered his village: "My heart is standing up! My heart is standing up (I'm excited; I'm excited)!" Where formerly we had met nearly 300 people now there remained only a dozen. Hanging about the houses were the net bags stuffed full of their possessions. "Why the net bags full and hanging thus?" I had inquired. "We are going to Mulia to get the Words of Life," they had told us.

We had trekked another three days down the valley; we had seen the same sights; had asked the same questions; had been given the same response: "We are going to Mulia to hear the Words of Life."

I remembered climbing over treacherous cane bridges swinging over canyons and turbulent rivers several hundred feet below; scaling 200-foot precipices on poles crudely tied together—so dangerous that even some of the Danis would not attempt the climb—and pulling leeches off my legs, one day numbering more than 25. I could not believe what I had seen: a vacated valley. Whereas on our first trip we had estimated a total population of perhaps a thousand people, now we could find no more than a couple of hundred.

"What are you going to eat when you get to Mulia?" I had asked. "At Mulia there is no pandanus fruit, no wild pig, no cassowary birds," I had reminded them.

"Tuan Kobo," they had replied, "if we stay here who will bring us the Words of Life? We will die here in our badnesses and go to the place of fire as our fathers have gone. We don't want wild pig; we don't want the pandanus fruit; we want eternal life," they had replied.

With a new appreciation in my heart for that distant valley tucked back in most difficult terrain, for the father and his kinfolk who would be gathering materials to help me replace the building, and for this lad who, though responsible for the fire, was in training to become a future church leader and pastor to his people, I climbed on that airplane and returned to our conference.

The event of the fire occurred in the latter 1960's. I want to record that we experienced a special joy when this lad, now married with five children, came to see us during our visit to Papua in the summer of 2006. Many years later, true to his father's words, Nigik, for that is his name, is head of several churches in that difficult Kiyage area. He spoke warmly of his love for the Lord, his eyes dancing with delight that we could meet again after so many years to renew our friendship—forged in the fire of my burned down workshop.

The stolen gun

One evening my colleague, Doug Hayward, who also spent several terms with us at Mulia, and I were sitting in the living room of his house, sipping cups of hot coffee prepared by his wife, Joanne, and discussing strategy. Suddenly, in a village fairly close to his house, we heard the sound of gunfire.

I mentioned to Doug that as I rode down through that village to his house on my motorcycle, I had noted something going on. Several armed police from the police post a short distance away, were mulling about in the village. Though this was a bit unusual, we figured it was none of our business, so carried on with our conversation.

All of a sudden, we heard this terrible clatter on the porch outside Doug's back door. As we got up to take a look, the door literally burst open and a young man, whose name was Kabu and well-known to us, stumbled inside dragging something underneath a large overcoat some missionary had thrown out. He was greatly agitated and was shouting: "Help me! Help me quick. Teach me how to use this. They are coming to get me. They are coming to get me!" By that time he had opened the front of his long coat to disclose a gun he was carrying, and pleaded with us to teach him how to fire it since the police were after him.

"O.K! O.K! O.K!" we said, "but what's happened?" And he blurted out the story. He had a beautiful younger teenage sister living with him, also well-known to us, whom the police wanted to take that evening to use for their sensual pleasures. They had surrounded his house in uniform and with their weapons to intimidate him, then to force him to release his sister to them. He refused.

When sweet-talking, then intimidation, would not produce the desired end, they resorted to getting physical. As one of the policemen raised the butt of his gun to whack him on the side of his head, he had ducked, grabbed the gun, wrenched it out of the policeman's hand and ran—with the gun! Following the stream down several hundred yards, he had surfaced in Doug's house with the gun, and now wanted to use it to protect himself.

Quickly we sized up the situation and said, "Get out of here quick—with the gun. We could be accused of aiding this perverse action. Get out quick and hide until we have time to speak to the chief of police. Wait for us to call you." And we nearly had to push him out of the house into the darkness, with the gun.

As other shots were being fired in the vicinity of Kabu's house where we knew those rogue police were still looking for him, we sent a runner over to the chief of police with the message that we needed to speak with him; would he have time this late at night to give us a hearing? In just a few minutes he was knocking on Doug's door, face ashen and body trembling.

Having heard the story, he pled with us to help him get the gun back. Promising Kabu protection and complete immunity from the law since what he did was in self-protection, he again asked our help in retrieving the gun or he would lose his position and probably his profession.

From that, knowing he was on the side of Kabu, we said, "O.K. You return to your home, and get your policemen under control; we will do what we can to find Kabu." With that he left and, after we were sure that the policemen had returned to their barracks, we started looking for and calling out for Kabu to come in. But nothing! We waited again, then, called. Again, nothing!

So I jumped on my big trail bike and, though without lights, headed upvalley in the beautiful moonlight, calling out for Kabu as I rode. I knew the sound of my near mufflerless motorbike could be heard all over the valley and that he would hear it if he had gone upvalley to his village. Again, nothing!

So I had returned to our house and, since it was nearly 11 p.m., I was preparing to slip between the sheets when a message from Doug arrived. "Dave," he said. "Come on down. Kabu is sitting here in my living room with me; I have sent word over to the chief of police to come."

I climbed on my bike and raced down to Doug's house just as the chief of police arrived. Together we went in and there sat Kabu with the gun! Thankfully, the chief of police did not rush over and grab the gun. He graciously sat down as Kabu simply told him the story he had related to us. When finished, after declaring before God that his only motive was to protect himself and his family from the rogue policemen, Kabu stood up, walked over and placed the gun in the hands of the chief of police!

The police chief graciously thanked him. And after profusely apologizing for the actions of his men, he promised protection for Kabu and his family, and severe discipline to the policeman who had threatened him. Kabu was given that, and the offender was sent out of the area. Life went on.

Missionary arrested

The months following the Indonesian takeover of Dutch New Guinea in 1963 were filled with unbelievable tension and incredible problems for missionaries and people. Having no experience in dealing with matters of culture, the Indonesian soldiers felt that since they were now in control, everything could be solved with a fist and, if that did not work, then with a gun.

A real person to these men was one who wore clothes, ate rice, could count over ten, spoke Indonesian and lived in a house in which he did not have to stoop to step inside! They had never worked with a Stone Age people such as they found at Mulia where their government finally opened a military post, complete with several soldiers, in the mid 1960's. Such a people were called *"oranghutan,"* the name given to apes in the forest, and they were treated as such. Stealing their potatoes was O.K; raping their women was O.K; extortion of their few vegetables and chickens was O.K. They were not truly human; they were only like the apes in the forest without a morality.

In addition, the Dutch were their enemies and white. Though we, the missionaries were not Dutch, we were white; we had the confidence of the people because we had been there longer and spoke their language. And we had the communication with the outside world through the single sideband radio and the small airplane. The soldiers were bitterly jealous of this and, initially, relationships were hostile and very fragile. They disliked us, but they had to live with us and often depended on us for their safety and survival in the interior. It was a tough slot which got better with time; nonetheless, those first years were full of tension.

****

A young man was involved in some offense—time has erased the detail from my memory—and in fear he ran over the mountain to his home where he was found and brought in to the government post to be questioned. He came willingly, and squatted down on his haunches, the position of respect and subordination in his culture. When ordered at gunpoint to stand giving respect to his superiors, since he could not understand Indonesian, nor was standing to give honor culturally acceptable, he remained in the squat subordinate position of respect. After the second command, which he did not understand so did not respond, the soldier pulled his gun and shot him in the leg. He died three days later, probably more of fear than the gunshot wound. But die an unnecessary death he did!

I myself saw an older man reluctantly release his live chicken to a soldier, for which he was given a handful of small bills. Not knowing the value of those bills, the old man quickly sought out his younger brother who helped him count the money he had been given. Realizing he had been grossly defrauded, he went back to the soldier who was still holding his chicken and, returning the money, requested that his chicken be given back to him. His answer was the stock of the soldier's gun along the side of his head. That old man staggered, fell to the ground then was helped to a sitting position on the rock fence nearby.

These were the day-by-day humiliating experiences the Dani endured as the Indonesian government took control of the interior. But they learned!

Early one morning, a young man came with news that the people had elected him to be their "plane watcher" so that soldiers leaving the area did not strip the Dani people of all their chickens, rabbits, fish, and vegetables to take out with them to sell on the coast, making a handsome profit.

The point of this information was to let us know that there could be a problem at the plane which was due in a few minutes. The people had made a ruling that chickens or rabbits raised by personnel leaving the area were O.K. to take out. If not, it was forbidden, since it was depleting the area of animals and vegetables necessary for their nutrition.

We watched with bated breath as the plane landed, unloaded its cargo, and the waiting passengers began to make their way to board the plane. Among them was a soldier carrying several net bags full of chickens and rabbits. So, this elected "plane watcher" went up to him, and reminded him quietly that the people were forbidding him to take out that meat because he had not raised it himself.

Angrily, the soldier brought his gun back to whack the young man on the head, but in just a split second about 20 Dani men moved in to protect their kinsman, the "plane watcher," and the soldier knew he was whipped. Had he dared strike this young man, those standing around the plane would have shredded him, with his gun, to bits! It was a very unhappy, angry soldier who got on the plane that day empty-handed. But it was a real victory for the people, who began to see that they were not animals of the forests, but human beings with rights which they needed to protect.

****

Now that you have the picture of what can happen by the little guy with a big ego and a big gun, let me tell you the story of the arrest of Doug Hayward, our colleague.

In those early days of the Indonesian takeover, officials were suspicious of everything. Permission for any travel and certainly for any special meetings had to be formally requested from the police; this included permission for any special church meetings. There was a large district-level pastors' conference planned to be held about three hours walk upvalley. The church had tried repeatedly to obtain the necessary letter of permission, and they had been promised repeatedly by the police that it would be given.

The day before, as some of the leaders left to go upvalley to begin preparations for this meeting, they had stopped again to obtain that permission, but the police had not yet prepared the necessary letter. The pastors were told to go on up, and, since Doug was going up the next day as the mission representative, the police would send it with him. With their bases covered, they went on up to the conference.

The next day, again, due to poor administrative practices, the police still had not prepared the letter and when Doug went over to get his own "travel permit," he also was told there was no problem and to go without it; they would send it with a couple of their own staff who would be going. So Doug went happily on his way and was enjoying the conference when a runner came with an order from the military contingent in the area that he was to return immediately and appear before, not the police, but the military. Doug had returned and had gone immediately to the military post where he was "questioned" and put under house arrest.

The most common form of torture by the military was to force-feed the accused a bowl of hot peppers which had the effect of a triple-size enema, reaming out one's entire digestive system. Then he was made to sit for several hours in a fish pond on their complex in chilly water with the level up to one's neck. Word had gotten out that the head of the military, who turned out to be a real rogue, had boasted that he intended to do this with Doug.

Doug went to bed that night in his own home, wondering what was going to happen the next day. During the night, he awoke to strange noises in the yard behind his house. Wondering what was happening, he took his flashlight, went to the door and played its light out over the yard. He was totally shocked to find his yard packed solid with literally hundreds of black bodies carrying bows and arrows, clubs, sharpened digging sticks, bush knives and steel axes.

When some of the pastors and community leaders stepped forward out of the dark, bewildered he asked them, "What has happened? What are you guys doing here?" "We heard you would be given the hot pepper treatment," they replied, "and we are here to see it does not happen. Indeed, blood will be spilt if they try that!"

Thinking quickly, Doug turned off the light of his flashlight and said to them: "My friends. It is best that you disperse; we will see what happens. If the military knew you were here, they would come with guns blazing and I really would be in trouble." Just as stealthily as they had arrived, these men slipped off into the darkness, reminding Doug that they would be standing by to see what would happen.

Word had gone out that night to the far corners of Daniland and, early the next morning from a village six hours trek to the east, came a group of warriors, fully painted and decked out, each of them carrying whatever he could lay his hands on: a club, a bush knife, a sharpened digging stick, a bow and arrow. As they neared the military complex, the "big man" of that area who had mobilized the group, and whom we knew to be a no-nonsense powerful chief, ran out ahead of his warriors, frantically waving his arms, and calling: *"Pok o! Pok o!"* "Stop! Stop!"

When the chanting had ceased and those steaming bodies had halted, he called out to his group of some 50 to 60 warriors: "My younger kinsmen," he said. "We are out on a mission of mercy to our spiritual father but in our excitement we have forgotten one important thing: we have not yet prayed; let us pray!" Whereupon all those warriors with the weapons of destruction in their hands squatted down on their haunches there in the middle of the road while this powerful, influential chief led them in a passionate prayer that God would go with them and hold on to their tempers lest more harm be created.

When the "amen" was sounded, all jumped to their feet and, minutes later, leaping over fences, streams, roads and rocks, they swarmed into the military complex brandishing their weapons. Those whom Doug had told to disperse, who were hiding out in the grass, were waiting for this moment. When it came, so did they! Out of the bushes, out of the grass, up from the riverbed came hundreds of black bodies merging with other warriors to form a formidable army which ran past the police—the police had secretly told the people that since this was a military problem they would not respond with their guns—and flowed into the yard of this military commander, who was still sleeping.

By this time, hearing all the noise, the soldiers on the military post had awakened and, frightened out of their skins, had locked the door of their flimsy dwelling. No matter, the Danis crashed through their door and politely asked for this one commander who was causing all the problems.

They were met with flying chairs and boards thrown at them from the soldiers inside the house. Not to be denied, the Danis picked up the chairs and boards and threw them back into the house, now demanding the rogue commander.

While this was going on out front, seeing that their request was not being granted, dozens of these Dani warriors slipped around behind the house, built several feet off the ground, and climbing up on one another's shoulders, sent their men through the back windows to find the man responsible. In just seconds the house was full of these painted, armed warriors who found the frightened commander hiding in a window curtain he had tried to wrap around himself.

Picking him up, they tossed him bodily out the window to the masses below. Before he hit the ground, several raised their clubs to give him a beating, and one man sliced his arm with a bush knife. Fortunately, before the masses could touch him to literally shred him to bits, several of the pastors and community leaders formed a corridor of bodies around him. They literally carried him over to the top of the airstrip where there were three MAF airplanes waiting for the weather to clear to begin their flying schedule for the day. These three planes with their pilots had spent the night at Mulia because of a meeting they were having.

When the group carrying this commander arrived at the airplane, the masses, still angry and hungry for blood, ran a short way down the airstrip and, after throwing long poles across the runway, sat down in the middle of the airstrip in front of the airplanes. The reason was obvious: they were blocking the airstrip from the plane taking off with this commander until they had a chance to unload their frustration.

While the pilots, roused from their pleasant night of rest by all the commotion on the airstrip, waited patiently by their airplanes, the church and community leaders gathered together all the government officials, including the police and military personnel, and led them to the group sitting there on the airstrip. Seating the officials in the center, one of the Dani leaders stood to speak the mind of the masses sitting about him.

"My fathers," he began. "What you have just witnessed is not an insurrection against the government. We are Danis and we are Indonesians. But above all we are real people who wish to be treated as such. Ever since your commander has come to Mulia, we have been treated with contempt by him. 'You are dogs; you are pigs; you are like apes of the forest,' we are told. Now his attitude has overflowed, touching the life of one of our spiritual fathers, and we have had enough. We have no gripes about the Indonesian government, but when the government sends us men like this, we will strike back. Take him out and never let him return. We don't need soldiers like him in our community."

In a mighty yell of triumph those hundreds of Danis sitting on the airstrip rose to their feet, rushed quickly off to the side taking with them the poles with which they had shut down the runway, and watched the departure of this commander in the small MAF airplane.

Case closed! Doug returned to his work and the masses drifted back to their villages. Life in the valley picked up its normal rhythm but added this dramatic story to be told around the fires at night.

Chapter 22:
The big catch: the amazing Danis

—ɯ—

It was a normal Sunday. Several hundred Danis had gathered for our Sunday service which we held out under a large tree. Had it eyes to see and ears to hear, that tree could have told us a lot of stories, and could have applied a lot of sermons. The space beneath it, and spreading out into the large open area beyond it where several thousand could gather at any one time, was our cathedral where we gathered, normally under the sun, but at times even in the rain, to worship our Lord.

This particular day was one of those beautiful, glorious days in the mountains when the sunlight warmed the valley and made everything glow with dazzling light. I was giving the message that morning, but at that particular moment I was disappointed that the interest of my audience had been interrupted. Most had turned their faces and eyes from following me to some movement on the mountain to the north. Noting my distress, one of the men yelled out, *"Tuan Kobo wae."* "Hey, Mr. Scovill. A runner is coming down the mountain trail!" My gaze followed the gaze of the group and, sure enough, from a distance we could see a man tripping down the mountain path, making all speed to reach us, and I knew immediately that we were in trouble!

About two weeks prior to that, a world-renowned mountain trekker and author, Mr. Harrer, with a friend, had arrived at Mulia, intent on organizing a trek which would take him to the source of the stone from which the Danis made their beautiful stone axes. He loved those firsts, and this was one of them. No white person had ever been there; he had come from Europe to Irian Jaya to put his flag on several yet unclimbed mountains, and to be the first white person to reach the stone axe source. That source was about ten days trek to the north of our airstrip and station of Mulia, and over a 12,000-foot-high mountain range. It was a brutal trek but he had done a lot of trekking and mountain climbing and he was ready to try it—if he could get carriers to go with him. And that was the problem!

He had pitched his tent in a small grassy area below Ralph's house. Though he knew none of the Dani language, he had tried very hard to sell his ambitious venture to the Danis, offering them axes, bush knives and anything else they wanted, but there was no response. We helped him as much as we could by explaining to the Danis where he wanted to go, and the price he was offering, but there was little interest. Finally he came to Ralph and me, suggesting that since he was a newcomer without credibility among the Danis, would we assist him in getting a small group of men to go with him. This we were happy to do.

We spoke in depth to several responsible men helping us in the work around the station and, probably in deference to us, they reluctantly agreed to go with him, guiding him to the axe quarry. Mr. Harrer was elated; his dream would be realized; he would add another first to his list! They had left on Friday, two days before this Sunday when we were interrupted by the runner.

There was little chance of continuing the morning worship service. All knew that something had happened to the group and, with the runner soon to arrive bringing news, we quickly closed the service with a word of prayer and waited. Aside from several women who had to slip out to care for the needs of their infants, the group did not move. I was still standing when the runner, dripping with perspiration, weary and footsore, walked briskly into the group and thrust a note into my hands. Indeed it was from Mr. Harrer, who had scratched a short message requesting our immediate help in bringing him out to get medical assistance.

On the way up the mountain trekking toward the 12,000-foot mountain pass, being quite a photographer as well as a trekker and author, he had cautiously made his way out to a large rock in the middle of a rather small stream to take a picture of a beautiful waterfall. From there he had slipped and fallen about 20 feet into the pool at the base of the waterfall. He was certain that he had broken several ribs in the fall, and needed help.

I explained the content of the letter to the Danis sitting around me, telling them that we had to retrieve Mr. Harrer from the place along the mountainside where he had fallen. If there were those who would be willing to come with me, they were to wait right there until I got my canteen and sleeping bag. Though it was already early afternoon, the weather was nice; I would leave immediately.

Fortunately, Dr. van Rhijn from Holland had been at Mulia several months doing research on the goiter problem in that area. I spoke with him, then sped up to our house, grabbed my canteen and sleeping bag, inhaled a couple of sandwiches Esther had quickly put together, kissed her goodbye, and ran back down to the gathering I had left. I remembered how difficult it was to get anyone to go with Mr. Harrer in the first place, and that now we needed men, good men, to volunteer to bring him out of that treacherous spot where he had fallen.

Approaching the group, my worst fears were realized. Most were still sitting where I had left them, and I thought to myself, *Oh, no! They are still thinking about it and probably do not want to go. I can't do this myself. Now what do we do*? I was ready to go; Dr. van Rhijn was already there and ready to go with a stretcher from the clinic, but where were the men to assist? We had to have men!

I walked into the group with the question, "Aren't there any who will go with me?" One man on the periphery heard my question and gave a circular motion with his hand, pointing to those sitting there, which I interpreted to mean, "I don't know; ask them." So, I did. With a note of desperation in my voice, I asked again, "Men, I need help. I can't do this alone. Is there no one to go with me?"

Sensing my miscalculation, the group rose as one, shouting, "We're ready. We've just been waiting for you! Let's go!" And they rushed forward, grabbing our sleeping bags, grabbing our canteens, grabbing the stretcher, and with a mighty shout of "We're-on-our-way!" we took off, running down the trail with nearly a hundred strong, able-bodied men carrying axes, bush knives, walking sticks and anything else they could get their hands on. Then it dawned on me that the gesture which I had interpreted as meaning, "I don't know. Ask them," was really, "What's the problem! We're all going." And I shook my head again at those amazing Danis! Whatever the impossibility, they would prove it possible.

We climbed fast that afternoon! We were soon topping the first small mountain range to the north of our Mulia station, and began working our way down to the large Yamo River. It was a long way down, and the problem was that we would have to climb all that way up again after crossing the river. From our side of the river, someone pointed out several old grass-roofed huts barely visible on the other side, which, they said, was our destination. It seemed utterly impossible, but we kept walking, down, down, down to the old rickety vine bridge which spanned the turbulent Yamo River.

Dusk was just setting in as I placed my foot on the hand-hewn long tongue of that bridge held in place by vines lashed to the handrails which would help propel us across. Night was coming on; it was beginning to rain; the huts of our destination were still a good way off and I was weary. At times like this, one does not think of what might happen!

Nor does one study the quality of workmanship in that vine bridge, nor contemplate its height above the turbulent waters below. One shuts all that off, grabs hard to the handrails and begins the journey across—one deliberate step at a time.

I encouraged myself. *Don't worry about the broken support vines; don't worry about the slippery boards; don't worry that the gentle sway of the bridge could dump you in the river! Just go, one foot after the other!* Dr. van Rhijn followed me across and we each breathed a sigh of relief to find our feet on solid ground on the other side. Then, shaking our heads in disbelief, we watched our Dani men literally trot across. Light was fading quickly now and we had to move fast.

Obviously this was a trail the Danis did not use much; it was almost entirely overgrown. So, some of the men went ahead, beating and breaking over the grass and shrubbery to make climbing easier for us who followed. And then the cicadas began chirping.

On the equator, as the sun sinks in the west, dusk arrives slowly. But having arrived at the horizon, it seems to slide very quickly over the rim and out of sight, with darkness falling very abruptly. The sign that darkness is just about to fall is that the cicadas hiding in the grass and underneath the leaves of the shrubbery begin their very loud chirping. This was the sign to the Dani that the evil spirits were leaving their abodes, venturing out to create havoc in the world of people near them. So, at dusk when the cicadas began their chirping, the Danis, fearing the evil spirits, would rush headlong to the nearest hut, where they would spend the night hours.

Though we were close to our destination, when the Danis with whom we were walking, many still in the seeker stage or new believers, heard the cicadas give forth their loud call, there was a moment of panic as these men raced around me, running ahead to the hut where we were to spend the night. When Dr. van Rhijn and I arrived a few minutes later, they were sitting warming themselves about the fire, embarrassed that they had fled, leaving us to come those last few minutes alone.

Someone had already started a fire; others had hunted for and brought in dead limbs or fallen trees to use for firewood. We were packed like sardines in that little round hut on the mountainside. Our bodies were steaming from the heat of the fire as we dried out from the rain; our eyes were watering from the smoke; our limbs were aching from the arduous walking we had done; and our stomachs were reminding us that we would sleep hungry—but the mood in the hut that night was delightful. In spite of the weariness and lack of food, there was laughter and there were chants which spontaneously broke out, with all joining in. I loved such moments with the men. We were truly entering into and enjoying their world, being Dani with them in their context. They loved it and so did we.

We did not know exactly where Mr. Harrer had fallen. However, we were on the same trail, so we would come upon him and his men the next day. After having prayer with the men, I slid into my sleeping bag with men stretched out on either side—feet toward the fire, head toward the wall—to catch some sleep. As I drifted off to sleep, I smiled contentedly when I remembered that we had covered the same distance in four hours that had taken our world-famous mountain climber, Mr Harrer, nearly eight hours to travel two days before. Those amazing Danis!

We spent a restless night fighting fleas and trying to get away from the heat of the fire. This had been stoked in the early morning to roast some sweet potatoes the men had managed to bring with them. At the crack of dawn, we rolled up our sleeping bags and were on the trail.

We climbed fast and we climbed far, pushing ourselves to the limit since we did not know how far up toward the pass Mr. Harrer with his men had climbed. We were hopeful that, having reached their group, we could carry him back down the mountain into a populated area by nightfall. However, the trail was getting increasingly difficult, with steep ravines and treacherous terrain to work our way across; it did not look too promising.

We had been climbing steadily for almost three hours when the runner, who had brought us the original note and who had returned as our guide, pushed himself alongside of me and said, "*Koorok yi aret.*" "It is just up ahead a little ways." So we powered up the limbs for the final climb, and sure enough, within a few hundred feet, we saw Mr. Harrer's blue tent pitched among the trees and Mr. Harrer himself lying outside in a flat area, cushioned by his sleeping bag beneath him.

Both he and his partner were glad to see us. While waiting for Dr. van Rhijn to catch up with us, Mr. Harrer told us the story: "Climbing was going well and the men were happy," he said, when he had seen this beautiful waterfall which he wanted to photograph. Calling a halt, he had pulled out his camera, and very cautiously made his way out to a large rock about midway down the waterfall; from there he wanted to capture the beauty of that scene. Unfortunately, his hold on the slippery rock had given way, and he had tumbled about 20 feet down into the rocks and water below fracturing, he thought, several ribs.

Dr. van Rhijn with some of the men arrived shortly, confirming the rib fractures. He then laced Mr. Harrer's upper torso to keep it as immobile as possible to prevent damage to the lungs in the challenge we now faced — getting him out of the mountains. Though we had brought the stretcher from the clinic, Dr. van Rhijn and I had both spoken of the near impossibility of carrying the injured man out on a litter such as that. But we were game to try.

While Mr. Harrer grunted and occasionally (and understandably), yelled out in pain, we positioned him on the stretcher as carefully as possible with plenty of padding around him, tying him to it with vines to prevent him from falling off. Our task was not an easy one in the treacherous terrain we had to navigate!

Then we sat down with our Danis and explained the delicacy and the difficulty of the situation; however, we had no choice but to take him out. The group was very somber as four men carefully lifted Mr. Harrer, on the stretcher, to their shoulders and started down that steep treacherous trail. Around these four men carrying the stretcher rallied other strong bodies to support and give assistance; the rest of the group, armed with axes, bush knives, and digging sticks, spread out ahead, widening and making the trail more user-friendly for the stretcher team. We followed more slowly but we could hear his cries of pain and, though not in their language, words of abuse Mr. Harrer was heaping on those men as they worked keeping the stretcher balanced, but also working it around trees, up steep banks, and over large rocks.

We had gone not more than several hundred yards when a couple of the leading men came back to explain their problem to me. "Tuan Kobo," they said. "There is no painless way we can get him out of here. Please tell him that we are here to help, but that he too must 'harden his liver' (get tough with himself) and bear with us so we can do that. We need his understanding! And furthermore," they went on, "if he hasn't killed himself falling down a waterfall, he will certainly kill himself falling off that litter! Can't we do with him like we do with our own sick people whom we bring over the trail to get help at the clinic?"

The question was a plea! And I knew that the only way we could ever accomplish our mission was to do it their way. Stretchers were not made for the trails we had to maneuver that day. The men had a better way, and I loved them for suggesting it. They take a long pole, three to four inches in diameter, to which they tightly bind the person to minimize sway and movement; then several men pick up one end and several men pick up the other end and off they go!

I knew Mr. Harrer would have problems with it; I also knew there was no way to snake him out of those forests unless we did it the Dani way. So I said to the men, "O.K! Several of you run on ahead, find a little clearing, and get the pole and the vine ready. When the stretcher arrives, without a word you move him from the stretcher to your pole, binding him as you would your own sick person. I will lag behind so that he has no one who knows the language to whom he can protest. He will fight, but do your thing!" And off they went, down the trail to cut the pole and to find the vine to ready it for the transfer.

Intentionally, I hung back. Several minutes later, I heard angry words of protest directed to the Danis, and then a call for me. "Mr. Scovill. Where are you? What are they doing to me? They will kill me. Where are you?" I hurried ahead to see him angrily hitting at my men, who were making the final loops of the vines securing him to the pole. That long pole, stretching out beyond his feet, came right up past his knees, on top of his sternum, and extended past his head another four or five feet. They had done a good job and had made a nearly painless transfer.

I approached his now immobile head—only his eyes could move—and told him what the Danis were saying, that this was the only way they were going to get him out of the mountains alive, and that he would just have to "grin and bear it," using one of my father's favorite sayings. While he spat and fumed in German, which I could not understand, I turned to the Danis saying, *"Nawi o!"* "Let's go!"

They grabbed that litter, hoisted it to their shoulders, and started moving down the trail so quickly that I could not keep up. Dozens were up ahead cutting down trees that were in the way, digging footholds in the banks of the streams we had to cross, felling trees across the streams or smaller

ravines to make simple bridges—all to assist the bearers of
the pole on which was tied this man with the broken ribs! I
have never seen such excitement, yet such order and careful-
ness, as I saw that day. Down, down, down we went: over
boulders, around trees, across logs, slipping and sliding
down ravines, wading streams, and climbing slippery banks.
When one team was exhausted, without stopping, another
was right there to take over.

Then, all of a sudden the trail leveled out and we found
ourselves in the tall grass of a large meadow, probably an
old garden site, for we could see quite a large village on the
other side of the river which separated us. We paused there
to rest, and as we did so, noticed the sun beginning to sink in
the west and a rain coming in over the mountains. We were
without food and without shelter for more than 50 men. We
had to make that village before nightfall.

Mr. Harrer must have read our thoughts for he informed
us that he had had enough for the day, and suggested that
we make camp, then go on the next day. Sheepishly, he
reminded us that he had his canned food and his little tent
where he could sleep. This so angered me, that, though I
held my tongue for a moment, I finally retorted in perhaps
not a very Christlike tone of voice, "And what about these
men? What will they eat, and where will they sleep?" Then,
without waiting for my questions to be answered, I turned to
the men and said to them in Dani, *"O mayu wage me, nawok
aret o."* "The rain is coming; we must go!" All had their eyes
on the village across the river, at least another hour away.

In a flash they had the litter hoisted onto their shoulders
and were moving rapidly down the trail in the direction of
the river. I prayed that the rain falling in the mountains would
not reach our crossing spot before we arrived. But it did! The
rain drenched us before we got there and alas, the river had
already risen considerably with flood waters from the rain
on the mountains above us. We paused on the banks of that

turbulent current for only a moment. All of us saw what had to be done. We waited until the entire group had arrived, then interlocking arms with one another and giving extra support to the men bearing the litter, we hit the water together.

Walking, swimming, drifting, pushing the litter ahead of us, we were able to break up the strength of the current and crossed without mishap, climbing out of the river on the opposite bank exhausted, yet thankful. We had made it! We paused just a moment to make sure our group was still intact. Then as we climbed up the steep terrain out of the river gorge, we heard the chirping of the cicadas, and knew we had just minutes to make it up to the village before darkness fell.

The litter with Mr. Harrer went first—the men bearing him literally running up the mountainside with their burden. We followed more slowly, our pace dictated by our weariness. Just as darkness blanketed the valley, we stepped up the short ladder, climbed over the fence, stepped down into the village yard, and made our way to the large men's house. The men had already untied Mr. Harrer from the pole and were helping him into the men's house, where we would all spend the evening.

We had done it! The worst was behind us; the morrow would be a hard day, but the trail was good and we would have lots of help from the villages along the way. There was no reason we could not get him back to Mulia. We ate happily and hungrily of the piles of roasted sweet potatoes the women of the village brought to us. We were among friends who opened their hearts in generous hospitality. Our stomachs full, our clothes drying out, our bodies soaking in the heat as we sat in front of the fire, one by one each of us found his spot on the floor of the Dani hut. And soon we were stretched out, submitting to the demands of our bodies calling for sleep.

It seemed but a few minutes later that we became aware of movement in the small hut and the noise of someone blowing on the coals to produce a flame. Another sleepy form was pulling firewood from the drying rack above the fireplace. Morning had come; one by one we sat up drowsily, yawned, and edged closer to the warm flame that was beginning to lick at the dry wood they had placed on the fire.

Someone pulled the boards from the doorway and the procession out into the grass and small brush around the village to relieve themselves began. We too, slipped out, and noticed that the sky was clear; the sun would soon break through those low-hanging clouds on the horizon to the east. We would have a good day.

An hour later, as the warmth of the sun began to invade that small valley, we were ready to go. Quickly, we finished our breakfast of roasted sweet potatoes, tied Mr. Harrer to his pole, and set off at a brisk pace, the men with the litter leading us. The trail was good and led us through several large villages on our way to the long vine bridge across the Yamo River. As we passed through those villages, not only was fresh help available in the form of strong able-bodied young men, but the women made sure we had ample provisions of food to eat on the return trip to Mulia.

By midmorning we had arrived at the long vine bridge and, as the men carrying the litter paused to rest and snatch a bite of sweet potato, I worked my way across the long tongue of that bridge and was regrouping on the other side when the Danis next to Mr. Harrer called out to me, "Tuan Kobo," they said, "come back across; he is calling for you." So I made my way back across the bridge to find out what Mr. Harrer had in mind.

He came right to the point. "Mr. Scovill," he asked. "Would you ask the Danis to untie me so that I can fake a walk across the bridge as you take my picture with my camera?"

What could I say? He was not only a world-renowned mountain climber; he was also a well-known author and was thinking ahead to what he would write in his book about this experience. In spite of his excruciating pain due to his fall and with at least three fractured ribs, he still wanted to be seen as the hero, walking across that vine bridge alone! What an ego!

When I mentioned his request to the Danis, they reluctantly conceded and, somewhat disgustedly, untied him from his litter, the pole. Then, I walked backwards out on the bridge with his camera and, as he stepped onto the tongue of that bridge and moved a couple paces toward me, I took several shots of him grimacing in pain as he made as if to walk across. The picture taken, he retraced his steps, laid down on his litter and the Danis tied him up again to the pole. His ego trip over, they once again hoisted him to their shoulders, carefully and sure-footedly crossed the bridge, and started up the mountain over which we had to pass to then move down into the Mulia valley and home. We were at least two hours away from that destination.

Though I had a bit of a head start, the men with the litter quickly narrowed the edge, passed me and were off, climbing rapidly with their load. Shortly, the momentum on the trail, the excitement of the group, and the toughness of the climb, reached the point where they broke out in their chants which they claim shortens the trail and gives them extra energy. And indeed they had it. My final glimpse was of them literally running up the mountain trail with their load, as fresh recruits quickly replaced those tiring under the weight and pace.

Though I tried, I could not keep up with them. Their speed, super endurance, and the dexterity of those bare feet left me far behind! An hour and a half later, when I topped the mountain over which we had to climb to move into the Mulia valley, the litter carrying Mr. Harrer was already entering the main floor of the Mulia valley and was heading for the final stop at the top of the airstrip.

By the time I arrived, the men had already loosed him from his litter, that glorious pole. Having been tied in one position, he was a bit stiff so was moving cautiously around, getting his limbs moving again while at the same time protecting himself from the pain of those fractured ribs. The Dani group was milling around with big smiles on their faces, eating some of the sweet potatoes the women along the trail had provided for them. They were supremely happy that their mission was accomplished!

As Mr. Harrer looked out upon them, realizing this was the group that had brought him so miraculously out of that tight spot high up in the mountains, he, too, was grateful and wanted to express his gratitude. So he said to me, "Mr. Scovill, I'm sure these men are tired and want to return home. Please ask them what payment I can give to them which will best express my gratitude. I have some steel axes and I have some bush knives, but there are so many of them. I would be happy to order more and when the order comes in on the airplane you could give them out."

I called to the Danis to come sit down; we needed to talk. They moved quickly and quietly into a huddle around me. I could see the question marks on their faces, so I quickly communicated to them what Mr. Harrer had said about payment for their incredible work.

It was a moment or two before anyone spoke, and when they did, it was in the person of one of the older men who had accompanied us. Looking around for confirmation from the group at what he was about to say, he turned to me saying, *"Tuan Kobo wae."* "Hey, Mr. Scovill. Who said anything about payment? We did not do this for payment. We did this because this man was in need, and we wanted to help you rescue him from where he had fallen. We will accept no payment except what God continues to give us by way of healthy bodies, productive gardens and pigs, and strong children. He needs medical help, and we need to be getting back to our homes. That's all we have to say."

Then, he turned to the group, shouting, *"Mi'nanip! Nawi aret! Nawi aret!"* "Arise! Let's go! Let's go! Night is coming." They jumped to their feet and went running back up the trail to their homes in the adjacent valley from which they had just brought Mr. Harrer. They wanted to sleep beside their own fires that night.

As they went back up the trail, chanting as they ran, I turned to Mr. Harrer and told him what they had said. He shook his head at their incredible response and flicked away the tears that began to form in his eyes. The amazing Danis!

On the single sideband radio, we called for an airplane the next day. It came and took Mr Harrer out to the hospital on the coast. There he spent several months before returning to Mulia to pick up his things, then to return to his home in Austria for long-term healing.

As I recall, after conferring with us, he did bring in several sacks of white rock salt which the people loved. We gave them to the villages which had helped bring him out of the mountains. In this way, he felt he had properly expressed his gratitude for their help, and they too were happy for the salt.

When leaving with his outfit, he promised he would be back in several months to complete his mission. And he did return! With several carriers, he made a second attempt to reach the stone axe quarry, but never got far enough to the west. His carriers took him to a smaller source of a softer blackish stone from which they make their axes and which he claimed was the main quarry but it was not. The main source was a mountain to the west from where they quarried a greenish very hard stone to make their finest stone axes.

Several years later our son, David Brian, and I made a special trip to that quarry, documenting its location, its history and the method of extracting the stone from the mother mountain. It was very fascinating. As the Danis themselves had often said, "If any foreigner has the right to be the first one to visit that quarry, it should be Tuan Kobo!" We fulfilled their wishes in making that trek and the following chapter records the story.

Chapter 23:
Our trip to the stone axe quarry

—ɯ—

In addition to our daughter, Dawn, my reader will have already learned that our loving Lord blessed our home with a son, David Brian, who was born in a mission hospital in the interior of Papua on May 13th, 1967. On the 28th of December 1983, sixteen and one-half years later, during our furlough, in a car accident on an icy road in Virginia, the same loving Lord snatched him away from us. His story I have written in a booklet entitled "DAVID, Beloved."

One of the stories in that booklet is of our trek to the source of the stone axes; I will reiterate that story here, because of its relationship to the Dani.

****

Many years after Mr. Harrer, came another ambitious Austrian — his name I have forgotten — but he was an anthropologist sitting on the couch in our living room at Sentani on the coast. He was responding to my surprise that he had arrived back so soon from his trip to the stone quarry, some 10 days arduous trek to the north of Mulia.

He had flown to Mulia two weeks before, with a note from me to several of my Dani friends, asking them to assist him in his preparation and trek to the quarry. As I heard the story from my Dani friends, the group was only two days out when the anthropologist and his partner got into a quarrel which grew to such proportions that they scuttled the trek, parted ways, and were returning to their homes. He had come to thank me for my help and to reassure me that he would be back next year to pursue his goal of being the first white man ever to have visited the famous Dani stone axe quarry.

Like fun you will, I thought as I shook hands bidding him a safe trip home, for there were other thoughts dancing at the periphery of my brain. As he walked out of the yard, I sat down allowing those thoughts to move across the screen of my mind. *Why should it be you?* I thought. *If anyone has the right to be the first white man to visit that quarry, it needs to be a missionary. And I'd like to be that missionary! I'll do it with David during his Christmas vacation coming up.*

Esther approved the plan and we wrote of it to David in high school at Ukarumpa in Papua New Guinea. His response was immediate and enthusiastic. Thus, we set plans for mid-January after the holidays, but prior to his return to school.

David arrived home for his 1982 Christmas vacation on schedule. And, since by that time UFM had an airstrip in the lowlands called Faui which was much nearer the stone quarry, our plan was to launch our trek from that airstrip. We would go downriver by dugout five hours to Dagai, another UFM station on the lower end of the river which drained the stone quarry area. Then we would follow that river upstream for at least two days to the stone quarry at its headwaters. For interest's sake, that river is called the *"Yeyi"* "the stone-for-the-axes-is-here" river!

Having arrived by plane at Faui, we made for the river where our dugout was waiting. As we walked, I noticed that David was favoring one of his shoes, the sole of which was beginning to separate from the body of the shoe.

"What pray tell happened to you?" I asked. "Aw," he said, "I ripped it loose playing soccer yesterday." "Keep your eye on your extra pair," I continued, "we will undoubtedly need it before this trip is over."

The blank look in his eyes told me all. "Dad, what extra pair?" he said. "I didn't bring any extra pair of shoes that

I know of." We had a hurried search, and sure enough, he hadn't. *Nice,* I thought, *real nice! I wonder how we will handle this one!*

We climbed into the dugout—two of them in fact since David had brought along two of his friends, Kevin Powell and John Lunow—and headed down the river. After four hours in the dugout and one hour's walking, we arrived at Dagai on the banks of the Yeyi River.

Here along this beautiful, clear, rushing river, we enjoyed a feast with the Duvle believers and their Dani missionary. Then we spent the night in the translation house of Char Murdoch, one of our UFM missionaries, whose house had been built near the Duvle village.

The next morning we awoke to the sound of rain pounding on the aluminum roof and looked out upon a steady downpour and a flooded river. By 8 o'clock, however, the rain had subsided to a gentle drizzle with the skies somewhat brighter. In that our schedule was tight, we decided to go for it.

We—one by one with our Dani guides—were literally launched into our trek across the flooded roaring river in a dugout canoe handled by a competent national who understood dugout canoes and the currents of roaring rivers! For several hours we walked in and out of the river climbing ever upward, soaked to the skin, for the rain had started again.

Shortly, the trail left the river, and conversation ceased as the pull of the muscles, the pace of the trek, the pounding of the heart, and the panting of the lungs took over. We climbed steadily, and I must confess, ever more slowly. After six hours of climbing, I was about ready to forget the adventure, to lie down alongside the trail and die. Shooing David on ahead of me to walk with his friends, I plodded on a step at a time. Four long hours later, totally spent, I arrived at the village where we intended to spend the night, the boys having already arrived.

We had a good time around the cozy fire in the Dani hut that night. The sole of David's shoe was just about totally separated from the body of the shoe. With the laces from another smaller pair of shoes Kevin had brought, and with David's famous Swiss Army knife, we laced it back to the body of the shoe over the toe, quite confident it would get him up to the stone quarry the next day.

We tried to determine how far the stone axe quarry was from that village. Late into the night we talked to men who had been there and learned that it was at least another day's trek upstream, and that the climb was steep as we would move up into the headwaters of the river.

Feeling so very weary and sore from 10 hours on the trail that day, I slid into my sleeping bag, having made the decision to forfeit my goal of being the first white man to visit the stone axe quarry; I would remain in the village letting the three young people have that privilege. And on that note, I fell asleep.

We awoke the next morning to the sound of a man blowing on the coals of our fire to restart it and to warm the house. A short time later, the boards of the door were opened and a big bag of steaming hot roasted sweet potatoes was pushed into the house. That was our breakfast.

Again, it was drizzling but shortly cleared and, as the fellows pulled on their wet socks and shoes, I could not resist. Flexing my arms and legs, I felt rather good. The soreness was gone; my strength was back; the day looked good; excitement was in the air. This was the day. I, too, pulled on my wet shoes; we bundled up our sleeping gear and took off.

Midmorning the sun came out in all its glory, warming and beautifying all nature around us. The sound of the rushing river in and often across which we walked, the richness of the smells of jungle life and foliage, the superb quietness broken only by the occasional cry of a bird of paradise—all were sights and sounds we will never forget.

All of us were enjoying the trip: skipping over rocks, wading across the streams, climbing the ridges, making good time which, according to our guides, would put us at the stone axe quarry in the early afternoon.

Rounding a bend in the river, we noticed our Dani friends up ahead felling a tree to make a bridge across the deep, rapid river we were following. Having placed the tree securely on each side, the nationals walked across it with ease. However, as Kevin made his way across, he slipped and fell into the river but, in the fall, grabbed the tree to prevent being pulled downstream. Our Dani friends quickly rallied around him and assisted him in getting across. Then, David and I made prepared to make our way across. David had taken off his shoes to get better footing on the log and to prevent the current from catching the sole—which was again loosening as rocks had cut the lacing—and dumping him into the river.

David's two friends were already on the other side when David, coming behind carrying his shoes, realized he needed both hands free to get himself across, so he tossed the first shoe across to John, who laid it out on the rocks, but the throw of the second was short. It dropped into the river and, before anyone could make a dive for it, was taken by the swift current past us and downstream.

I gasped as I realized our predicament and, at the same time, bit my tongue. David had no other shoes with which to finish the trip, let alone return two days trek down the mountainside. Without a word we crossed the stream and sat down on the rocks to think through our next move. "Kev," I finally said. "I think you have the answer in that extra pair of shoes. Would you mind us cutting them up for this need?"

Without a question, he handed me the shoes and, with David's knife, we cut the toe out of the one we needed. David slipped it on, tried it successfully, and we were off again with David's toes hanging out over the end of the shoe, but at least with a sole beneath. As we walked on, I sensed David's deep hurt that he had "blown it," especially in front of his friends. How could I build up the kid's ripped up self-image? We talked as we walked, and I shared with him several experiences in my life when I, too, had blown it.

Getting it off his chest must have helped, for I felt the tension subside and noticed his steps picking up. A few moments later he sped around me shouting back, "Thanks, Dad," and up the steep climb he went. He made his way through some brush and roots at the side of a huge waterfall, into a cave on the upper side out of which dozens of bats fled when he ducked inside, around one more bend in the river, and there was the stone axe quarry.

Following only a few minutes behind, I was awed at the mammoth rockface under which we stood. That face rose probably 80 feet into the air. It was at least a hundred feet long and, due to the hundreds of fires that for generations had burned away at its face splitting off slices of rock to be later polished into stone axes, it slanted back into the hillside probably another 75 feet. It was under this overhanging rock that we slept that evening around four fires in a space that would have easily accommodated several hundred people.

Late into the night we talked about the history of the rock, the wars that had been occasioned because of it, the lives fallen in battle over it, the method of extracting a piece of it, and the significance it had within the Dani culture. It was a memorable evening. Finally, we drifted off to sleep to the roaring sound of three rivers converging and pounding past us, the screaming silence of God's great outdoors around us, the massive rock jutting out above us, and the history and foundations of the Dani culture making deep impressions within us.

Burning the special axe stone from the mother lode

The next morning, we photographed the steps taken in extracting a sliver of the rock: A scaffold was built high up against the cliff. Upon this was placed a bundle of firewood which was eventually ignited. The fire heated the rock, causing expansion. When cooling, the rock contracted, popping off thick slivers of rock which one then chipped into the rough form of a stone axe. This he would take home to grind and polish against a sandstone, whetting it as necessary in the water of a small stream along which he would sit. While this was going on, he would prepare a hardwood handle into which the axe would be fitted. The grinding-polishing task took months to complete, but when finished this unique stone axe was a useful tool, a valuable barter product, and a true symbol of the Dani culture of which he was intensely proud.

The photography completed, we picked up some rough samples of the stone—which some have said is a type of jade—as evidence, bundled up our sleeping gear and made our way back in the direction we had come. Two days walk and one day in the dugout placed us again at Faui where, the following day, right on schedule, the MAF airplane arrived to take us back to our homes and families.

We were happy to be home, but happier still with the distinction of being the first and, as of this writing, the only outside foreign people who have experienced this part of the world of the amazing Dani.

Chapter 24:
Opening the T-valley

—⟋⟍—

The trek in

The clouds were hanging low that morning as we circled above the Angguruk airstrip looking for a hole through which to slip to make our landing. Already the single side-band radio at Angguruk had advised us that the airstrip and its approach was free of fog. But we needed a hole through the layer of clouds hanging on the tops of the surrounding mountains. This was the aftermath of a storm which had dumped its moisture on that area during the night; we had to descend through it to reach that fog-free approach area. The pilot also was a bit jittery because the airstrip at Angguruk was below the normal specifications of length for that altitude; I noticed his hand on the throttle had a funny tremor to it. But there was our hole in the cloud layer and the pilot put that little plane into a steep dive to then level out, making the approach. Our wheels touched, and we raced up to the end of the airstrip where he swung it around and hit the brakes.

We had arrived with our trekking gear and three strong Dani men from Mulia plus a young man Esther had trained to cook some of our special dishes. A second plane was soon enroute from Ilu with my colleague, Stan Sadlier, and several other Dani men. Our destination was the T-valley, at least five days trek to the east over incredible terrain. We were on our way into an area we had seen only from the airplane.

In preparation for our trek, several times we had flown low over the T-valley as well as over the possible ground route we would be taking. From the Angguruk airstrip we would be following the flow of the rivers through several valleys, and then we would be climbing up into a high, forested but uninhabited, area. There the headwaters of the rivers began, fanning out in a northerly direction from the mountain range along which we would be trekking, to the valley known in missionary jargon as the T-valley.

The area received its name because of two rivers flowing toward one another from opposite directions, eventually joining. We were to find the headwaters of the western arm and to follow it down to where it joined with the eastern arm, then, made its way north into the lowlands. The T-valley had never been entered by the outside world; we were to be the first expatriate people to walk its paths. As we had noted from the air, there was a sizeable population, estimated by the number of houses we could count in the numerous villages throughout those valleys.

And this area had a special connection to us. Many new missionaries coming out to the field dream of discovering their "unreached tribe," then giving themselves to the activities necessary to see a church planted among that people. And we were not immune!

Following our arrival at Mulia in 1960, we began to hear that UFM's next pioneering effort would be a focus on a new area called the "T-valley." Never had white man been there, and we listened with rapt attention to the stories being told, the strategies being discussed, and the prayers being offered for the people along its mountainsides. Esther and I had dreamed and had shared the secret thought that though we were new missionaries, perhaps we would be the ones asked to pioneer that area. For a few months this obsession dulled our attempts to learn the Dani language.

Well do I remember the day when we paused in our busy lives to discuss our future. Dani language learning was coming well; relationship building was very fulfilling. The more we learned of the language, the greater was our ability to understand and communicate, the more we were accepted and appreciated and the deeper our roots reached into Dani soul and soil. So much so that following our discussion, we had made a deliberate decision to forget about living in a future possibility: T-valley!

We were among the Dani; it was our responsibility to give ourselves 100 percent to living in the NOW as God's place for us. And we had done that. Feeling that the Dani was indeed "our tribe," we had put the T-valley on the shelf and waited further developments. And this was it. We were asked to go with our colleague, Stan Sadlier, into the T-valley to assist him in building an airstrip and perhaps a simple house, so his family could join him as soon as possible after the airstrip was officially opened.

At that moment, we were waiting there at Angguruk among the Yali people. The Yali people, though distantly related to the Dani in language and culture, are, by linguistic standards, considered a different tribe and thus, people group. Language comprehension between the two is minimal. Neither we, nor our Dani men, could understand them.

We were waiting for the second plane bringing Stan and other Dani men so we could be on our way into the T-valley where Stan would begin work among yet another tribe, the tribe populating the T-valley. However, the weather was not cooperating.

But wait! There it was. We heard the sound before we saw the airplane. Moments later it had landed and, after chatting briefly with the staff at Angguruk, we divided our packs and set off up the path, heading east, each of our men carrying a 40 to 50 pound pack in a light rain.

Poor weather had delayed Stan's plane and had put us several hours behind schedule. However, we felt we could make up some of that distance by pushing off immediately, which we did. We trekked all that day, ever climbing, and ever moving out to the fringe of the Yali people being reached by the mission personnel living at Angguruk.

That night we slept in one of the Yali villages; my only remembrance of that village was of the fleas that literally ate us alive in our sleeping bags. Running the beam of my flashlight over the bottom of my sleeping bag, I could see them jumping, waiting for their meal, my feet, to slip back into the bag. I unzipped my bag and beat out as many as I could, but even the thought that there were probably others still there in the bag kept me awake and my feet moving!

Fortunately I had written the following entry in my diary before climbing into my sleeping bag.

This has been a big day! We arrived here in the village about 5:30 this afternoon having walked for over 5 hours. The Yali people along the way were quite excited. Communication is less than poor. We are always searching for words or gestures to be understood.

We didn't think we would make it due to weather but Stan finally arrived at Angguruk at 12:30. Then, we walked in light rain for several hours. We are sleeping in the mouth of the valley into which we will move tomorrow. Seems like we will get up to the pass tomorrow.

God has been good to us. Our hearts rejoiced all the way along the trail at what He has done and is doing. We look forward with real anticipation to the coming days. These people will do anything for salt. They are even now begging us for more.

Early the next morning, having had our breakfast—an all-in-one granola mix which our wives had prepared—and the sweet potatoes for the Danis traveling with us, we were off. We had not traveled far before we noticed one of our men lagging behind. Upon questioning him, we learned that he was sick upon arrival, and the trek the previous day had further weakened him to the point where it was hard for him to keep up. What were we to do?

One of our men, Tibenok, already introduced in our story, had the answer. "Tuan," he said. "Let me have his pack. I will carry his as well as mine. But I would like your small axe to go on ahead and cut trail for you to follow." I gave him my small axe and picking up his double pack, he was gone.

All through that day his work on our behalf was evident. We would come to a small ravine, and there would be steps dug into the cliff to make it easier to climb out; there would be small bridges across the streams. Up ahead we could hear trees falling; one time we came upon a fire he had made with several ears of corn roasting in it—for us as we came along. And late that afternoon, when we knew we had to build a simple bivouac over which to spread our tarp to sleep, he had the poles already gathered and was tying them together when we arrived. What a man! I'll never forget the strength in that muscular frame which God used then, and later, in the extension of His kingdom throughout those mountains.

By midday, we had walked through the Yali populated valleys and, that evening, we had made camp high up in the headwaters of those rivers on a plateau-like area running along the backbone of the mountain range. Around the fire that night, we talked about how much further it might be before we arrived in the valley running eastward where, from the air, we had seen a sizeable population. My diary brings back the realism of that night:

We are somewhere over the pass. We walked 10 hours today and they were not the easiest. This afternoon was cold and wet. The fellows are most gracious.

Never a murmur! There are no houses here in these forests so we built a kind of shack of poles and branches we gathered together. We are going to TRY to sleep though the fellows say they will just doze around the fire.

Tomorrow we think we will come into the main valley. We had quite a bit of help today from the locals along the way. They are mad for salt. Hope the people in the T-valley will be salt-hungry as well.

We also voiced our fears at the possibility of not being received, or perhaps even ambushed, and how we would handle such a situation. Knowing we were on a mission for the King of Kings, we had prayed and then tried to sleep; now another day was ours. Would this be the day we would slip out of the forest into a village? We grabbed our packs and moved off—a single thread of 10 human bodies weaving our way through the forest, following wild game trails.

About midafternoon our lead men stopped and pointed to some footprints on the trail and some disturbance of the brush in that area. "We are getting close," they said. "Here is where they have been splitting trees to make boards for their houses." We moved on with care, our anxiety level rising as we noted more footprints as well as activity where they had been gathering poles for their houses and wood for their fences and fires. A few minutes later, we rounded a bend in the trail and there right ahead of us was a village.

Quickly we retreated and found a place under some trees to rest. Stripping ourselves of our bags, we squatted down, and raised our hearts to the Lord in a round of prayer, first in Dani, then in English. Feeling so very helpless in that situation, we wanted no misunderstanding in our praying! Indeed, for this we had come, but we sort of wished it would go away!

After digging out the small bags of salt and some matches we had brought along for contact gifts, we again shouldered our packs, and walked down the trail a few yards into the village.

First contact

There was not a sound! The entire village was deathly quiet! We stood around in the yard, speaking with one another waiting for something to happen. Nothing! Not even the cry of a baby! Then, we noticed two old men and a couple of children cautiously eyeing us from behind one of the huts. Signaling to and smiling at them we waited, seated there on our packs.

When they saw we were not out to attack them, to ask for their women, or to shoot their pigs, they slowly slipped around in front of the hut, still carefully watching us. Shortly, we began to hear the murmur of voices in some of the other huts and the muffled sounds of the boards of the doors being lowered. Then, faces began appearing at the doors; other men slipped out and stood in front of the houses; pigs began to run freely; and our anxiety level began falling back to normal.

With our matches, we made a simple fire; we sprinkled some salt in our hands, and licked it up making pleasant gestures and holding these things out to them to come to us so we could give those gifts to them. Slowly, ever so slowly, they began to gather around us, tasting our salt and trying the matches. Someone had gone out to a nearby garden and cut some sugarcane. This they placed before us—their symbol of hospitality and acceptance of us.

Don't forget that neither of us knew the other's language, so all we could do was to use gestures. The Danis, who were also dark-skinned, were a real help, but neither could they communicate with the people of the T-valley. Their languages were totally unrelated. Through gestures, we told them we were on our way down river to build an airstrip so the airplane could land bringing in things like salt, steel knives and axes, which we showed them.

There seemed to be a positive response to this as they began pointing to a nice level spot quite close to their village and indicated their displeasure that we go down river to build. They wanted us to build the airstrip at their site to be able to cash in on goods the plane would be bringing in as well as to have the white foreigner living among them. Undoubtedly the occasional traveler from the T-valley had made his way to Angguruk and, after seeing with his own eyes the airstrip and the plane bringing in goods which they, too, could use, had brought back the story to his village.

Again, with sign language we made it known that we would have go on the next day, but would they have a hut in which we could sleep, and maybe some sweet potatoes we could purchase for food? They obliged us by bringing in food for which we paid them our salt. Then they pointed out a hut at the edge of the village where we could sleep. And it was not long until we were sitting around the fire our Dani men had built, warming up, drying out and roasting our sweet potatoes purchased from them. Except for millions of fleas taking their midnight snack from our blood, we were able to get some rest before the new day dawned bright and clear above the ground fog which had not yet lifted.

When it did, we were on our way after giving a couple of steel knives to the one who seemed to be the leader of the village. Again, there was some disturbance and the rattle of arrows among them to hold us there, with a lot of chattering and gesturing about what we assumed was the airstrip which they wanted us to build there instead of down-valley. They also feared for us, since we were heading into their enemy area where we would certainly be killed. But we pushed on since we wanted to find land and build the airstrip near the center of the population, which was further east. Again, an entry in my diary gives us the dynamic of that day:

We were on the trail by 7:15 and met our first large group of people midmorning. What a time we had! Some were a bit afraid to shake our hands, but when they did, they would jump up and down. They met us with bows and arrows, but seeing we were unarmed, many hid them in the brush along the trail.

They did their best to stop us at another possible airstrip site in that area telling us we would get killed if we went on. They wanted to give us pig, probably to persuade us to change our plans. Even though we rejected that idea, they were generous with sugar-cane and sweet potatoes which encouraged us.

We had no problem trekking that day though we did see them fighting in one of the large treeless areas above our trail which later we learned was their normal, formal fighting arena. The one thing I remember was that our trail took us up a fairly steep mountain from which, when we reached the top, we could look down upon the potential airstrip site seen from the airplane. We were excited that we could at last SEE our destination. However, since it was some three to four hours' trek away, we opted to make camp that evening in a little grove of trees and to go on the next day.

Alas, we did not know what was between that which we saw in the distance and where we were on that small razor-back mountain. We had come up on the backside which was steep upwards but, with care, navigable. Now from the top we looked into an abyss of nearly a thousand feet. It seemed that a geological phenomenon had pushed this razorback mountain right up out of the innards of the earth. And we were on the crest, wanting to find our way to the bottom. Eventually we worked our way nearly straight down with some hair-raising places which we had to navigate by clinging to roots and rocks. A fall would have been fatal and we were not inviting that!

We also met some local people of the T-valley working their way up who seemed a bit hostile but warmed up as we sought to communicate with them. Once down, the path led us in the direction of the area having the most potential for building the airstrip, and our gait quickened. Three hours later we were standing in the long grass at the top of that piece of ground, sorely disappointed.

We had arrived

We had imagined a relatively level piece of ground which would be easy to work into an airstrip by felling the trees on it, by digging out the roots and the rocks, by shaving off the top soil down to hard ground, and by filling in any holes or small ravines. This was going to be a real challenge. The one thing that pleased us was that the local people seemed to indicate their acceptance of us by bringing in food and hanging around engaging in friendly banter which, of course, we could not understand.

In the middle of this area was a nice grove of trees, so we picked this as the most ideal place to pitch our tent—a large tarpaulin which we hung over a 12-foot-long ridge pole placed in the crotch of two 6-foot posts. This would be our home for several months, and we all slept fitfully that night around two fires we made under the tarp.

Culture clash

Early the next morning, our Dani men with their axes headed for a grove of trees about 10 minutes' walk away. Their first priority was to build themselves a small round house, Dani-fashion, in which they could sleep and function in reasonable comfort. Not long afterwards we heard the sounds of their axes at work and the fall of several trees; we knew they were busy making the boards and collecting other materials to build their house.

Stan and I were out with our measuring tapes staking out possible airstrip boundaries when we looked up to see our Dani men running toward us. Greatly exercised, Tibenok told us what had happened.

They had seen a nice tree, just the size they were looking for to split into boards for their house, and had laid their axes to it when suddenly they were accosted by the local chief, who came yelling at them to stop. "What you have done is *'memo'* 'forbidden in every way,'" he said.

Though he was very agitated, he understood that the men had not done this wittingly and, through gestures, communicated to us that our men had cut down a sacred tree in which lived the spirit of one of their ancestors. It was a tree through which this ancestor related to the local community, and very special.

We ended up paying for the tree. Then, the local shaman killed a pig and planted a sapling of the same type of tree with a piece of pig fat next to the base of the tree our men had chopped down. This he did while repeating certain spirit phrases to nullify our desecration of the tree. Payment made; spirit placated through correct ritual; consequences negated; the tree was ours.

Initiated into the tribe

While all this was going on, we became aware of a lot of activity in the three villages nearest the potential airstrip site and smelled the aroma of meat being cooked. With a tinge of anxiety, we continued measuring the site, wondering what would be our next experience. We did not have long to wait.

Shortly down the trails from these villages came several groups of men carrying something in their hands—all making their way toward us in the grove of trees under which we had pitched our tarp. Stan and I had stepped in under our tarp and had seated ourselves by the fire, waiting.

Immediately one of the chiefs of the area slipped in under the tarp and sat down close to Stan, and a second chief slipped in and sat close to me. Seeing what was beginning to take place, one of our Dani men sneaked up behind us and whispered: "Just do what they ask; we will explain it when they are finished." So we did!

The two chiefs each took from his net bag a small piece of pig fat and, as they began to render it over our fire, told us to take off all our foreign clothing. So, shoes, socks, pants, shirts, tee shirts—everything we had on we took off down to our inside shorts; leaving these on seemed O.K. to them. Then, they began systemically rubbing us with that handful of rendered fat, from the top of our heads right on down to the soles of our feet as well as between our toes, repeating over us words we could not understand.

Having finished that, they told us to stand up. In the spot where we had been sitting, they dug a small hole in which they placed the remains of that piece of pig fat, covering it carefully—first with a leaf, then with dirt—after which we were told we could sit back down.

Then, the two men assigned to us each took another piece of fat and, having warmed it over our fire, placed it to our lips indicating we were to eat it along with a piece of their sugarcane. But it was *"memo"* "forbidden" to strip off the hard outside layer of the sugarcane with one of our knives; we had to peel it with our teeth as they did. After they had taken a bite of the cane with the pork, we were given the same to eat, alternating back and forth between them and us.

Following this, each of the two chiefs took a new net bag of the type worn by the men, placed a small piece of pig fat wrapped in leaves in each bag, and hung the bags on our necks telling us in no uncertain terms that the net bags were never to come off. Those bags, they indicated, would ensure that our wives would bear healthy children; they would guarantee bountiful gardens; they would make our pigs have large litters; and they would keep us in health.

I can still remember them hanging the bags, with the pig fat in them, in front of us, covering our chests, saying, "That's O.K."; hanging them over our backs, saying, "That's O.K."; hanging them over our shoulders on either side, saying, "That's O.K."! But it was *"memo"* "forbidden" to take them off. And just as I was thinking, *Like fun I will. As soon as you leave, I'm heading for the stream,* he said, "Now that we have anointed you with this pig fat you will be accepted as one of us; however, you must never bathe in the stream!" Obviously they had seen that after working all day, we always headed for the stream for our evening baths.

Following that ritual we were asked to stand up outside, near our tent, along with the Danis. Again these two chiefs each produced a special sandwich they had made from certain, normally uneatable, parts of the pig, and a starchy food called "taro." They stood in front of us, pushing into our mouths that special sandwich, then the taro food; the sandwich, then the taro food, until we had eaten probably half of what was in their hands. Following this, they moved down the line, making the Danis eat the same sandwich. Having finished that little ritual, they reiterated that we were not to bathe. Then, since it was getting dark, they returned to their villages leaving us with bodies covered with pig grease and stomachs that wanted to rid themselves of whatever it was they gave us.

We waited our chance to slip off to the stream, wondering what our sleeping bags would look like had we slid into them with all that pig fat. Feeling it time to move, we had no sooner headed toward the stream to bathe when we heard a lot of commotion and yelling up in the village. Looking up that way, we saw the people waving their hands and yelling, *"Memo! Memo!"* "It's forbidden! It's forbidden!" so we retraced our steps to our tarp tent to find another group of men waiting for us with several brand-new gourds. Through gestures, we realized we were being asked to take off our foreign clothes and put on the gourds. We already had been initiated and anointed into their world, and now they wanted us to look like them by wearing their clothes, with everything else that putting on those gourds could signify.

Well, it was getting dark and we were getting weary of this ritual. After speaking among ourselves, we felt it was time to draw the line. Through gestures we tried to make them realize that we were different from them. We were white-skinned because that is what the Creator Spirit in the heavens made us; they were dark-skinned. We ate different food; our houses were different; we spoke a different tongue; we wore different clothes; and just to make a point, since we had brought along an old rifle, we pointed to our gun and told them that our weapons were also different from their weapons. They seemed to understand and accept our explanation, for they soon drifted back up to their villages overlooking our tarp tent. Neither did they create too much of a fuss when we slipped off to the stream to have our baths.

The frustration begins

Let me share with you some entries from my journal written on Sunday, the 3rd of November 1963 which indicate our increasing disappointment and frustration with the local T-valley people.

People were in and out all day. Seemed real friendly and seemed to be interested in working. I was blessed as Stan read from Isaiah 55 following which we claimed some of those promises in prayer for the valley. We trust the Lord to do great things for us.

On Monday, the 4th of November:

A very trying day! We had drops today (supplies tossed out of the airplane as it flew low over the area). We were glad to get all the goodies from home plus a long letter from my sweethearts. I'm finding I miss them very much.

We moved our camp up to a more permanent site where we set up our tent. Our men will finish their small round house tomorrow. We were a bit down-cast this morning—so much to do and many to do it, yet they don't understand. We speak and gesture; they nod and seem excited. We'd like to brain them, but we don't. So it goes. Yet we are rejoicing at what appears to be a desire to help us build the airstrip.

On Tuesday, the 5th of November:

Woke up with expectancy! On a hunch I went looking for and found the drum top (our stove) and four more pick axes from the drop. Tried working on the airstrip

*today. One by one the locals left and did not come
back until tonight.*

*Midday found us both discouraged and racking our
brains to know how to motivate the local people to
help. In the afternoon we worked with our men, the
Danis, to get their house up. Then, we read, brain-
stormed and prayed. By tonight we felt somewhat
revived by His Word and the realization that we have
only been here 4 days. We spoke to the men tonight
when they brought food to us. It seems they still seem
anxious to help. It will not come without some lessons
for us, I'm sure.*

On Wednesday, the 6th of November:

*Slept in until 6:30 at which time a fellow from the
nearby village came dragging in a pack dropped from
the plane which someone had run off with. They had
opened it and dug through its contents. Seems like
some books may be gone but don't know what else.*

*We worked hard making an outline of the airstrip
today. We are a bit disheartened but my soul found
encouragement in Him throughout the day. Then
tonight I was blessed by reading Luke 5:1-11. Days
like this I miss my family terribly. I have sacrificed the
thought of being home by Christmas. The Lord knows
best. I must get at learning some of the language.*

And so it went: work, rain, disappointment that only a
few people turned up, then again encouragement when they
did. Most days we were working by 5:30 in the morning,
taking a break for breakfast, then back at it until we either
ran out of strength, or it started raining by 2 or 3 o'clock.

Some days we worked with only one or two locals; other days we had 15 to 20. Obviously we were too optimistic regarding our ability to mobilize the local folks to work building the airstrip. In the back of our minds, we probably felt they would respond like the Danis by turning out by the hundreds and completing the airstrip in a matter of weeks. They did not!

It was slower than we had anticipated but, little by little, we stripped the proposed site of its topsoil, exposing the hard turf beneath it; we dug out the wet spots, filling them with rocks; we cut down a small hill in the middle of the site, making the ascent more gradual; we cut into the hillside of an old garden site, moving tons of dirt to the lower side of the site to make it level; and we dug ditches on either side of the airstrip to handle the drainage. Slowly, ever so slowly, the site began to look like an airstrip and we began counting the days until the airplane could land.

Christmas on the trail

Over the Christmas holiday we did a limited exchange of personnel, bringing in several other Danis, and I ended up trekking out with a couple of our Dani men, arriving home the day after Christmas. I include a final journal entry made on my way out. It was Christmas Eve, 1963.

This is a indeed a strange way to spend Christmas eve! We are only a couple of hours out of Angguruk. I started to settle down for the night in a house here in the village, but it was full of fleas, so I put up the tarp outside from where I am now writing.

Last night was a terrible night—cold and fleas biting. I went flea-catching half a dozen times during the night and killed 8 to 10 fleas in my sleeping bag each time I hunted. Then this morning I opened it up and did those fleas move—dozens of them. I shook it out hoping I won't be bothered with them this evening.

We had a good day, trekking out in 9 hours what took us 15 hours coming in. We will get into Angguruk quite early tomorrow.

That inglorious first landing

Stan, with most of the Dani men, dug his heels in for the entire time; eventually he began to work on a small house which, at least temporarily, would accommodate his family who were to join him as soon as the airstrip was ready. And he was there for that inglorious first landing the last of January.

First landings are always risky: winds, surface hardness, possible soft spots, approach and takeoff distance—are all factors which the MAF pilots work with and this particular airstrip was above average in these potential risks. A mountain off the end of the runway could scare you spit-less unless you knew the distance would allow you normal approach and takeoff.

While the center of this airstrip had dried out and hardened satisfactorily, a spot off to the left on touchdown and another near the top were the two questionable soft areas. On making that initial landing, the plane, assisted by some contrary crosswinds, drifted left just enough for its wheels to bore into that spongy area near the top, dragging it to an abrupt stop which flipped the airplane on its back, damaging the propeller. Of that horrific moment, my colleague, Stan, has shared this bit from his diary:

*I ran and helped Don, (the pilot) out of the plane;
he was not scratched. Then I sat down and wept.
Heartbroken and numb. . . is how I felt. The fellows
sat and cried with me. I cannot express my pain of
heart over it all.*

Early the next morning, a second plane was in the air,
bound for the new airstrip site in the T-valley with tools and
a new propeller as its cargo. It was piloted by the then head
of MAF, Hank Worthington. Stan continues:

*Hank flew in from Sentani, rolled down the airstrip
several times radioing us that it was as hard as rock.
Then he dropped a new securely crated propeller and
returned to MAF base at Sentani. That day we installed
(the propeller) on...Don's plane. It seemed ready to
fly out as there was no other serious damage.*

Hank was a very capable, cautious, yet confident pilot;
he was fairly sure he could land his plane on the bottom two-
thirds of the airstrip below the plane which Stan, Don and
the men had flipped back on its wheels and pushed up to the
top of the airstrip out of the way!

And the following morning, he did. But unfortunately,
he too, pushed off center by those same contrary crosswinds,
got too close to that soft area. Into it his wheels sank, dragging him also to an abrupt stop with the momentum standing
his plane right up on its nose. It teetered there a moment,
then fell back on it own wheels with a bounce that buckled
the fuselage.

Now there were two damaged planes on the airstrip.
But this was no problem to Hank. Using a length of 2 X 4
in which the crate for the new propeller had been dropped,
Hank, assisted by Stan and Don, reinforced the damaged
fuselage of his plane, cranked it to life, went through the

takeoff procedure, gave Stan the thumbs-up sign, then pushed the throttle full forward, released the brakes, and sped down that shortened runway in pouring rain on his way to Sentani followed by Don in the other disabled, but flyable, aircraft. And both arrived without problems. Stan writes of that moment:

> *It was painful watching (the two crippled planes) take off. When they got airborne, we all sat around relieved but numb with grief (at the failed landing attempts).*

The glorious unfolding of ministry

In spite of its inglorious beginning, the subsequent unfolding of the ministry in the T-valley, later to become known as Nalca, has brought much fruit. Nalca now boasts a church numbering into the thousands through the combined efforts of our Dani missionaries and our UFM staff serving there over the years. Perhaps unknowingly, this ministry was launched through a brief confrontation by one of our Dani men with the main spirit shaman of the area during those initial days.

As I mentioned above, shortly after we arrived, one of the first things our Dani men felt necessary was to build themselves a small round grass-roofed house at the top of the airstrip.

I remember the day it was finished. They had brought in grass for the roof and, after securing it, at its very peak they had placed a large flat stone to hold the grass in place.

While the Dani men were standing back enjoying the finished product, one of the local shamans came up to them gesturing that he needed to properly complete the process by invoking the protection of the area spirits on the occupants of that house. Whereupon he climbed up on the roof, reached over and lifted up that large flat stone the Danis had placed there to hold the grass in place. Taking a piece of pig fat from his net bag, he placed it in the apex of the roof, mumbling some secret words over it after which he returned the rock to its original position.

Crawling back down the roof, he stepped over to where the Danis stood watching him and said to them, "Don't meddle with that piece of pig fat. That sacrifice to our spirits will guarantee your gardens at home will produce big potatoes; it will protect the health of your children while you are away; and it will ensure that your pigs have large litters."

Tibenok, a strong believer, listened with a big smile on his face. Then stepping back a few feet, he made a running leap up onto the roof, lifted that large flat stone, reached in, grabbed the piece of pork, and stuffed it into his mouth.

That local shaman, greatly exercised, ran about saying, *"Memo! Memo!"* "Forbidden; that is totally forbidden. You will die; your wives will give birth to stillborn children; your pigs will abort; your potatoes will shrivel up." Tibenok walked over to him, and pointing to himself then up to the sky, said, "My friend. I used to do all these things but now I have a heavenly Father who watches over me. He gives me my pigs. He makes my potatoes grow large for me; I have many children. And we have come to tell you about this Creator God so that you will not have to live any longer in fear of those spirits."

And that is what transpired subsequent to that initial brief power encounter between light and darkness; between life and death. The light of the Gospel shone in that dark area. Today there is a virile, vibrant church among the Nalca people with the Dani missionaries having had a major role in seeing that people transformed by the power in the Gospel message.

Chapter 25:
Missionaries in bare feet!

—ᄴ—

D oug Hayward, one of our colleagues who later came
and worked with the Danis for a number of years,
wrote a small booklet entitled *Missionaries in Bare Feet*.
I will borrow the title of that little booklet for this chapter,
since it so graphically pictures for us the simple, yet fervent,
missionary activity of the Dani church in those early years.

Some years ago, one young expatriate missionary family
arrived on the field with 31 maximum-size footlocker type
suitcases filled with their "outfit" and costing several thousand dollars of the church's funds to get them there. The sad
part was that four months later, finding themselves unable
to face the rigors of the field, they had returned home! This
is in contrast to the following stories of our missionaries in
bare feet! Let me pen for you the following stories of the first
missionary efforts of the Dani church in the Mulia-Ilu area.

I was upstairs in our home at Mulia working on language
and preparation of materials for our literacy program. We
were trying to keep up with the hundreds who wanted to
learn to read. Suddenly, Esther called up to me, "Dave,
there is a man down here who wants to see you. He says it
is urgent." I quickly finished whatever I was working on,
tripped down the stairs and opened the door. There stood
one of our pastors who was very excited. He burst out with
his news: *"Tuan Kobo wae."* "Hey, Mr. Scovill. There is a
group of men from the Koyan tribe who have come asking to
speak with you. They are waiting for you down at the place
where we have the Sunday services. Can you come now?"

The Koyan tribe is a small people group inhabiting the vast jungle plain which stretches from the foothills of the mountain ranges where we were located, down, then out to the coast, approximately ten days walk from our station at Mulia. In these thousands of square miles of terrain threaded by slow-moving, crocodile-infested rivers, many smaller tribal peoples roamed in search of food and fought over land rights and women. On some of my treks out to the villages in the peripheral valleys populated by the Danis, we had talked about the Koyan people.

One night high up on the 12,000-foot mountain pass, we had bedded down for the night under a large overhanging rock which protected us from the wind and the rain. In the light of our fire, the Dani men with me had made rough drawings in the ashes to indicate where these peoples were located. They estimated that it would take another full week's walk to reach them from where we were. By the flickering light of that fire, I saw in their eyes and facial expressions the yearning to share with those tribes the message of LIFE which we had given to them. I, too, was moved! Now, these men had come to us!

We hurried down to where they were waiting and, after greeting them Dani-style (since we did not know their greeting), we joined the circle, sitting down on the ground in the space they had made for us. All was quiet for a few moments as we looked at one another, smiling.

These were a tall people, much taller than the Danis. Their skin was dry and scaly due to infestation of the small mite which burrows under the skin, causing unbearable itching. They were naked except for large leaves or pieces of old cloth covering their private parts and various ornamental pieces of attire around their waists and chests. Their noses boasted three-inch-long upright bone needles, while from their ears hung other interesting objects. Their hands gripped their bows and arrows with which they hunted food, protected themselves, and engaged in intertribal trade. This was a rare encounter and we savored the moment. Never in my wildest thoughts on missions had I imagined I would experience a situation like this.

We were still wondering how to communicate with them when one of the older men of their group, a very charismatic man and obviously their leader, jumped to his feet and began his story. There was some confusion since he thought I could understand him, but the Danis seated there with me quickly took care of that by finding two other men in the group through whom his story could be transmitted to me. So, there we were in a lineup of four: the Koyan chief communicated in his language to one of the men in a Dani-related but distinct dialect which I could not understand; that man then conveyed the message, in his dialect, to one of our Dani men who knew it; then our Dani man, who was fluent in both dialects, communicated the message to me. And what a message!

There he stood in a loin-leaf, body painted with exotic colors, bones in his nose, bow and arrows in hand, his eyes burning with intensity, his voice passionate as he spoke: "Tuan Kobo," he said. "We are from the Koyan tribe, the people who live along the large rivers in the coastal plain many days walk to the north from your valley of Mulia. We left our hunting grounds and fishing waters over a month ago, arriving in this area several days ago. We have been walking through the valleys and sleeping in the villages here at Mulia for three days. We have seen the steel axes and steel knives you have given to the people here; we have bathed with the soap given to us by your people and find it very soothing to our skin disease; we have tasted the white salt which you have distributed; we have seen the animals which you have flown into this valley. And we say, 'Incredible! Awesome!' but we have not come to ask you for these things. We have our bows and arrows and our long spears with which we hunt the crocodiles and the wild boar. We have our knives to prepare our meat. We have our fruit and nuts to roast and eat. Our forests are full of wild boar, and our rivers full of fish.

The Koyan chief minus some of his normal dress

"As we have wandered through this valley, we have seen your people reading some marks on banana leaves (paper) which they say are words from the Creator God and which we note have changed their lives. They are no longer fighting and killing one another; they no longer steal from one another; they no longer fear nor sacrifice to the spirits residing in the trees and the mountains. There is joy! There is laughter. We want that kind of life and we have come to ask that you return with us to share those words with our people as well. We are leaving tomorrow and will take you to our people if you can come." And he sat down.

No one moved! I sat with my head down and tears running down my cheeks. This was why we had come to Papua! Here was another tribe begging us to come share the Words of Life with them. Where were the young people in the churches and Bible Schools at home who should hear this? What should I do? We were within a few weeks of returning to the States on our first furlough. I could not go.

I heard the sniffles of the men around me as they flicked away the tears. The request required an answer. What should I tell them? As I pondered that question, Tibenok, sitting on my right, could contain himself no longer. He jumped to his feet and, with tears running down his cheeks, said, "Tuan, it is true! It is true. We lived the way these men are now living. We know the fear of the spirits. We know the darkness and the hopelessness of which they are speaking. I know we are still like newborn infants in understanding these new words, but we have firmly set our hearts on them (believed) and our lives are changed! Fear is gone! Hopelessness in death is gone! If you can't go at this time, please let me go. We know that of which he speaks. Please let me go."

At the same time and before I could respond, another man from our "witness school" stood to his feet. On his neck hung a long string of beautifully-colored beads, the value of many days of hard work. In one swift motion he swung them off his neck and handed them to Tibenok, saying, "Here! I'd like to go with you, but I can't. My wife is deaf and needs me to help her in the duties about the village. But you will need goods to barter for food on the trip. Take and use them as you need them." By this time all of us were weeping, but the decision had been made. Tibenok would go with them.

That next Sunday I made my way to Tibenok's home church in a valley three hours trek away. There we commissioned him to go with these Koyan men to their homes and hunting grounds in the Great Plains area. Following the service and special prayer for their protection, we bid them farewell as they picked up their few belongings and headed for the trail which, after many days, would take them to the lowland people.

Tibenok on his way to the Koyans

Many were the tears; many were the gifts their friends showered upon them. But as they left the village, one man ran out ahead of the group and, standing aside on a small knoll, cried out his parting words: "My kinsman, Tibenok. You are a leader among us. You have unselfishly shared your potatoes and your pigs. Your physical strength has assisted us in building houses and fences around our gardens. Your fearlessness in times of war has often brought us victory. And now you are leaving us. We will never see you again.

Yours is the death of a good man. For on your way to the lowlands where live this Koyan people, you will descend to a place in the trail where, it is said, if a man passes that point he never returns. Goodbye, Tibenok, goodbye. We will never see you again." And he sank to his knees in heart-wrenching sobs as the group, with Tibenok in the lead, climbed over the village yard fence and moved down the trail—a missionary in bare feet.

It was all heart-wrenching to me as well! Seeing some of the older men sitting around, I asked them concerning the words of the speaker. Whereupon they reiterated the story circulating among them that on the backside of that mountain which descended slowly to the Great Plains area, there was a dangerous place in the path, in their words (and imagination) a barrier of huge rocks, which with difficulty a man could make his way through, but once on the other side of that "doorway to the lowlands," those who passed through never returned. They believed that Tibenok would never return and grieved his demise even though he was very much alive.

They went! After many months, word drifted back that they had arrived. Once there Tibenok had combed the forests, gathering the local people together, and they were working hard to build an airstrip. This airstrip was eventually finished and opened with the first landing of the small airplane. Tibenok spent several years there, encouraging the people to a more sedentary way of life, with houses built closer to the airstrip and periodic trips into the forests to hunt and to fish. His ministry was very productive but his health was beginning to fail due to malaria in his blood.

One day he returned to his home at Mulia. I was not there when he returned, but some days later as I walked down the path to the clinic, I saw this oldish-looking man scuffling ahead of me, very much dependent on his *wanggun,* his "walking stick." Coming up alongside him, I turned to greet him and was astonished to see that the man was Tibenok. His muscular frame was now emaciated and weakened by sickness. Many of his teeth were missing and his skin was dry and covered with sores. I embraced him, asking, "What has happened to you?"

He leaned on his walking stick, flicking the tears from his eyes, and said, *"Nogoba Kobo o!"* "My father, Kobo! I left all — my wives, my children, my village, my gardens and my pigs — to take those eternal words to the lowland people. We gathered the people together from their nomadic wanderings; I helped them build new houses closer to the airstrip. The airstrip is finished and the plane is now able to land. The people are meeting together to recite the Bible stories I have told them. Now, I have come home.

"Arriving home, I find that one of my wives has died, along with two of my children. My garden has been taken over by the pigs. I have no sweet potatoes. My house recently burned to the ground, and my health is broken. I am an old man, and perhaps I, too, will soon be gone." What was I to say? We stood weeping together there on the path.

Then he looked past me up into the sky where dark clouds hung low, blotting out all except a few patches of blue sky, and said to me, "But look, my father. Look beyond those dark rain clouds. Is not that blue sky which we can see beyond the clouds? Those heavy clouds will soon be replaced with blue sky and warm sunshine. God is still caring for me; my faith is strong. I shall continue to trust in Him." We hugged each other again, then walked together down to the clinic where he received the necessary medical help which eventually restored him to health. Tibenok did live many more years with strong step and unfaltering faith in the Lord. And the work he began there in the lowlands during the latter part of the 1960's continues to this day, with daughter and granddaughter congregations all through that vast area. A missionary in bare feet!

****

During the latter '60's and into the '70's, many were the Dani believers who, released from their bondage to the spirit world and driven by the joy of their newfound faith, literally went everywhere sharing the Gospel with other tribes throughout Papua. Stories abound of missionaries in bare feet riding risky rafts down turbulent rivers; of their dugout canoes smashed to bits in the rapids and their lives lost to crocodiles, to malaria, to exposure to the weather, to sicknesses, and to enemies. I salute them!

In a very real sense, the isolated unreached tribes of Papua have been found and evangelized by Dani believers. Very generally speaking, I view the decade of the '60's as the years of the conversion of the Western Dani tribe and, subsequently, the consolidation of those thousands of new believers into local churches throughout Daniland. The decade of the '70's I see as the decade when this young church, motivated by their love for the Lord and extreme happiness that they had found again the secret of eternal life, went everywhere throughout Papua sharing that message. At one time a quick count documented that more than 250 national missionary families within the Evangelical Church of Indonesia—the denomination founded by three missions: UFM, RBMU, and APCM—had left their home areas to move out to reach other isolated tribes all over Papua.

These Dani missionaries had left with only a net bag or two filled with their personal possessions, a handful of seeds, a bundle of sweet potato sprouts, and a pair of piglets, to plant their feet in hostile territory to share the Gospel with those of another culture and another language. On unfamiliar soil and, at times, in an unfriendly environment, they built their homes; they made their gardens; they bore, and often buried, their children; they learned the language of the peoples among whom they lived and served; and they have left congregations of strong believers and indigenous Bible Schools among most of these peoples. I say it again: I salute them!

And they are still doing it. In 2003 during one of our trips back to Papua for the dedication of the printing of the Old Testament in Western Dani and to initiate the revision of the New Testament, I was standing with some of my Dani brethren watching the plane take off. I noticed that very close to me, leaning on the wooden fence, was a good-looking younger Dani man who was eyeing me as though he wanted to make contact. So we introduced ourselves—his name is Les Kogoya—and I began asking questions about what he was doing. I was not prepared for the story which he shared with me.

He had just arrived back in his home area at Ilu to recruit his own people to return with him into an area called "The Bird's Head," the far northwestern part of the island, and to place them among three smaller unreached tribes he had discovered in the forest.

That evening he came with maps, showing me where these tribes were located and sharing with me his vision for pioneering in that area. Years before, with intent that UFM would eventually establish a work there, I had flown over the area noting the villages literally in and among the trees of that large swampy region. Now before me sat a man who had walked their paths, who had waded their streams, who had ridden in their primitive dugout canoes, who had slept in their shabby houses and eaten their food, and who had promised he would return with recruits to work among them.

Overwhelmed by his simple story, I asked who had motivated and sponsored him on these trips into that area. He was a long way from his home in Daniland and he was moving about in a very distant, difficult, and depressing area of Papua. His answer, with the flick of his hand and a teary eye, was, "No one!" Then he went on to tell me that when he attended the Dani Bible School at Mulia, while studying the life and missionary journeys of the Apostle Paul, his heart had been so stirred that he had cried out, "My heavenly Father. Is there no place in Papua to which I can give my life to reach other peoples with the Good News?"

And God had laid on his heart to take the Light of the Gospel into that darkened area. He had sold several of his pigs to get his initial boat fare there, then, he had lived with and like the people for nearly a year, building relationships, learning the language, and thinking through a strategy for reaching them. Even as he spoke with me, I learned he was penniless but depending on God to supply the need for funds and for men to return with him. And that ministry is currently one of the foci of the church as it continues to find peoples and to develop its mission ministries.

My dear reader, this is missions in the raw — without any foreign interference, fussing or funding. He is another one of those precious "missionaries in bare feet" taking the message to the ends of the earth.

Chapter 26:
Stories that live on!

—m—

Kinogowa and the axe

Kinogowa is gone now, but he was one of the first older men in the valley who, years ago, slipped into our house one late afternoon, sitting down in front of our woodstove, the equivalent of the fireplace in the middle of his own hut. (With no clothes, these tribespeople were most comfortable squatting around our warm woodstove in the late afternoon and evening.)

Kinogowa's body was greased with the normal pig fat and soot mixture; his hair was done up in a net bag. After chatting for a few minutes, he reached into his net bag, pulling out a big, beautiful stone axe, and slid it over to me where I was seated facing him with my back to our kitchen wall.

I picked it up and ran my fingers over the perfectly polished stone and the sharp edge he had honed. "Wow!" I said. "You have worked months on this axe to have it so beautifully polished. My friends in America have never seen such craftsmanship. Could I purchase this to take to my village in America? I'll give you a brand-new steel axe in payment for it."

He grinned—a toothless grin—and shook his head. "No, Tuan," he said, "I have not come to sell that axe."

I knew it was priceless to him, so I doubled my offer: "I'd really like to have it to show my people. Would you take two steel axes for it? I really want it!"

Again, his head nodded a negative so I slid the axe back to him, our eyes meeting. And as they met, I noticed that his were full of tears, just ready to overflow and run down his greasy cheek. Then he said, "Tuan. This axe is not for sale. I am giving it to you." And he gave the axe a little push back in the direction of where I was seated.

"My father, Kinogowa," I said. "Why do you want to give me this stone axe? I have offered to purchase it for the price of two new steel axes and you have refused. Now you tell me you want to give it to me. I do not understand!"

He looked at me again, and I can still see those tears running down his greasy cheeks as he said: "Tuan. I was like a wild pig up in the forest, scrounging for my food among the roots and the vines, with only death and the cremation fires to end it all. You came from your village of America. You tied me up and fed me those sweet potatoes from heaven so that today my life and the lives of all my people are changed because of those Words. That axe is a symbol of my appreciation to you. Take it and, as you show it to your family and friends in your village, tell them how much we appreciate your coming to share with us those eternal words."

Then, picking up his net bag and walking stick, he slipped quietly out the door, going back to his village. We still have that big, beautiful stone axe reminding us of the Dani lives touched by the words of that Big Book.

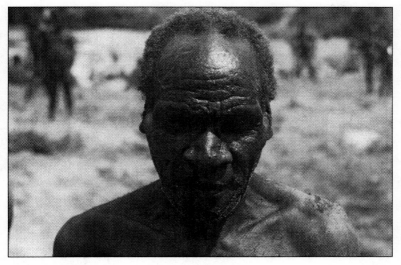

Kinogowa

Aromare'lek

It was a finger-smudged, dirty piece of folded paper—a note tied with a piece of grass—the young runner thrust into my hands. Carefully, I untied it, and slowly made my way through the misshapen letters and misspelled words of the message. A man named Aromare'lek, in charge of our road building project, had written it. I read it again, asked a few questions of the young runner, and then turned away with tears in my eyes.

Though somewhat of a newcomer in the Mulia area, Aromare'lek was a very charismatic figure. He dressed with pomp and splendor in terms of Dani dress, and carried himself with a regality which made you turn your head to look when he walked by. He had made a name for himself in the community as a leading shaman in the spirit ritual; also he had become a friend to the first missionaries into the Mulia valley, and particularly of Ralph and Mel Maynard.

317

Forgive the mundane, but my first encounter with Aromare'lek was watching him speak with Ralph the morning after the logs across the opening of the hole in the ground into which drained the septic from Ralph and Mel's home had rotted and caved in. This had left a big hole and a very pungent odor wafting into the air.

Ralph was asking him to round up some men to bring in bigger logs to repair the cover on the hole. He was also reminding him that the rotten ones, which had fallen into the hole, needed to be pulled out before the new ones were laid across the opening.

With a shake of his head, and a rattle of his beads, Aromare'lek had answered Ralph, "My father. I will take care of it. I have already eaten some of your feces. I will get to work immediately." And that was pretty graphic, considering the context!

Let not my reader feel disgusted at the imagery conveyed in this language. I have given you the literal phrase which he used. However, you should know that, contrary to our understanding, embedded in this phrase was the very highest expression of Dani relationship that exists! He was saying, "I am your humble servant, willing to do the most menial task because of my love and respect for you."

I have heard Dani pastors, tears running down their faces, plead with God to grant them help in some desperate situation. They will use all the normal terms; then, feeling them all inadequate they will often burst out with, "My loving heavenly Father, please. Oh, please help. Let me cook and feast on your feces!"

Those early days of ministry were greatly complicated by distortion of teaching. One day Ralph and I heard that two of our leading men in the community were going around baptizing sick pigs so those pigs would return to health, and they were receiving payment for their services. We were very disappointed to hear this, since both of the men were close friends, one of them being Aromare'lek. We knew this was probably a spin-off from our teaching on salvation, and eventually the public testimony of that decision in water baptism.

So Ralph and I hiked upvalley to find out what was going on. Slipping through the small doorway of that round hut, we were a bit surprised to find both men seated comfortably near the fire, sheepishly waiting for us like guilty children. After the normal greeting, we explained what we were hearing, and why we had come. Then we launched into our tirade on the evil of what they were doing—our passion and intensity making up for any lack of language finesse and indicating that unless such actions stopped immediately, the God of that Big Book would certainly rain terrible judgment on them!

They listened with eyes staring into the fire and heads nodding their approval. "And on top of all this false teaching, we hear you are accepting payment for your services. Is that true?" we asked sternly. Without a word, Aromare'lek stood up, reached up through the hole in the loft through which they climbed to sleep, pulled down a net bag bulging with "goodies" and placed it in front of us. "We can't deny it," he said. "Here is the loot!" In the net bag were all sorts of shells, beads, and exotic things that were valuable simply because they were exotic. And that was the end of their health-and-wealth effort. Looking back, we recognize that payment for such services from the shaman was totally within the realm of reason, but of surprise to us was their acceptance of our remonstration of their actions.

It was partly Aromare'lek's charismatic influence which had resulted in the burning of fetishes. As mentioned earlier, at that burning he had stood before all, stripping himself of each item of his spirit paraphernalia. Then pulling the long dagger from his arm band, he had shouted, "My fathers and mothers, my brothers and sisters! With this I have killed over 10 men, and today because I choose eternal life, I am tossing it into the fire," which he did, then had spat in contempt on those things before walking back to his group.

Aromare'lek at the burning

Friendship and appreciation of Aromare'lek's superior skill in motivating people was so apparent that we put him in charge of the motorbike road building project with its goal of joining our station of Mulia with Ilu, some 25 miles upvalley.

And he was in a village somewhere along that road when he wrote the note just delivered to me. "My fathers!" it read, speaking to Ralph and me, "I, Aromare'lek, am writing this note with my own shaking hand. The road building has come along quickly; the people are enthusiastically working, but I have been ill for several weeks, unable to eat sweet potatoes and coughing up blood. I am far too weak to come and get pills. Perhaps it is my time to die. When you hear that Aromare'lek has departed from his old skin, do not mourn me. My heart has been firmly placed on God's Word (their word for 'believe'); we will meet again, dressed in our new skins in that fair land about which you have told me." And it was signed with a smudged finger!

Aromare'lek had passed away that night, with the runner bringing me the note the next day. We mourned his passing, but rejoiced at his transition into real LIFE.

They called him "Beardless"

As I recall, my initial meeting with *Amborolek* "Beardless" was the day I looked out the window to see him sitting with our son, David, on a large rock near the small duck pond we had off to the side of our yard. Together they were watching the mother duck swimming around with her newborn ducklings. Even at that time, Beardless seemed ancient. He walked with a stick, his back hunched over, his step slow, his skin dry, his naked body creased with age, his cheeks gaunt and his nose continually running.

He sat chatting with David, who was about 3 years old at that time and sported a nice brush cut his mother had given him because she feared he, too, was infected with the prover-bial head lice so easily picked up through our interaction with the Danis. This was a small price to pay for the pleasure of our personal relationships that we and our children have enjoyed with the Danis over these many years.

It was years later that Beardless came noiselessly by our house and sat down on the grass outside our door. I knew he was waiting to speak with one of us, so I slipped outside and sat with him there on the grass. Shortly he began his explanation of the pain he was experiencing in his stomach. He had tried everything but the pain continued, especially when he ate the sweet potato, their main food. Then, he voiced his fear. "Is the spirit called the *'Kuguruwo'* eating on my insides?" he asked.

In the Dani mind, all sickness is caused by a spirit. A common flu or cold is said to be caused by a spirit: *"Kugi nookerak"* "a spirit has struck me." Pneumonia, bringing pain in the region of the lungs, is caused by a spirit that shoots an arrow into one's side. The greater the pain, the further in that arrow is said to have penetrated. The Kuguruwo is the feared female spirit often accused of bringing death by gnawing on the insides of her prey; this is what Beardless feared.

After speaking more in depth with him, we felt he probably had a stomach ulcer; and it was certain to act up after eating the sweet potato or sweet potato vines which often brought about indigestion in sensitive stomachs. So Esther encouraged him to lay off the sweet potato, eating only a bland type of banana which they grew, and which had worked with some of her other patients. Even though she knew he would be reluctant to do so since milk is for babies, she also mixed up a bottle of powdered milk for him, telling him to drink it. He did, rather reluctantly; then went on his way home.

That seemed to help, for the next afternoon, and for several weeks, each afternoon he would come by for his bottle of milk. Esther would vary the taste by one day giving him just the milk then the next day she would mix it with a couple of eggs in a sort of "eggnog" which he liked. One afternoon when he came by, Esther was busy with something else in her line of duties, so I mixed it up myself. Trying to be a bit creative, I added a touch of mashed potato left over from our table; I also put in a dash of peanut butter—peanut butter was good in everything, was it not?—and gave it to him. He walked on down the trail to his home to drink it as per usual, but the next day when he came back he said, "Tuan. Who made up my medicine yesterday?" Expecting to get a bit of the glory, proudly I said, "I did. How did you like it?" He was quiet for a moment then said, "Tuan. Let my mother, Esther, make it after this!"

He continued to come by for several weeks; then one evening, since I had not seen him for several days, I said to

Esther, "Did Beardless come for his milk today?" When she answered in the negative, I responded, "I wonder if he is losing hope. I think I should go see him at his house."

I knew where his village was, so grabbed my flashlight and was off down the trail to his village which was only about fifteen minutes away. The entrance door to his small house was open and, as I approached, I could see across the fire where he was lying with his face to the wall. I maneuvered my frame through the small doorway of his house then called to him, "Hey Beardless. I'm Tuan Kobo and I've come to see you. How are you doing? You haven't been by for your bottle of medicine lately."

When he heard my voice, he rolled over then slowly pulled himself up into a squatting position on the opposite side of the fire. I could see that he was emaciated and terribly weak. "No," he said, "you are right. I haven't been by for a few days. Milk is for babies; if a man can't eat sweet potato he can't survive."

"What do you plan to do?" I asked, fearing the worst. Without looking across the fire at me, he replied, "I'll just drink water when I am thirsty and sip on sugarcane when hungry, then one of these days I'll slip out of this old body like a man slips out of his old gourd and be gone." "Wow!" I said. "Aren't you afraid?"

Beardless looked across the fire at me, then past me to the light of our house on the horizon and said, "No, Tuan. I'm not afraid. You see, between the light of my small fire here and the light of your big lamp there on the horizon, there is a valley of darkness, but I'm not afraid to walk through that darkness because you have given me a LIGHT to guide me to my eternal home in heaven."

I sat with head bowed, tears flooding my eyes! What more could I say or do? I prayed with him, asking that God would take him quickly, reached for my flashlight and made my way home. Several days later, his friends came and told us that Beardless had gone. He had slipped out peacefully; the LIGHT had guided him safely HOME.

A man called "Big Mouth"

His name was *Ambenggwok* "Big Mouth." And he was one of the "big men," the chiefs of the Western Dani tribe living in the Mulia valley in the interior of Papua when we arrived in 1960.

He was a powerful, proud sort of man, with his long hair, greased with pig fat and soot, falling past his waist and made ankle-length by tying the strands of his deceased father's and grandfather's hair on to his. At the very tip, as the Dani men did, he had tied a colorful tuft of feathers so that, when walking, the tuft at the end would bounce against his ankles, creating the Dani macho male figure effect.

He was also very interested in the *Obeelom Wone* "Good News" we brought and was one of hundreds of Danis who would come to the Sunday morning church services. His very presence seemed to motivate his people to join him in these services where we sat under a large tree in an open area. Very faithfully, and with a certain amount of quiet pomp, he would arrive with his three wives walking obediently single file behind him in the order in which he had wed them. As they slipped into the women's section of the group, their grass skirts rustling as they sat down, Big Mouth would walk to the very front of that large group where we were normally seated as we waited to begin the service.

As many of them did in those early days, Big Mouth was always chewing the red betel nut, a mild drug which necessitates occasional spitting. So you would see this red spittle along the path, on the rocks, and also on the boards of their houses

And Big Mouth was constantly chewing. He would come to the Sunday services laboriously chewing the red betel nut.

Walking right up to where we were sitting under that big tree, he would take careful aim, and shoot (read spit) that red juice as high up as he could on the trunk of that tree, then watch it run down for a few seconds before slipping into a space near the front where normally those most interested in hearing the message positioned themselves.

That was Big Mouth, but I enjoyed him, and he enjoyed coming to our home in the afternoon, slipping in to sit in front of our woodstove. Normally, after chatting about the affairs of his people, I would give him a newly translated Bible verse, or a story for him to take back to his village. And he liked that.

Big Mouth preparing the red pandanus fruit

One evening, just before we were to leave for our second furlough, he had come in. We sat chatting about things in America—my village, my parents. Finally he asked, "Will it ever be possible for your mom and dad to come here to Mulia so I can meet them before I go the way of my ancestors?"

He had asked this several times before, but a bit casually, and I was able to give him a very general answer and move on. But this evening he was boring in and wanted me to take his question seriously.

"No," I said, "I doubt that such a visit of my parents would be possible." I went on to say that we were a poor family, and mom and dad just did not have funds to pay the airplane fare to make such a trip.

"Well, how much does it cost?" he asked. Since they did not know money at that point in time, I quickly groped for a concept that would make sense and, once and for all, lay the matter to rest. "Big Mouth," I said, "it would cost every pig in this valley!"

But instead of bemoaning that fact, or at least shaking his head in disbelief, he looked up at me saying, "Is that all?" Then, he reached for his walking stick and slipped out into the dark evening with a final word, "I'll be back." And I sat wiping my brow, wondering what on earth I had done.

It was several days later when, in the dusk of the evening, I heard his familiar step on our porch. He burst into the house, seating himself again in front of our woodstove. With an obvious I've-got-this-one-solved smirk, he reached into his net bag, pulled out two bundles of sticks about three inches long and thrust them into my hands saying, "Here, is this enough?"

I looked from the sticks, now in my hand, to his eyes, now impatiently waiting my answer, and asked, "What pray tell are these for?" With a touch of exasperation in his voice, he said, "Well, what do you think I have been doing the past few days? I have been up and down this valley getting promises of pigs from my people so that your father can come to visit us!"

Stalling for time, I counted out the sticks in those two bundles. There were 36 sticks and they represented 36 pigs his people had pledged to him for the purpose of bringing my father to Mulia. I turned to him, and said, "But how are you going to do this?" And again with a touch of scorn at my obvious stupidity, he said, "Well, when the plane brings your father here, we will have all these pigs waiting at the top of the airstrip and give them to the pilot!"

Now, indeed it is funny, but don't laugh, my friends. He was straining all this through the grid of his own very limited worldview and seeking a solution. But what would one pilot flying a small Cessna aircraft do with 36 pigs, dead or alive?

I finally said, "Big Mouth, it can't work," and tried to explain why, but he left disappointed and crestfallen.

Several days later, as we were readying ourselves to leave, I heard the familiar footsteps on our porch. Again the door burst open, and in came Big Mouth. As usual he sat down in front of the stove, and I sat down with him, chatting about this and that.

Finally he said, *"Tuan Kobo wae,"* "Hey, Mr. Scovill. Is it true you are going home?" And I answered, "Yes."

"Are you coming back to us after several full moons?" And I answered, "Yes, indeed! Our hearts are here with you."

"When you get home will you see your parents?" he asked. Again, I said, "Yes."

"Is it true they are not able to come to visit us here at my village?" he asked. And I had to answer again that they had no plans to come to Mulia.

Having heard that, he reached into his net bag and pulled out a large stone axe, beautifully sharpened and polished, slid it over to me, and said, "When you arrive at your father's village, I want you to give this stone axe to him. Tell him there is a chief among the people here at Mulia, whose name is Big Mouth, who wants to thank him for releasing his son so that he could come to tell us the message of Good News. Tell him that I and all my people have heard and accepted that message of eternal life." Then, flicking the tears from his eyes, he picked up his walking stick and slipped out the door. And I was left holding that big beautiful stone axe.

Though rather heavy, I brought it home and put it in the trunk of our car where I could easily get it when we arrived at my parents' farm, now in Wisconsin. As we pulled into the yard that afternoon, mom came out of the house to greet us and dad, in his overalls, came out of the barn where he was tending the cattle. After giving them both a hug, I said, "Dad, I've got something for you." And I opened the trunk lid, pulled out that axe, and handed it to my astonished father, saying, "Dad, there's a chief in Papua named Big Mouth who wants you to have this axe. It is a symbol of his appreciation to you for willingly allowing me, your son, to go share the message of the Gospel with him and his people."

Dad looked from me to the stone axe he now held. Then, overcome with emotion, he sat down on a rock there in our yard, turning that beautifully polished axe over and over in his hands. The years he had farmed without his boys, the mortgage on the farm that he had never been able to pay off partly due to the support he and mom had faithfully given to us, the prayers they had sent heavenward every morning for us—these had suddenly taken on a new significance with that stone axe from Big Mouth, and dad wept.

This must have been on his mind, for when we prepared to return to Papua a year later, dad pulled out a large hunting knife he very much treasured and asked, "David, (he always called me David) would Big Mouth enjoy a knife like this?" I assured him that Big Mouth would think the world of it. So, he gave it to me. And when we returned to the field, I took it back and gave it to Big Mouth who genuinely appreciated it, showing it off at the pig feasts they had.

The years continued to slip by and Big Mouth's role, being an older man, was beginning to fade. He was around, but rather sickly, and one day I heard that he had died peacefully in his village down at the end of the airstrip. Though it was dusk and I would have to return in the dark, I grabbed my flashlight and raced down to his village, about 20 minutes away.

Arriving at his small round house, I twisted my large frame through that little door and seated myself in front of the fire in the center of the house. Looking across the fire, I saw the little old lady we had named "Oma"—who, like a Dorcas in the community, always carried a smile, and gave an encouraging word or a baked sweet potato to you—seated opposite me on the other side of the fire. She immediately stoked the fire into a blaze to provide some light in that dark little house as I said to her, "Is this Big Mouth's house and is it true he has passed away?" "Yes," she answered, "This is his home and he passed away early this morning."

"Oh," I said, "I'm sorry that I missed seeing him before he died. Where is he?" With a twinkle in her eye, she looked across that fire and said quietly, "Tuan, he is not here!" "Oh," I said, disappointedly. "You have already cremated him! I came to pay my respects to this man whom I loved very much!"

By that time my eyes were becoming accustomed to the darkness of that little house, and I noticed movement behind me, to my left. Turning more fully around, I saw Big Mouth's body, propped up on a simple pole chair they had made, and his wives, with small leafy twigs in their hands, waving them about to keep the flies away.

I turned back to Oma, saying, "What do you mean, he is not here? Here he is!" Those eyes turned to me again, with a twinkle in them as she said, "Tuan. That is not Big Mouth. That is only the hut in which he lived for the few days of his earthly life. Big Mouth has gone to be with Jesus. Even though I am older and wanted to get to heaven first, he beat me there!"

And I remembered that a few months before, indeed Oma had been deathly sick. The young men trained by Esther had ministered faithfully to her, bringing her back from the brink of death with the right amounts of medicine mixed with tender loving care. When Oma was able to walk about again, she had slipped into our house one afternoon and said to Esther, "My mother. It was fine that you cared for me so I can walk about again, but if I get sick another time, please don't give me any medicine. Just let me go."

Esther was taken aback just a bit, so asked her, "Why would you want us to do that? We love you and want you to stay with us." Then Oma, her face radiant, went on to tell us her story. During her sickness, a personage in white had approached her and, taking her by the hand, had led her down a long trail. At the end of the trail, she could see a brilliant light toward which they were moving. She experienced no fear, she said, just overwhelming happiness and anticipation to get to the end of the path so as to be a part of that glorious place. As they were about to break out into that incredible brilliance, the personage in white had said to her, "You must return now. Your day is not yet."

Deeply disappointed, she turned to retrace her steps, and immediately found herself lying on her mat beside the fire in her little grass-roofed house by the bank of the river. Weak and emaciated was she from her sickness but alive and coherent. Weeks later, hands and face animated, light shining in those aged eyes, she had looked at Esther and said, "Please, my dear mother. Next time I get sick, just let me go. I don't want any more medicine; I've seen what is at the end of that path, and I want to be a part of that as soon as possible."

Now, looking across that fire in Big Mouth's hut and seeing the light radiating from Oma's aged eyes, I knew that Esther and I had made the right decision as young people. Here was another people, another culture and another language group, reaching out and finding LIFE. The mortal was putting on immortality. This was the heart of why we had come; this was Mission Accomplished!

After a short prayer with them in that little hut, warmed by their fire as well as deeply moved and further motivated by the assurance of their hope, I made my way by flashlight back to our house at the top of the airstrip, rejoicing that Big Mouth was one, with many others, who was finally HOME.

Epilogue:

—ᗡᗡᗡ—

I conclude the recording of these memoirs by suggesting to my reader that perhaps an appropriate subtitle would have been **This Is HIS Story**, for our story really began long before we were knowledgeable participants in its unfolding.

Prior to missionaries entering the Mulia valley with the message of the Gospel, an old man called his two sons to him one day and, as he lay dying, said to them: "My sons. I am going the way of our ancestors. But I have a feeling that within your lifetime strange men will be coming into our valley. When they come, do not harm them for they bring with them a message that will change this valley." And he passed away.

One of those brothers was four full days' walk to the west over unbelievable terrain, preparing a supply of the cylindrical native salt blocks to bring back to his family, when news reached him that strange men had arrived at Mulia. Remembering his father's words, he had bundled up the salt blocks already cured and headed for home. There he had found these strange men, the missionaries, about whom his father had spoken years before. The subsequent unfolding of this story, as it has affected us, I have written in this volume.

And the story continues to unfold! I would be remiss if I did not mention some of the current challenges with which the church is wrestling.

Given the foundational ideology that physical well-being (health and material prosperity) is a fundamental component of the Dani *nabelan-kabelan* "eternal life" mentality, there is a strong drive for materialism coupled with a desire to chuck the image of having had Stone Age, uneducated parents and grandparents. These drives propel him past his commitment to Christ, allowing compromise of calling (pastors who aspire to become salaried government servants); lowering of Biblical standards (young people in search of better educational opportunities who fudge on witness and religious conviction in a predominantly Muslim society); and rejection of the restraints of parents, kinsfolk and home church (school dropouts drifting out to coastal towns and cities who fall into a life of carousing and womanizing).

Such challenges are correctly driving the church to tears and to prayer. And, to the Glory of God, I must record that I believe the church with its leadership is dealing maturely with these issues. Let me cite several illustrations.

During our visit to Papua in 2005, one late starlit night I was walking up the airstrip at the station of Ilu. Coming toward me were three forms who emerged out of the darkness as three mothers with small children on their shoulders. Genuinely frightened at my dark form which they supposed was a *kugi* "spirit/ghost," from a short distance away they cried out, *"Kat ta o?"* "Who are you?"

I responded that I was Tuan Kobo just taking a walk on a beautiful evening. "And where are you mothers going?" I asked. Relieved, they quickly responded, "Oh, we are going down here to the church for a night of prayer." "Really," I said, "I will stop in to pray with you on my way back to the house," and went on as they hurried a few hundred yards further to the church building.

Minutes later, in the darkness, I found the path to the church and headed in that direction. Nearing that large building, I heard this strange rise and fall of sounds emanating through the walls and windows. Rather than disturbing them with my presence, I peeked though the window; I was staggered at what I witnessed.

Though late at night, that large building was crowded to the doors with several hundred men and women sitting on the floor in small circles, heads bowed and voices raised to God in passionate prayer and praise. Solemnized by the felt presence of God in that building, I made my way quietly down the trail to our home. The Dani church was interceding for the spiritual needs of her people.

Wa'lambuk, the pastor in a church up on a high plateau called Kwiyawogi, was approached by a group of men who were pushing ahead of them a woman accused of murdering one of their kinsmen through sorcery. The men were wild with anger; the woman was weeping in fear; the husband followed a short distance behind. The woman knew she was only a breath away from being publicly humiliated by being stripped of all her clothes followed by a horrific death beneath the stamping feet of her angry accusers.

Praying desperately for wisdom because there were elements of the population wanting to return to some of the practices of their past, Wa'lambuk asked them to sit down around him. Heated words from the woman's accusers followed as they told him of the death of their kinsman, and the evidence pointing to the woman who had killed him through her sorcery. "And here is the evidence," they said, after rummaging through their net bags to hold up part of a dried weed for Wa'lambuk to see, which they claimed the woman had sprinkled on cooked potato vines eaten by the man.

"You are sure this was what was used?" he asked bluntly. When they responded confidently, he said, "Very well. I am going to eat the remaining part. If I die, you have my permission to take the woman and kill her. If not, we will agree that she is not guilty and release her, knowing that the power of darkness is a liar with no authority over the believers in our valley and that this ritual out of our past way of life is not of God."

Faith bound his own fear; he placed the weed in his mouth, chewed it up and swallowed it. Fearfully they witnessed it; uncomfortably they waited!

One hour turned into two; two into three. The sun began to set as one by one, somewhat humiliated, they drifted off to their villages leaving the woman with the pastor and his wife. The ministry of the church continues.

In 2002, I was asked to be one of the speakers during a spiritual renewal emphasis at Mulia which was attended by several hundred young people, many of them high school graduates and younger university-level men in government positions in the area. The large building, constructed by the church, accommodated over 600 men and women seated on the floor. Great was the interest; eagerly they listened to the Word which we were able give to them in their own Dani language.

The closing service touched me deeply. A formal gathering such as this required an official closing during which those having had a part were properly thanked. The head of all the churches in the area, numbering nearly 75 at that time, was the final one to speak. He was, by that time, bilingual and began his little speech, in proper Indonesian, thanking all for their participation in the meetings.

Then, he turned to his younger kinsfolk seated on the floor before him. Several were Bible School graduates with secret thoughts of becoming salaried government workers; others were young people pursuing education at the expense of their relationship with the Lord; still others were dropouts causing concern in the community because of their irreverent life style. To them he directed his remarks, exhorting them in the Indonesian language to repent and return to their first love for the Lord.

No sooner had he begun to speak to his own people when the pent-up dam of his emotions broke! Unable to control himself, he slipped into his own mother tongue and, in literal torrents of grief, opened his heart to his younger brothers and sisters. Weeping, he challenged them to return to their first love; to return to the deeds of those claiming to be sons of God; to resist compromise and to get back on the rail of truth. It was very moving.

I sat there feeling the emotion of the moment. I heard him expose the deep burden of his heart for his people; I saw the tears running down his face and the faces of those who sat at his feet, and I thought, *He's got it; the burden of ministry has been transferred to these our spiritual children. With men like this replacing us, our mission has come full circle; my story is complete!* And I thanked God that we could leave certain that the church was alive; it would prevail against those outside influences threatening its existence and questioning its future.

We have had an unusual, joy-filled and fruitful ministry. Looking back over our missionary career of nearly 50 years, we have only one regret: It is that we do not have 50 more years to give to that which is most dear to the heart of God: MISSIONS!

Dave and Esther Scovill

—m—

You can contact Dave and Esther Scovill at:

109 Wild Goose Road
Blythewood, SC 29016

Printed in the United States
81802LV00003BB/1-87

9 781602 661172